BEYOND

THE

CODE

BEYOND

THE

CODE

Applying Real-World Ethics in School and Mental Health Counseling

BY: DANIEL STEWART, PHD

DISCLAIMER: This book is intended for informational purposes only and does not constitute legal or ethical advice. The information contained herein is based on publicly available sources and is believed to be accurate at the time of publication. However, ethics, laws, and regulations are subject to change, and the information presented may not reflect the most current legal or ethical developments. This book is not a substitute for professional legal advice. Readers are strongly advised to consult with a qualified attorney licensed in their jurisdiction for legal advice regarding their specific circumstances. The author and publisher of this book disclaim any and all liability for any actions taken or not taken based on the information contained herein. Any reference to individuals by name or case scenarios provided are fictitious and do not represent a real individual or actual client data.

The information provided in this book should not be relied upon as a definitive statement of the law or ethics. It is essential to refer to the official ethical standards, statutes, regulations, and case law for complete and accurate information. Specifically, this book is not intended to provide guidance on clinical decision-making, specific ethical, legal cases or situations, the application of the law to individual circumstances, the interpretation of specific legal terms or provisions, or any legal strategy or course of action. Readers are solely responsible for their own ethical decisions, legal decisions, and actions. The author and publisher make no representations or warranties, express or implied, regarding the accuracy, completeness, or suitability of the information contained in this book. The views expressed herein are those of the author and do not necessarily reflect the views of any organizations or institutions. By reading this book, you acknowledge and agree to this disclaimer.

ISBN-13: 979-8-9929732-0-4

TABLE OF CONTENT

1

---ｏ（ ᘓ ᕤ）ｏ---

ETHICAL FOUNDATIONS IN
COUNSELING

THE ROLE OF ETHICS IN COUNSELING

E thics is at the heart of professional counseling, shaping the way counselors interact with clients and guiding the therapeutic process. You might already know this, but in simple terms, counseling ethics refers to a set of principles that ensure responsible decision-making, professional conduct, and the well-being of clients. These ethical standards are not optional guidelines but essential rules that uphold the integrity of the profession.

A strong ethical foundation is key to building trust in the counselor-client relationship. It ensures that clients receive care that is safe, respectful, and free from harm. Ethical counseling practice includes maintaining confidentiality, respecting client autonomy, avoiding conflicts of interest, and working within one's professional expertise (ACA, 2014, A.4.b.; AMHCA, 2020, 1.3; ASCA, 2022, B.1). By following these principles, counselors create a supportive and secure environment where clients can heal and grow.

Beyond individual client care, ethical practice strengthens the credibility of the counseling profession as a whole. When counselors consistently uphold ethical standards, they foster public trust and confidence in mental health services (ACA, 2014, A.1.a.; AMHCA, 2020, 1.4). On the other hand, ethical violations can have serious consequences. A single instance of misconduct can harm a client and damage the profession's reputation, discouraging people from seeking the help they need.

Unethical behavior in counseling can take many forms, each with potentially serious consequences. For example, violating a client's confidentiality can not only breach their privacy but also damage the trust that is essential for effective therapy (ACA, 2014, B.1.c.; AMHCA, 2020, 2.1). Engaging in dual relationships, such as developing a romantic relationship with a client, can exploit the inherent power imbalance and lead to significant psychological harm (ACA, 2014, A.5.a.; ASCA, 2022, A.8). Similarly, working outside one's area of expertise can result in misdiagnosis or inappropriate treatment, worsening a client's mental health rather than improving it (ACA, 2014, F.3.d.; AMHCA, 2020, 1.2). These topics are explored more deeply in Chapters 5 and 15.

Ethical standards in counseling are not fixed rules but an evolving framework that adapts to societal changes and advancements in therapeutic practices (ACA, 2014, A.1.b.; AMHCA, 2020, 1.1). With the rise of new technologies, counselors face fresh ethical challenges, such as ensuring confidentiality in online therapy, responsibly managing electronic records, and maintaining appropriate professional boundaries on social media (ACA, 2014, H.2; AMHCA, 2020, 5.2). As cultural diversity increases, ethics must include cultural responsiveness. Chapter 4 will explore how culture intersects with ethical standards in counseling (ACA, 2014, C.2; ASCA, 2022, A.2).

One common misconception about counseling ethics is that good intentions alone ensure ethical practice. While counselors may believe they are acting in their clients' best interests, ethical decision-making requires more than just goodwill (ACA, 2014, A.4.b.; ASCA, 2022, B.2). It demands ongoing education, self-reflection, and consultation with colleagues to navigate complex situations responsibly. Counselors must be willing to critically examine their own biases, values, and limitations to provide the highest standard of care (ACA, 2014, A.4.c.; AMHCA, 2020, 4.1).

Adhering to ethical standards protects both clients and counselors. For clients, these guidelines ensure they receive competent, respectful, and beneficial care. Ethical principles safeguard their rights, including informed consent, confidentiality, and protection from exploitation (ACA, 2014, A.2; AMHCA, 2020, 1.3). For counselors, ethical standards provide a clear framework for making tough decisions, helping them navigate complex situations with confidence. Following these guidelines also shields counselors from potential legal or professional consequences that could arise from unethical behavior (ACA, 2014, F.3; AMHCA, 2020, 1.1).

Beyond individual counseling sessions, ethical responsibility extends to society as a whole. Counselors play a crucial role in promoting mental health and well-being, and their ethical conduct shapes public perception of mental health services. By upholding high ethical standards, they reinforce trust in the profession, encouraging more people to seek the help they need without fear or hesitation (ACA, 2014, A.1.d.; AMHCA, 2020, 1.2).

CORE ETHICAL PRINCIPLES UNVEILED

The core ethical principles in counseling have deep roots in ancient philosophy, with modern interpretations taking shape in the mid-20th century. Organizations such as the American Counseling Association (ACA), the American Mental Health Counselors Association (AMHCA), and the American School Counselor Association (ASCA) have refined and codified these principles to fit the specific needs of the counseling profession. While their origins lie in moral philosophy and medical ethics, the foundational principles of autonomy, beneficence, non-maleficence, and justice have been adapted to address the unique challenges counselors face (ACA, 2014, A.4.a.; AMHCA, 2020, 2.1; ASCA, 2022, A.5).

Autonomy, a concept championed by Greek philosophers and later emphasized by Enlightenment thinkers like Immanuel Kant (Kant, 1785/1993), underscores the importance of self-determination. In counseling, this principle marked a shift away from paternalistic approaches, recognizing a client's right to make informed decisions about their own treatment. During the 1960s and 1970s, autonomy gained even greater prominence in counseling ethics, with a stronger focus on informed consent and client rights (ACA, 2014, A.2.a.; AMHCA, 2020, 4.2).

Beneficence (promoting well-being) and non-maleficence (avoiding harm) can be traced back to the Hippocratic Oath in ancient Greek medicine. In counseling, these principles reinforce a counselor's duty to act in a client's best interest while minimizing potential risks. Their importance became even more apparent following controversial psychological studies in the mid-20th century, such as Stanley Milgram's obedience experiments, which led to a reexamination of ethical guidelines for both research and therapy (ACA, 2014, B.1.d.; AMHCA, 2020, 1.4).

Justice, a principle explored by thinkers from Aristotle to John Rawls, is centered on fairness and equal treatment (Rawls, 1958). In counseling, this principle has evolved to address access to mental health services, cultural competence, and the prevention of discrimination (ACA, 2014, C.2.a.; ASCA, 2022, A.7). The civil rights movement of the 1960s played a key role in shaping this aspect of counseling ethics, paving the way for a greater emphasis on multicultural counseling and social justice advocacy (ACA, 2014, C.2.b.; AMHCA, 2020, 4.3).

The American Counseling Association (ACA), founded in 1952, has played a key role in shaping ethical standards for the counseling profession. The publication of its first Code of Ethics in 1961 was a milestone in establishing clear, standardized guidelines for professional conduct. Over the years, revisions to the ACA Code of Ethics have reflected the profession's response to societal changes, emerging challenges, and advancements in counseling practices (ACA, 2014, A.1.d.; AMHCA, 2020, 1.1).

A major turning point in counseling ethics came in 1976 with the landmark case of *Tarasoff v. Regents of the University of California*. This case redefined the boundaries of client confidentiality by introducing the duty to protect, requiring counselors to take action if a client poses a serious threat to others (*Tarasoff v. Regents of the University of California*, 1976). As a result, ethical guidelines and legal standards were revised to clarify when confidentiality can, and must, be breached to prevent harm.

In recent decades, ethical considerations in counseling have been influenced by technological advancements, societal shifts, and new therapeutic approaches. The principle of autonomy now extends to client privacy in the digital age, addressing concerns such as electronic record-keeping and online therapy. Beneficence and non-maleficence have been reexamined in the context of evidence-based practices, reinforcing the need for interventions that are both research supported and tailored to individual client needs. As the profession responds to new technologies, questions around digital boundaries, online confidentiality, and virtual service delivery continue to emerge. These topics will be explored in greater depth in Chapter 7.

The principle of justice has also evolved, emphasizing diversity, inclusion, and cultural competence. Ethical codes now require counselors to develop the awareness and skills needed to work effectively with clients from different backgrounds. This shift acknowledges the profound impact of social and cultural factors on mental health and the counseling process.

Today, ongoing debates in counseling ethics revolve around issues such as the ethical use of social media, artificial intelligence in mental health care, and balancing individual rights with public health concerns in crisis situations. These emerging challenges demand a continuous reassessment of core ethical principles to ensure they remain relevant in a rapidly changing world.

Alongside the ACA, organizations such as the American Mental Health Counselors Association (AMHCA) and the American School Counselor Association (ASCA) have developed their own ethical codes. The AMHCA Code of Ethics provides guidance for mental health professionals in clinical settings, while the ASCA Ethical Standards focus on the specific challenges faced by school counselors.

As the counseling profession continues to grow and adapt, ethical principles remain the foundation of responsible practice. While the application of these principles may change over time, their core purpose remains the same: ensuring client welfare, professional integrity, and a commitment to social responsibility.

PERSONAL VALUES IN ETHICAL DECISION-MAKING

Counselors often find themselves balancing personal values with professional ethics, a challenge that requires careful navigation. While both shape behavior and decision-making, they come from different sources and serve distinct purposes. Personal values develop over a lifetime and are influenced by upbringing, culture, and personal experiences. In contrast, professional ethics are structured guidelines shaped by collective expertise, research, and societal expectations (ACA, 2014, A.1.a.; AMHCA, 2020, 4.2).

The roots of personal values stretch back to ancient philosophy and religious teachings. Thinkers like Aristotle, with his focus on virtue ethics, and Immanuel Kant, who introduced the concept of the categorical imperative, have shaped moral reasoning for centuries (Kant, 1785/1993). Meanwhile, professional ethics in counseling are a more recent development, with formal codes emerging in the mid-20th century. The American Counseling Association (ACA), founded in 1952, has played a key role in defining and refining these ethical standards (American Counseling Association, 2014).

In practice, personal values and professional ethics can sometimes align but may also create tension. For example, a counselor who values honesty might find this principle reinforcing the ethical duty of client confidentiality. However, conflicts arise when personal beliefs contradict professional responsibilities. A counselor who personally opposes abortion, for instance, may struggle when working with a client considering this option. In such situations, ethical guidelines require professionals to set aside personal views and provide impartial, client-centered support.

Relying on personal values in decision-making has its strengths, particularly in fostering authenticity and moral conviction. Counselors who align their actions with their personal values may feel more genuine in their interactions and find it easier to empathize with clients who share similar perspectives. However, this approach also has notable risks, including potential bias, inconsistency among counselors, and the danger of imposing personal beliefs on clients.

On the other hand, adhering to professional ethics ensures consistency, objectivity, and a shared decision-making framework across the profession. Ethical guidelines provide clear direction for handling complex situations, protecting both clients and counselors. However, a strict reliance on these rules can sometimes feel rigid, leaving little room for nuance or cultural considerations.

In some cases, personal values can complement ethical decision-making. For example, a counselor's strong commitment to social justice may enhance their advocacy for marginalized clients, aligning with the ethical principle of promoting client welfare. However, personal values should never override fundamental ethical principles such as respect for client autonomy, non-maleficence, or justice.

To effectively integrate personal values with professional ethics, counselors must engage in continuous self-reflection and ethical decision-making. This process can be supported through several key strategies:

1. **Ethical Decision-Making Models** – Using structured frameworks that consider both personal and professional perspectives can help counselors navigate complex ethical dilemmas with clarity and consistency.

2. **Supervision and Consultation** – Regular discussions with supervisors and colleagues provide valuable insights, helping counselors balance personal values with professional responsibilities.

3. **Continuing Education** – Ongoing learning about ethical issues and cultural competence enhances a counselor's ability to integrate personal and professional ethics thoughtfully.

4. **Personal Therapy** – Engaging in therapy can help counselors explore their own values, biases, and emotional responses, leading to greater self-awareness and ethical practice.

5. **Cultural Humility** – Maintaining an open, reflective approach allows counselors to recognize the limitations of their personal values and embrace diverse perspectives in their work.

By thoughtfully examining the relationship between personal values and professional ethics, counselors can develop a more balanced and effective approach to ethical decision-making. This integration strengthens the quality of counseling services, promotes client well-being, and contributes to the continued evolution of ethical standards in the field.

ETHICAL THEORIES IN COUNSELING PRACTICE

Ethical theories provide a foundation for decision-making in counseling, offering structured approaches to navigating moral dilemmas. Some of the most influential ethical theories in the field include deontology, utilitarianism, virtue ethics, and care ethics. Each of these perspectives shapes how counselors approach ethical decision-making and professional conduct.

Deontology, developed by Immanuel Kant in the 18th century, focuses on the idea that actions are inherently right or wrong, regardless of their outcomes. This theory argues that moral behavior stems from adherence to universal moral duties (Kant, 1785/1993). In counseling, deontological ethics is reflected in absolute principles such as respecting client autonomy and maintaining confidentiality. Its strength lies in providing clear, consistent ethical guidelines. However, its rigid nature can create challenges in situations where ethical duties conflict or when complex cases require flexibility.

Utilitarianism, introduced by Jeremy Bentham and John Stuart Mill, takes a different approach by emphasizing the consequences of actions. According to this theory, ethical decisions should aim to produce the greatest good for the greatest number (Mill, 1863/2007; Bentham, 1789/1988). In counseling, this perspective encourages professionals to consider the broader impact of their decisions on clients, families, and communities. While utilitarianism allows for flexibility in unique situations, it also raises ethical concerns, particularly when prioritizing the majority's well-being could lead to harm or injustice for an individual.

Virtue ethics, rooted in the teachings of ancient Greek philosophers like Aristotle and later expanded by modern thinkers like Alasdair MacIntyre, shifts the focus from actions to moral character (Aristotle, trans. 2009; MacIntyre, 1981). This theory emphasizes the development of personal virtues such as compassion, integrity, and wisdom. In counseling, virtue ethics encourages practitioners to embody these traits in their professional conduct. Its holistic approach fosters ethical behavior as part of a counselor's identity, but it may lack clear guidelines for resolving immediate ethical dilemmas.

Care ethics, developed by Carol Gilligan and Nel Noddings, emphasizes relationships, empathy, and context in moral decision-making (Gilligan, 1982; Noddings, 1984). This theory aligns closely with counseling, reinforcing the profession's focus on therapeutic relationships and individualized care. By encouraging counselors to consider each client's unique needs and circumstances, care ethics promotes a more personalized approach to ethical dilemmas. However, critics argue that this perspective may lead to inconsistent decision-making and could blur professional boundaries.

The Influence of Ethical Theories on Counseling Standards

These ethical theories have played a significant role in shaping professional counseling codes of ethics. For example, the American Counseling Association's Code of Ethics integrates elements from multiple frameworks:

- Deontology – Seen in clear ethical rules and professional duties.

- Utilitarianism – Reflected in the emphasis on client welfare and the broader impact of ethical decisions.

- Virtue Ethics – Encouraging professional values such as integrity and compassion.

- Care Ethics – Highlighting the importance of the counseling relationship and individualized client care.

By incorporating these diverse ethical perspectives, professional guidelines create a well-rounded framework that acknowledges the complexities of ethical decision-making in counseling. Counselors often draw on theories like deontology, utilitarianism, and virtue ethics. These frameworks provide useful lenses and will be explored in practical contexts in Chapter 8.

STRENGTHENING THE APPLICATION OF ETHICAL THEORIES

Counselors often rely on ethical decision-making models that integrate multiple theoretical perspectives. These models provide structured guidance for identifying ethical issues, applying relevant principles, and evaluating potential actions. While useful, they can sometimes be time-consuming and may not fully account for the nuances of complex cases.

To enhance the practical application of ethical theories in counseling, three key strategies can be considered:

First, interactive workshops can help counselors apply ethical theories to real world scenarios, strengthening their critical thinking and ethical sensitivity. While effective, this approach requires time and resources to implement successfully.

Another way to enhance the integration of ethical theories into counseling is by incorporating ethical theory modules into continuing education requirements. This approach ensures that counselors remain engaged with ethical frameworks throughout their careers, promoting lifelong learning and ethical competence. However, challenges may arise in standardizing these modules and effectively assessing learning outcomes across different professional settings.

A third strategy involves establishing ethical consultation teams within counseling organizations. These teams would provide a collaborative space where counselors can apply ethical theories to real time dilemmas, benefiting from collective wisdom and diverse perspectives. While this approach fosters deeper ethical reflection, concerns regarding confidentiality and decision-making efficiency must be carefully addressed.

Each of these strategies comes with challenges, including resource allocation, logistical coordination, and potential resistance to change. Additionally, their long-term impact on counseling practice and client outcomes requires careful evaluation. While enhanced ethical reasoning may improve client care and professional fulfillment, it could also increase decision-making complexity and potentially extend treatment timelines.

DECODING THE ACA CODE OF ETHICS

The American Counseling Association (ACA) Code of Ethics has played a crucial role in shaping the counseling profession since the mid-20th century. Its origins date back to 1961 when the American Personnel and Guidance Association (APGA), the predecessor to the ACA, introduced the first Ethical Standards. This document was a response to the growing need for a unified set of guidelines to ensure ethical and professional conduct across the field.

Early Development and Key Contributors

The initial development of the Code was led by influential figures in counseling, including Nicholas Hobbs, who chaired the committee responsible for drafting the first set of ethical standards. Hobbs and other leading practitioners recognized the necessity of a structured ethical framework to guide decision-making and uphold professional integrity (Hobbs, 1948).

Major Revisions and Their Impact

Over the years, the ACA Code of Ethics has undergone several major revisions, adapting to new challenges and societal changes:

- 1974 Revision – Expanded the Code's scope, introducing more detailed guidelines on confidentiality, client welfare, and professional competence.

- 1988 Revision – Addressed the increasing diversity of client populations by incorporating multicultural considerations and recognizing the role of technology in counseling.

- 1995 Revision – Introduced a more structured approach to ethical principles, emphasizing client autonomy, non-maleficence, beneficence, justice, and fidelity. It also provided expanded guidance on ethical decision-making to help counselors navigate complex dilemmas.

One of the most significant ethical controversies that shaped later revisions of the ACA Code of Ethics was the debate over conversion therapy. Concerns about its harmful psychological effects led to an explicit prohibition in the 2005 revision, reinforcing the counseling profession's commitment to client diversity, autonomy, and non-discrimination.

Current Structure of the ACA Code of Ethics

The most recent revision, completed in 2014, organizes the ACA Code of Ethics into nine key sections:

1. The Counseling Relationship
2. Confidentiality and Privacy
3. Professional Responsibility
4. Relationships with Other Professionals
5. Evaluation, Assessment, and Interpretation
6. Supervision, Training, and Teaching
7. Research and Publication
8. Distance Counseling, Technology, and Social Media
9. Resolving Ethical Issues

Each section provides detailed guidelines to ensure ethical and professional conduct across different aspects of counseling practice.

Key Principles and Their Impact

At the core of the ACA Code of Ethics is the principle of client welfare, emphasizing that counselors must prioritize clients' best interests while respecting their autonomy and self-determination. Another foundational principle is maintaining professional boundaries, which is highlighted in multiple sections to prevent ethical violations.

The 2014 revision introduced critical updates that significantly impacted counseling practice and ethics education:

- Ethical Use of Technology & Social Media

    o Addressed the rise of digital communication in counseling.

    o Led many counseling programs to expand training on technology-mediated counseling ethics.

- Cultural Sensitivity & Competence

    o Strengthened the requirement for counselors to develop multicultural competencies.

    o Encouraged professionals to adapt their practices to meet the needs of diverse client populations.

The ACA Code of Ethics Today

The current ACA Code of Ethics remains a dynamic and evolving guide for ethical decision-making in counseling. It continues to provide clear direction on complex ethical challenges, such as:

- Navigating dual relationships

- Confidentiality in the digital age

- Ethical standards in research and publication

By staying responsive to emerging ethical dilemmas, the Code ensures that counselors uphold professional integrity while meeting the changing needs of society.

NAVIGATING ETHICAL DILEMMAS IN COUNSELING

Ethical dilemmas in counseling often involve complex and conflicting principles, requiring careful judgment and ethical reasoning. Consider the case of a 16-year-old client who confides thoughts of self-harm but insists that their parents not be informed. Here we can see the tension between client autonomy and confidentiality versus the counselor's duty to protect and legal obligations.

As you will see repeated over and over, confidentiality is a cornerstone of counseling, fostering trust and open communication. While this chapter introduces its importance, we will revisit its complexities in later chapters, including digital counseling, group work, and crisis response. By respecting the client's request for privacy, the counselor strengthens the therapeutic alliance, encouraging continued disclosure and engagement in treatment. However, prioritizing confidentiality could pose serious risks, if the self-harm thoughts escalate, lack of intervention might endanger the client's well-being.

On the other hand, disclosing the information to the client's parents ensures that immediate safety measures can be implemented, aligning with the ethical principle of beneficence, acting in the client's best interest. Yet, this decision could damage trust, leading to withdrawal from therapy and a reluctance to seek future help.

The Role of Ethical Guidelines and Legal Considerations

The ACA Code of Ethics provides guidance on navigating such dilemmas, emphasizing that confidentiality has limits when there is a serious risk of harm. Additionally, state laws vary, some allow minors over 12 to consent to mental health treatment independently, further complicating the decision-making process. These nuances are explored further in the context of consent (Ch. 11) and crisis care (Ch. 17).

Ultimately, counselors must carefully weigh ethical, legal, and clinical factors to arrive at the most responsible and compassionate course of action. Employing ethical decision-making models, consulting supervisors or colleagues, and considering alternative support strategies can help ensure the best possible outcome for the client.

The American School Counselor Association (ASCA) Ethical Standards emphasize that school counselors must balance students' rights to privacy with their duty to protect them from harm. While this case does not explicitly involve a school counselor, the principles still apply, particularly the importance of considering the client's age, maturity, and capacity for independent decision-making.

Similarly, the American Mental Health Counselors Association (AMHCA) Code of Ethics stresses the importance of informing clients upfront about confidentiality limits. By establishing clear boundaries from the beginning, counselors can prevent misunderstandings and reduce ethical dilemmas.

One potential strategy is negotiating a limited disclosure plan with the client. This involves a collaborative discussion where both parties agree on specific conditions that would require parental involvement, such as an increase in self-harm thoughts or an ineffective safety plan. This approach respects the client's autonomy while ensuring their safety, making them an active participant in the decision-making process.

By integrating ethical guidance with compassionate, client-centered care, counselors can navigate these dilemmas in a way that fosters trust, empowerment, and well-being.

Alternatively, the counselor could opt to intensify treatment and implement a comprehensive safety plan without immediate parental disclosure. This approach respects the client's confidentiality while actively addressing the risk of self-harm. However, it requires careful monitoring and may not sufficiently mitigate long-term risk if the client's condition deteriorates.

The potential long-term implications of different courses of action are significant for all parties involved. For the client, maintaining strict confidentiality might preserve trust in the therapeutic process but could result in inadequate support systems if their mental health worsens. Conversely, breaching confidentiality could lead to improved safety measures but might deter the client from future help-seeking behaviors. For the counselor, adhering to confidentiality in this high-risk situation could result in professional and legal repercussions if the client engages in self-harm.

On the other hand, disclosing information against the client's wishes might be viewed as an ethical violation, potentially damaging the counselor's professional reputation and the broader public trust in mental health services. The counseling profession as a whole faces ongoing challenges in navigating these complex ethical scenarios.

Cases like this underscore the need for continued professional development, robust ethical guidelines, and interdisciplinary collaboration to ensure that counselors are equipped to make sound decisions in high-stakes situations.

ETHICAL DECISION-MAKING FRAMEWORK

Making ethical decisions in counseling can be challenging, as it requires careful thought and a structured approach. A commonly used framework consists of eight interconnected steps, helping counselors navigate ethical dilemmas with confidence. The first and most crucial step is identifying the ethical issue, which lays the foundation for all further decisions.

To pinpoint the ethical issue, counselors need to clearly define the problem they are facing. This can be tricky, as ethical concerns often overlap with clinical and legal issues. The American Counseling Association (ACA) Code of Ethics is a key resource at this stage, offering clear guidance on professional standards. Seeking supervision or consulting with colleagues can also provide valuable insights and help clarify the situation.

Once the issue is identified, the next step is gathering relevant information. Counselors must consider all aspects of the case, including client records, legal requirements, and cultural factors that may impact the situation. This step requires a thorough, unbiased approach to ensure nothing important is overlooked. Using checklists or structured formats can help counselors stay organized and avoid personal biases when evaluating information.

The third step involves reviewing ethical guidelines and laws. It's essential to ensure that any decision aligns with professional standards and legal requirements. While the ACA Code of Ethics serves as a primary guide, state laws and other professional regulations may also apply. Sometimes, these sources may offer conflicting advice. In such cases, counselors must carefully analyze the different perspectives and determine which guidance takes priority.

After reviewing the guidelines, the next step is to explore possible solutions. This involves brainstorming different courses of action and evaluating their potential outcomes. Ethical decision-making models can be helpful here, as they provide structured methods for assessing options. However, counselors must remain aware of how personal biases might shape their choices. Considering both short-term and long-term consequences ensures a well-rounded decision that prioritizes the client's well-being.

The fifth step in the ethical decision-making process is evaluating possible options using core ethical principles. Counselors must weigh principles such as autonomy (respecting the client's choices), beneficence (acting in the client's best interest), non-maleficence (avoiding harm), and justice (ensuring fairness) to determine the most ethical course of action. Ethical theories and the ACA Code of Ethics provide useful guidance, but a key challenge at this stage is balancing competing principles. Some options may support one principle while conflicting with another, requiring thoughtful analysis.

The sixth step is consulting with colleagues or supervisors. Seeking external input can provide fresh perspectives that help clarify ethical dilemmas. Resources like clinical supervision, ethics committees, or peer consultation groups can be invaluable. However, counselors must ensure they maintain client confidentiality by sharing only the necessary details to receive guidance.

Once all options have been carefully considered, the seventh step is making and implementing the decision. Counselors must choose the best course of action and put it into practice. This often includes creating an action plan and considering how to communicate the decision to the client. Doubts and anxiety about the chosen path are common, so documenting the decision-making process and rationale is essential for both ethical and legal protection.

The final step is reflection and evaluation. Counselors must assess the results of their decision and reflect on what they've learned from the experience. Tools like self-reflection, supervision, and outcome assessments can help. However, it can be difficult to evaluate one's own decisions objectively, making external feedback particularly useful at this stage.

This structured framework provides a clear process for navigating ethical dilemmas, ensuring that decisions are made thoughtfully and with consideration of ethical principles, relevant factors, and potential consequences. Taking the time to put these into practice, counselors can strengthen their ethical practice and make decisions that serve the best interests of both clients and the profession.

In some cases, counselors may need to act quickly, especially when a client is at risk of imminent harm. In these situations, a streamlined version of the framework may be necessary.

Instead of lengthy deliberation, counselors may need to:

- Quickly identify the ethical issue and gather only the most critical information.
- Focus on key ethical guidelines, especially those related to safety and harm prevention.

- Condense brainstorming and evaluation into a rapid decision-making process.
- Limit consultation to a brief phone call or, if time does not allow, rely on professional judgment.
- Implement the decision immediately while ensuring proper documentation as soon as possible afterward.

Even in urgent situations, it remains essential to document the thought process behind the decision to maintain ethical accountability and professional integrity.

CASE STUDIES IN ETHICAL ANALYSIS

Ethical dilemmas in counseling can be complex, often requiring counselors to carefully analyze multiple ethical principles before making a decision. The following case studies highlight common challenges in the field and demonstrate how ethical decision-making frameworks can be applied in real-world situations.

Case 1: Confidentiality vs. Duty to Warn

A counselor meets with a client who reveals plans to harm a specific individual. This situation creates a direct conflict between two ethical responsibilities: maintaining client confidentiality and protecting others from harm. The American Counseling Association (ACA) Code of Ethics stresses the importance of confidentiality but also recognizes exceptions when there is a clear and imminent danger to the client or others.

Using the ethical decision-making framework, the counselor's first step is to identify the core issue: balancing client autonomy and confidentiality against the duty to protect potential victims. The next step is to review ethical codes, state laws, and professional guidelines, as many jurisdictions have specific regulations on a counselor's duty to warn or protect in cases of potential violence.

The counselor must then evaluate possible actions:

Option 1: Maintain confidentiality to preserve trust in the therapeutic relationship but risk potential harm to others.

Option 2: Break confidentiality to warn the potential victim or authorities, prioritizing safety but possibly damaging the client's trust.

Each choice comes with significant ethical and professional implications, requiring careful consideration of the client's well-being, legal obligations, and the broader impact of the decision.

From a utilitarian perspective, the best course of action would be the one that results in the greatest good for the greatest number of people. In this case, warning the potential victim or authorities would likely be the most ethical choice, as it prioritizes preventing harm. A deontological approach, on the other hand, would emphasize the counselor's duty to protect life as a moral obligation, which may override the duty to maintain confidentiality in extreme situations.

Case 2: Multiple Relationships

Imagine a counselor is invited to a client's wedding. While this may seem like a harmless social interaction, it raises important ethical concerns about boundaries and dual relationships. The ACA Code of Ethics advises counselors to avoid nonprofessional relationships with clients whenever possible, as these can blur professional boundaries and create risks of exploitation or harm.

Applying the ethical decision-making framework, the counselor must weigh several factors:

- Potential Benefits: Attending the wedding could be seen as a way to validate the client's progress and show support for their personal growth.

- Potential Risks: It could also confuse the professional relationship, leading to unrealistic expectations or complications in future therapy sessions.

To make an informed decision, the counselor should consider:

- The current stage of therapy and whether the client is at risk of misinterpreting the relationship.
- The client's understanding of professional boundaries and how attendance might impact the therapeutic dynamic.
- How might the situation be perceived by others, including colleagues or future clients?

Consulting with colleagues or an ethics committee can provide valuable insights before making a final decision.

From a virtue ethics perspective, the best choice would be the one that demonstrates key counselor qualities such as wisdom, integrity, and care for the client's well-being. A care ethics approach would focus on maintaining the therapeutic relationship while ensuring that professional boundaries remain clear and respected.

Case 3: Cultural Competence

Counselors have an ethical responsibility to provide competent and culturally sensitive care to all clients, regardless of their background. The ACA Code of Ethics underscores the importance of cultural awareness and the need for ongoing professional development in this area.

In this example, the counselor faces a key ethical challenge: recognizing the limits of their cultural competence and taking steps to address them. The ethical principles of beneficence (doing good) and non-maleficence (avoiding harm) must be balanced with a commitment to equitable, non-discriminatory care.

To navigate this situation, the counselor has several options:

- Seek additional training or supervision to improve cultural competence.
- Consult with culturally knowledgeable colleagues for guidance and support.
- Refer the client to a counselor with more relevant cultural expertise, if necessary.

Each choice carries ethical and professional implications, influencing both the client's experience and the counselor's growth.

From an ethics of care perspective, the focus would be on building a genuine, empathetic relationship with the client while making an active effort to understand and respect their cultural background. A principlist approach, on the other hand, would weigh key ethical principles, autonomy, beneficence, non-maleficence, and justice, to determine the most ethical course of action.

Case 4: Technology and Confidentiality

In the digital age, maintaining professional boundaries can be more challenging than ever. Imagine a counselor receiving a social media friend request from a client. This scenario raises ethical concerns related to confidentiality, dual relationships, and the integrity of the counseling relationship.

Using the ethical decision-making framework, the counselor must carefully assess the potential risks and consequences:

- Accepting the request could blur professional boundaries, making it difficult to maintain the therapeutic relationship. It might also expose the counselor to personal client information that could impact the counseling process.

- Declining the request without explanation might be misinterpreted by the client as a personal rejection, potentially affecting their trust in the counselor.

A thoughtful approach involves reviewing existing social media policies and, if necessary, establishing clear guidelines for online interactions. Counselors can also take a proactive stance by discussing social media boundaries at the beginning of the therapeutic relationship.

From a social contract theory perspective, the counselor's response should align with the implicit agreement that professional relationships prioritize the client's well-being (Rousseau, 1762/1974). A feminist ethics approach would examine the power dynamics at play, ensuring that social media connections do not create unintended hierarchies or undermine transparency in the therapeutic relationship (Gilligan, 1982; Held, 2006).

These case studies highlight the complexity of ethical decision-making in counseling and the value of applying structured frameworks to navigate challenging situations. They reinforce the need for counselors to:

- Reflect continuously on their ethical responsibilities.
- Seek consultation when faced with difficult dilemmas.
- Prioritize client welfare while upholding professional integrity.

By thoughtfully addressing ethical challenges, counselors can provide effective, ethical, and compassionate care in an ever-evolving professional landscape.

SELF-REFLECTION ON PERSONAL VALUES

Self-reflection on personal values is a crucial aspect of ethical counseling practice. It helps counselors understand their motivations, biases, and decision-making processes, ultimately shaping their interactions with clients. This process begins with identifying core values, which often stem from cultural background, life experiences, and personal beliefs. For example, a counselor may prioritize values such as integrity, empathy, respect for autonomy, social justice, and professional competence.

These values are deeply influenced by personal history. A counselor who highly values empathy may have developed this trait through personal adversity or exposure to diverse perspectives. Similarly, a strong commitment to social justice might stem from witnessing or experiencing systemic inequalities. These values shape everyday choices, interactions, and ethical decision-making in the counseling profession.

The Role of Personal Values in Counseling

In counseling, personal values inevitably influence practice:

- A counselor who values autonomy may strongly support the client's self-determination, even when their personal beliefs differ from the client's choices.

- A counselor with a deep commitment to social responsibility might struggle with remaining neutral when working with clients whose actions they see as harmful to society.

Potential conflicts between personal values and ethical responsibilities can arise in various scenarios. For example, a counselor with strong religious convictions might find it challenging to work with clients whose lifestyles conflict with their personal beliefs. In such cases, it is essential to navigate these differences professionally, always prioritizing the client's well-being and right to self-determination over personal views.

Cultural background plays a significant role in shaping personal values and ethical decision-making. Counselors must recognize how their own cultural perspectives may differ from those of their clients.

- A counselor from an individualistic culture may need to adjust their approach when working with clients from collectivist cultures, where family and community obligations take precedence over individual desires.

- Awareness of these cultural differences allows counselors to provide more effective and culturally responsive care.

By engaging in ongoing self-reflection, counselors can enhance their ethical awareness, minimize personal bias, and ensure they uphold professional values that support client well-being.

Navigating value differences in a culturally sensitive way requires an open mindset. Counselors can develop cultural humility, seek ongoing education about diverse perspectives, and practice active listening to understand clients' worldviews without judgment. By doing so, they create a more inclusive and supportive therapeutic relationship.

Ethical decision-making in counseling often presents complex challenges when personal values intersect with professional responsibilities. For example, a counselor who deeply values honesty may face a situation where full disclosure could harm a client or others. In such cases, they must carefully balance their personal beliefs with ethical principles like beneficence (acting in the client's best interest) and non-maleficence (avoiding harm) (ACA, 2014, B.1.d.; AMHCA, 2020, 1.4). The goal is to find a thoughtful and responsible approach that protects the client while upholding professional integrity.

When personal values conflict with ethical obligations, counselors can use several strategies to navigate the situation. Seeking supervision or consultation can provide fresh perspectives (ACA, 2014, F.3.a.; AMHCA, 2020, 4.4). Engaging in continued ethical education reinforces professional standards while using a structured decision-making model helps counselors integrate both personal and ethical considerations into their choices (ACA, 2014, C.2.b.; ASCA, 2022, A.3).

Professional growth in counseling is an ongoing process that requires self-reflection. This means being willing to examine and, if necessary, adjust personal values that could interfere with effective practice. For instance, a counselor who strongly believes in self-reliance might need to rethink this perspective when working with clients who rely on strong support systems (ACA, 2014, A.2; ASCA, 2022, B.1). Growth comes from being open to new viewpoints and adapting when needed (ACA, 2014, F.3.c.).

Regular self-assessment enhances ethical awareness, cultural competence, and decision-making skills. Counselors can incorporate this into their practice by journaling, joining peer supervision groups, and engaging in personal therapy (AMHCA, 2020, 5.1; ASCA, 2022, B.3). These methods help them understand how their values shape their work and ensure they are providing the best possible care to clients.

Reconciling personal values with professional ethics isn't always easy. Counselors may experience internal conflict when their personal beliefs clash with ethical responsibilities, face countertransference issues, or struggle with tough decisions where multiple ethical principles seem to be at odds (ACA, 2014, F.2; AMHCA, 2020, 2.3). The key to handling these challenges is a commitment to continued learning, supervision, and self-growth (ACA, 2014, F.2.a.; AMHCA, 2020, 4.4).

Self-awareness is at the heart of ethical counseling. Recognizing personal biases and understanding the limits of one's competence allows counselors to make informed, ethical decisions (ACA, 2014, A.4.b.; AMHCA, 2020, 1.3). By maintaining clear boundaries and seeking guidance when needed, they can refine their practice and better serve their clients (ASCA, 2022, A.6).

AMHCA DECODED

The American Mental Health Counselors Association (AMHCA) Code of Ethics has played a crucial role in shaping the profession since AMHCA's founding in 1976. Recognizing the need for clear ethical guidelines, the organization developed its first Code of Ethics in 1979. This marked an important step in defining professional standards for mental health counselors.

The original Code was relatively brief, focusing on fundamental principles like client welfare, confidentiality, and professional competence. Since mental health counseling was still an emerging profession, these early guidelines provided a necessary ethical foundation. The Code's development was influenced by AMHCA's founding members, who adapted ethical standards from related fields such as psychology and social work to meet the unique needs of mental health counselors.

As the profession evolved, so did the ethical code. The 1987 revision brought a more comprehensive approach, expanding sections on counselor-client relationships, assessment procedures, and research ethics. These changes reflected the increasing complexity of mental health counseling and the need for more detailed ethical guidance across different practice areas.

A major overhaul of the AMHCA Code of Ethics took place in 2000, driven by rapid technological advancements that were reshaping counseling practices. This revision introduced guidelines on electronic therapy, online counseling, and the ethical use of technology in client communications. It also expanded its focus on multicultural competence, acknowledging the increasing diversity of client populations and the need for culturally sensitive approaches.

Another significant update came in 2010, reflecting the profession's evolving landscape. This revision addressed new ethical concerns, including social media use, distance counseling, and the role of personal therapy for counselors. The profession had begun placing greater emphasis on self-care and personal development as essential to ethical practice. Additionally, informed consent guidelines were strengthened to account for the complexities of modern treatment methods.

Today, the AMHCA Code of Ethics is organized into key sections covering critical aspects of professional conduct:

- The Counseling Relationship

- Confidentiality and Privacy
- Professional Responsibility
- Relationships with Other Professionals
- Evaluation, Assessment, and Interpretation
- Supervision, Training, and Teaching
- Research and Publication
- Resolving Ethical Issues

Each section provides detailed ethical standards to navigate the complexities of modern mental health counseling. At its core, the Code emphasizes five fundamental principles:

- Beneficence – Promoting client well-being
- Non-maleficence – Avoiding harm
- Autonomy – Respecting client's self-determination
- Justice – Ensuring fair and equitable treatment
- Fidelity – Honoring commitments to clients and the profession

This structure ensures that counselors have clear ethical guidance while adapting to the ongoing evolution of the field.

The evolution of the AMHCA Code of Ethics has had a profound impact on counseling practice and ethics education. The 2000 revision's focus on multicultural competence, for example, led to enhanced training programs and continuing education requirements emphasizing cultural sensitivity. More recent updates addressing digital counseling ethics have spurred the development of specialized courses and best practices for working with clients online.

Today, the AMHCA Code of Ethics remains a pillar of professional standards for clinical mental health counselors. It provides a structured framework for ethical decision-making, helping practitioners navigate complex dilemmas in their work. The Code also plays a crucial role in shaping licensure requirements, continuing education programs, and overall professional development.

As the field of counseling continues to evolve, the Code will likely undergo further revisions to address emerging challenges. Potential areas of future focus include:

- Artificial Intelligence in Counseling – As AI becomes more integrated into mental health assessment and treatment, clear ethical guidelines will be needed.

- Genetic Counseling and Personalized Medicine – With genetic data playing an increasing role in mental health care, new ethical considerations may arise.

- Climate Change and Mental Health – The psychological impact of environmental crises may require counselors to consider new ethical responsibilities.

- Intersectionality and Social Justice – Ethical guidelines will likely continue evolving to address systemic inequalities and the complex interplay of multiple identities affecting mental health.

As new challenges emerge, the AMHCA Code of Ethics will remain a living document, adapting to ensure that counselors uphold the highest ethical standards in an ever-changing world.

ASCA DECODED

The American School Counselor Association (ASCA) Code of Ethics has evolved over several decades, growing alongside the profession of school counseling. Its origins date back to the 1950s when school counseling began to take shape as a distinct field within education. As counselors worked to define their roles in supporting students' academic, personal, and social development, the need for a standardized ethical framework became clear.

ASCA published its first formal ethical guidelines in 1965, marking a significant step in the profession's development. This initial document provided a foundation for ethical practice, covering core issues such as confidentiality, professional boundaries, and the counselor's role in the school system. Though relatively brief, it set the stage for future revisions.

As the profession expanded, the Code of Ethics was updated to address new challenges. The 1984 revision reflected changes in education, offering more specific guidance on student records, testing, and the counselor's duty to report child abuse and neglect. It also reinforced the importance of cultural sensitivity and non-discrimination in counseling practice.

Further refinements came in the 1990s, with updates in 1992 and 1998. These revisions responded to ethical dilemmas arising from new technology in schools, such as computer-based counseling tools and the protection of electronic student records. The 1998 version also strengthened the Code's emphasis on advocacy, reinforcing the counselor's role in protecting students' rights and well-being.

A major overhaul in 2004 reflected a shift toward a more comprehensive, data-driven approach to school counseling. This revision aligned the Code with the ASCA National Model, which emphasized accountability and the use of data to guide counseling practices. It also addressed emerging issues such as social media ethics and online communication with students.

The most recent major revision of the ASCA Code of Ethics occurred in 2016, with minor updates in 2022. The Code is organized into eight main sections:

- Responsibility to Students
- Responsibility to Parents/Guardians
- Responsibility to Colleagues and Professional Associates
- Responsibility to Schools, Communities, and Families
- Responsibility to Self
- Responsibility to the Profession
- Maintenance of Standards
- Resources

Each section provides specific ethical guidelines to help school counselors navigate their professional responsibilities.

A key principle woven throughout the Code is the prioritization of students' welfare and rights (ASCA, 2022, A.1). School counselors are expected to act in students' best interests while balancing relationships with parents, administrators, and the broader community. The Code also underscores the importance of cultural competence and equity, reflecting the growing diversity of student populations (ASCA, 2022, A.2).

Revisions to the Code have significantly influenced counseling practice and education. The 2004 emphasis on data-driven approaches led many counselor education programs to incorporate more coursework on research methods and program evaluation. Similarly, evolving guidance on technology and social media has reshaped how school counselors navigate digital communication with students. Today, ethical considerations surrounding electronic interactions are essential components of professional development and training.

The ASCA Code of Ethics stands as a go-to-guide in the school counseling profession, shaping both daily counseling practices and broader school policies. As the field continues to evolve, future updates will likely address new challenges such as remote counseling, artificial intelligence in education, and the rising mental health needs of students in a post-pandemic world.

2

THE EVOLUTION OF

COUNSELING ETHICS

EARLY FOUNDATIONS

The roots of counseling ethics trace back to the early 20th century when psychotherapy emerged as a distinct field. Initially, ethical principles were heavily influenced by medical ethics, which had long followed traditions like the Hippocratic Oath. However, as psychotherapy developed, practitioners saw the need for ethical guidelines tailored to the unique nature of the therapeutic relationship and its potential for psychological harm.

Sigmund Freud played a key role in shaping early ethical considerations, even though he never formalized an ethical code. His emphasis on confidentiality and professional boundaries in psychoanalysis set an important precedent. His concepts of transference and countertransference underscored the power dynamics between therapist and client, laying the groundwork for later ethical discussions (Freud, 1912/1958).

Carl Rogers further contributed to ethical thinking in counseling. His person-centered approach emphasized genuineness, unconditional positive regard, and empathy, core conditions that implicitly addressed ethical concerns like respect for client autonomy and the therapist's responsibility to create a safe, nonjudgmental environment (Rogers, 1957).

THE PUSH FOR FORMAL ETHICAL STANDARDS

By the mid-20th century, counseling had begun to establish itself as a profession distinct from psychology and psychiatry. However, without a unified professional identity, developing a standardized ethical framework was challenging. Different theoretical orientations and societal norms influenced mental health practices, sometimes leading to ethically questionable approaches, such as involuntary institutionalization or treatments without informed consent.

In the 1950s and 1960s, professional organizations like the American Counseling Association (ACA) (founded in 1952) took the lead in shaping ethical standards. These organizations recognized the need for formalized guidelines to protect both clients and practitioners.

One of the biggest debates in early ethical development was how rigid these guidelines should be. Some professionals argued for detailed, enforceable rules, while others favored broader principles that allowed for professional judgment in complex situations. Striking a balance between protecting clients and preserving counselor autonomy became a key challenge, one that continues to shape ethical codes today.

The societal landscape of the mid-20th century played a crucial role in shaping ethical considerations in counseling. The civil rights movement, for example, heightened awareness of discrimination and cultural sensitivity in mental health care. This shift led to the inclusion of ethical principles emphasizing respect for diversity and non-discrimination in early counseling codes.

Another significant development was the growing recognition of informed consent as a fundamental ethical principle. Borrowed from medical ethics, this concept was adapted to the counseling field, where treatment often involved exploring deeply personal issues rather than physical interventions. Ensuring that clients fully understood the counseling process became a core ethical responsibility.

As the field of counseling matured, so did its ethical framework. What began as informal ethical practices gradually evolved into structured ethical codes developed and published by professional organizations. These codes not only provided guidance for practitioners but also served as a means of public accountability.

This transition from informal ethics to formalized standards marked a defining moment in the professionalization of counseling. It was a collective effort to establish clear ethical responsibilities, reinforcing counseling as a distinct profession with its own guiding principles. The foundational work of this era paved the way for today's comprehensive ethical codes, which address key issues such as confidentiality, professional competence, informed consent, and managing multiple relationships.

ETHICAL CODES THROUGH THE AGES

The evolution of ethical codes in counseling reflects the profession's deepening commitment to client welfare and professional integrity. The first formal ethical code for counselors emerged in 1961 when the American Personnel and Guidance Association (APGA), now the American Counseling Association (ACA), established its initial ethical standards. This foundational document set the stage for future guidelines, addressing core principles such as confidentiality, professional competence, and client autonomy.

As the counseling profession expanded and societal norms evolved, ethical codes underwent significant revisions. The mentioned, ACA has updated its code approximately every seven to ten years, with major revisions in 1974, 1981, 1988, 1995, 2005, and 2014. Each update has reflected new challenges in the field, from shifting cultural expectations to advancements in technology and clinical practice.

A comparison of ethical codes across different counseling organizations reveals both shared values and unique emphases. The ACA Code of Ethics, widely regarded as a comprehensive framework, provides broad guidelines applicable to various counseling specialties. In contrast, the American Mental Health Counselors Association (AMHCA) Code of Ethics delves deeper into issues specific to clinical mental health counseling, such as the ethical use of technology and managing multiple relationships. Meanwhile, the American School Counselor Association (ASCA) Ethical Standards for School Counselors focus on dilemmas unique to educational settings, including the balance between student confidentiality and parental rights.

While all three codes uphold fundamental ethical principles, their differences highlight the specialized nature of each counseling discipline. The ACA's broad framework serves as a foundation for the profession, while the AMHCA and ASCA codes tailor ethical guidance to the distinct challenges faced by clinical mental health counselors and school counselors, respectively.

Over time, ethical codes have adapted to address contemporary challenges in the counseling profession. One of the most significant shifts has been the integration of technology into counseling practice, prompting the inclusion of guidelines on electronic record-keeping, online counseling, and social media interactions. The ACA's 2014 revision notably expanded these sections, reflecting the profession's ongoing adaptation to digital advancements.

The effectiveness of each iteration of ethical codes can be measured by their responsiveness to emerging issues. For example, the 1995 ACA Code of Ethics introduced more specific guidelines on multicultural competence, acknowledging the increasing awareness of diversity in counseling. This update demonstrated the profession's commitment to adapting ethical standards in response to societal changes and professional needs.

Several pivotal figures have shaped the development of counseling ethics, including Gerald Corey, whose work on ethical decision-making has had a lasting influence. Corey's emphasis on self-awareness and continuous ethical reflection has been incorporated into various ethical codes and training programs, reinforcing the importance of thoughtful, ethical practice.

Different ethical codes balance specificity and flexibility in various ways, each with its strengths and weaknesses. Highly detailed codes, such as AMHCA's, offer clear guidance on specific scenarios but may require frequent updates to stay relevant. In contrast, broader frameworks, like the ACA's, allow for flexibility in interpretation but may leave counselors with less concrete direction in complex situations.

The prominence of certain ethical guidelines often reflects broader societal trends. For instance, the increased focus on informed consent and client rights in the 1980s and 1990s paralleled a growing emphasis on individual autonomy in healthcare ethics. Similarly, today's heightened focus on cultural competence mirrors broader conversations about diversity, equity, and inclusion.

Ethical codes are likely to converge around universal challenges such as technological integration and cultural competence, as these issues impact all counseling disciplines. However, divergence may persist in areas specific to different counseling contexts, for example, school counselors must navigate ethical considerations related to working with minors and educational institutions, while clinical mental health counselors may face distinct challenges related to diagnosis and treatment planning.

LANDMARK CASES SHAPING COUNSELING ETHICS

The evolution of counseling ethics has been profoundly influenced by landmark legal cases that have redefined professional responsibility and client rights. One of the most pivotal cases mentioned earlier is *Tarasoff v. Regents of the University of California* (1976), which fundamentally reshaped the ethical and legal boundaries of confidentiality in therapy.

The case involved Prosenjit Poddar, a graduate student at the University of California, Berkeley, who confided to his therapist that he intended to kill Tatiana Tarasoff, a woman who had rejected his romantic advances. Although the therapist expressed concerns and attempted to have Poddar detained, no direct warning was given to Tarasoff or her family. Tragically, Poddar carried out his threat and murdered Tarasoff two months later.

The *Tarasoff* ruling presented a critical ethical dilemma: balancing a therapist's duty to maintain client confidentiality with the responsibility to protect potential victims from harm. The California Supreme Court's decision established the *duty to protect*, requiring mental health professionals to take reasonable steps to prevent foreseeable harm when a client poses a serious threat to another person. This ruling created an exception to therapist-client confidentiality in cases of imminent danger.

The court's reasoning centered on the concept of foreseeability and the special relationship between therapist and client. It argued that mental health professionals, given their training and expertise in assessing dangerous behavior, have an obligation to act when a threat is credible. This decision had immediate and far-reaching implications for counseling practice, prompting the development of risk assessment protocols and procedures for handling threats of violence.

The *Tarasoff* decision also influenced ethical guidelines across professional organizations, leading to revisions in ethical codes that clarified when and how confidentiality may be breached in cases of imminent danger. Additionally, many states enacted laws codifying the *duty to warn* or *duty to protect*, ensuring that counselors and therapists had clear legal obligations in such situations.

Expanding the Duty to Protect: Ewing v. Goldstein (2004)

Building upon the *Tarasoff* precedent, the case of *Ewing v. Goldstein* (2004) further expanded the concept of duty to protect. This case involved Keith Ewing, a police officer who died by suicide after his therapist failed to warn Ewing's parents about his suicidal intentions. The key distinction in this case was that the therapist had not received this information directly from Ewing but rather from Ewing's father.

The California Court of Appeal ruled that the duty to protect extends to information received from third parties, not just from the client. This decision broadened the scope of the *Tarasoff* warning, requiring mental health professionals to consider collateral information in their assessment of potential threats. The *Ewing* case underscored the complexity of risk assessment and the need for therapists to gather and evaluate information from multiple sources.

The impact of *Ewing v. Goldstein* on counseling ethics was substantial. It reinforced the importance of a comprehensive approach to threat assessment, urging clinicians to weigh information from family members and other third parties when determining risk. This ruling also highlighted the ethical challenges of balancing confidentiality with the duty to protect, particularly when the information does not come directly from the client.

Protecting Confidentiality: *Jaffee v. Redmond* (1996)

While *Tarasoff* and *Ewing* expanded the duty to protect, the case of *Jaffee v. Redmond* (1996) strengthened confidentiality in counseling. This case arose when a federal court sought to compel the disclosure of therapy notes from counseling sessions between Mary Lu Redmond, a police officer, and her therapist following a fatal shooting incident.

In a landmark decision, the U.S. Supreme Court ruled in favor of protecting the confidentiality of these therapy sessions, recognizing, for the first time, a federal psychotherapist-patient privilege. The Court reasoned that effective psychotherapy relies on trust and confidentiality and that the mere possibility of disclosure could discourage individuals from seeking treatment or fully engaging in therapy.

The ruling in *Jaffee v. Redmond* had profound implications for counseling ethics, reinforcing the legal foundation for protecting client privacy. It established a strong precedent for maintaining the confidentiality of therapeutic communications in federal courts, ensuring that clients could speak openly without fear that their private disclosures would be used against them in legal proceedings.

The *Jaffee* decision had a lasting impact on ethical guidelines, reinforcing the critical role of confidentiality in therapeutic relationships. It provided counselors with a stronger legal foundation for protecting client privacy, even in the face of legal challenges. However, the Court also clarified that, like other testimonial privileges, psychotherapist-patient confidentiality is not absolute and may need to yield in certain circumstances, such as when there is an overriding public interest.

These landmark cases illustrate the evolving nature of counseling ethics and the intricate relationship between legal decisions and professional standards. *Tarasoff* and *Ewing* underscore the ongoing challenge of balancing client confidentiality with the duty to protect, while *Jaffee v. Redmond* affirms the fundamental importance of trust and privacy in the therapeutic process. Together, they highlight how ethical principles in counseling are not fixed but continuously adapt to legal interpretations, societal changes, and the realities of clinical practice.

SOCIETAL INFLUENCES ON ETHICS

The evolution of counseling ethics has been deeply influenced by broader societal movements, reflecting the dynamic interplay between social progress and professional standards. The civil rights era helped push the profession to address systemic bias and promote equitable care, which had been largely shaped by a white, middle-class perspective.

As issues of racial bias, cultural competence, and equitable access to mental health services gained attention, professional organizations responded by revising ethical codes. The American Counseling Association (ACA), for example, incorporated explicit guidelines on cultural sensitivity and non-discrimination. These changes were not without resistance, some practitioners viewed them as the politicization of professional ethics. However, multicultural competence has since become a foundational principle of ethical counseling practice.

Feminist theory has also played a critical role in shaping counseling ethics, particularly regarding power dynamics in the therapeutic relationship. Feminist critiques of traditional psychotherapy highlighted concerns about the misuse of authority and the reinforcement of gender inequalities. These insights prompted a reassessment of ethical standards related to client autonomy, informed consent, and the responsible use of counselor influence.

In response, counseling organizations integrated feminist principles into ethical codes, emphasizing the need to recognize and address power imbalances, promote client empowerment, and adopt a more collaborative approach to therapy. While these changes have led to a more egalitarian counseling model, ongoing debates continue about the balance between counselor expertise and client self-determination.

The LGBTQ+ rights movement has also shaped counseling ethics, particularly regarding sexual orientation and gender identity. As societal acceptance has grown, ethical codes have evolved to explicitly prohibit discrimination and require counselors to develop competence in working with LGBTQ+ clients. These guidelines acknowledge the unique challenges and mental health concerns faced by this population.

However, this ethical shift has sparked controversy, especially among counselors whose personal or religious beliefs conflict with affirmative approaches to LGBTQ+ counseling. This tension has led to legal challenges and ongoing debates about the balance between counselor autonomy and client welfare, with a grown push to ensure equitable services for all individuals (Alegria et al., 2018).

Similarly, disability rights advocacy has influenced ethical standards, driving the push for more accessible and inclusive counseling practices. Ethical codes now emphasize equitable access to mental health services, including considerations of physical accessibility, communication accommodations, and adaptive therapeutic techniques. Counselors are expected to develop competence in working with diverse abilities and to advocate for the rights of clients with disabilities.

These societal influences have fostered a more culturally sensitive and inclusive approach to counseling ethics. However, they also highlight ongoing challenges, such as addressing the intersection of multiple identities, race, gender, sexuality, and disability, and ensuring ethical guidelines remain adaptable across diverse cultural contexts.

Additionally, the rapid pace of technological change presents new ethical dilemmas. Issues such as confidentiality in online counseling and the impact of social media on client-counselor boundaries underscore the need for continuous ethical development. As society evolves, so too must the ethical frameworks guiding the counseling profession.

TECHNOLOGY AND ETHICAL EVOLUTION

Technology has changed the way counselors work, bringing both benefits and challenges. Online counseling and telehealth make mental health care more accessible, especially for people in remote areas or those with physical disabilities. But at the same time, these digital tools raise important ethical questions, how can counselors ensure confidentiality, and does virtual counseling offer the same quality of care as in-person sessions?

Social media also complicates things. Should a counselor accept a friend request from a client? How should they handle online reviews? The internet blurs the lines between personal and professional life, and counselors have to be careful about how their digital presence affects their work and their relationships with clients. Navigating social media boundaries is increasingly important. Chapters 1 and 13 offer examples of how this issue plays out across settings.

Electronic health records (EHRs) have made it easier to keep track of client information, but they also come with risks. Cybersecurity threats, data breaches, and evolving privacy laws mean counselors must be extra cautious about protecting sensitive client information. Ethics in counseling now extend beyond face-to-face interactions to include online security and responsible record-keeping.

Artificial intelligence (AI) and machine learning are changing the way mental health care works. These tools can help detect mental health issues early, suggest personalized treatments, and even enhance therapy sessions. But they also bring ethical concerns, how much should we rely on machines for mental health decisions? Can AI be biased? And how might it affect the relationship between counselors and clients?

One of the biggest concerns is confidentiality. In traditional counseling, privacy is protected by strict rules, but digital tools introduce new risks. Sensitive information shared online must be carefully protected with strong security measures. Counselors need to explain the limits of confidentiality in digital spaces and make sure they're using secure communication platforms.

Informed consent also becomes more complicated with technology-assisted therapy. Clients need to understand the benefits and risks of online counseling, like possible technical issues, data storage policies, and the differences between virtual and in-person sessions. Counselors must ensure that consent is not just a one-time agreement but an ongoing conversation as technology evolves.

In today's digital world, being skilled with technology is no longer optional for counselors, it's an ethical responsibility. As technology evolves, counselors must continuously update their knowledge, from using digital platforms effectively to understanding cybersecurity risks and the ethical dilemmas that come with emerging tools.

The impact of these changes on society is complex. On the positive side, online counseling and telehealth have made mental health services more accessible, helping people in remote areas or those who might struggle to get in-person care. However, the digital divide remains a challenge, some individuals lack the technology or digital literacy needed to access these services, potentially worsening existing disparities.

To address these ethical challenges, professional organizations have updated codes of ethics, developed specialized training, and provided guidelines for using technology in counseling. While these efforts help counselors navigate new digital realities, they also have limitations. Technology changes rapidly, making it hard for guidelines to stay relevant, and overly rigid rules can become outdated before they are widely adopted.

To keep up with rapid technological changes, the counseling profession must adopt proactive solutions to evolving ethical concerns. Several key strategies could help ensure ethical standards remain relevant and effective:

1. A Continuously Updated Ethical Framework
A dynamic, regularly revised ethical framework could provide up-to-date guidance on technology use in counseling. A multidisciplinary panel, including experts in counseling ethics, technology, and law, could oversee this process. While this approach ensures adaptability to new challenges, it would require ongoing resources and could create confusion if guidelines change too frequently.

2. Integrating Ethics and Technology in Counselor Training

Embedding technology ethics into counselor education would equip future professionals with both technical skills and a strong ethical foundation. This proactive approach prepares new counselors to handle digital challenges from the start. However, it would require significant updates to training programs and constant curriculum adjustments to keep pace with technological advancements.

3. A Centralized Technology Ethics Resource Center

Creating a dedicated resource center could provide counselors with real-time guidance on ethical dilemmas related to technology. This center could offer expert consultations, best practices, and the latest updates on ethical technology use in counseling. While it would be a valuable support system, challenges include securing funding and ensuring the center's recommendations remain widely recognized and accepted.

As you consider implementing these solutions, the counseling profession can better navigate the ethical complexities of an increasingly digital world while maintaining its core commitment to client well-being and professional integrity.

GLOBALIZATION OF COUNSELING ETHICS

As the world becomes more interconnected, counseling ethics must adapt to diverse cultural perspectives. While certain ethical principles, such as respect for clients and professional integrity, are widely accepted, their interpretation and application can vary across regions.

In Western countries like the United States and much of Europe, ethical standards emphasize individual autonomy and confidentiality, reflecting societies that prioritize personal rights and independence. These ethical codes are shaped by legal precedents, professional organizations, and academic research.

In contrast, many non-Western cultures prioritize community well-being and family harmony. In these settings, ethical decision-making may involve family members or community leaders, which can sometimes conflict with Western counseling norms that stress client privacy and self-determination.

Global institutions like the World Health Organization (WHO) and the United Nations (UN) play a crucial role in promoting universal ethical principles for mental health care. The WHO's *Mental Health Action Plan 2013–2020*, for example, highlights human rights and evidence-based care as global priorities.

However, applying these international guidelines is challenging, as cultural values and local practices often differ. Balancing global ethical principles with cultural sensitivity remains a key issue in the evolution of counseling ethics worldwide.

One big challenge in counseling around the world is finding a balance between rules that everyone agrees on and rules that fit different cultures. For example, ideas like "doing good" (beneficence) and "not doing harm" (non-maleficence) are accepted almost everywhere, but how people actually use these ideas can change a lot from one place to another. In some cultures, the idea of informed consent, where someone agrees to treatment after learning all the facts, is understood differently because decisions are made by families or groups instead of just one person.

In Western countries, counseling ethics developed a lot in the mid-1900s. Leaders like Carl Rogers helped shape ideas that focus on treating each person with respect and letting them make their own choices (Rogers, 1957). On the other hand, many non-Western countries mix counseling ethics with their own cultural and spiritual traditions. For example, in many Asian cultures, ideas like harmony and respect for elders (influenced by Confucian thinking) guide how counseling is done, which can be quite different from Western practices (Chen & Davenport, 2005; Tu, 1998).

Global guidelines, like those from the International Association for Counselling, try to create a common set of rules for counselors everywhere. They stress the importance of human rights, understanding different cultures, and being good professionals. But sometimes, these rules can be too general and might miss important details that are special to certain cultures. This shows that we need rules that are both universal and flexible enough to respect local traditions.

In some situations, local ethical standards may be more effective than global ones. For example, when dealing with family relationships or spiritual beliefs, ethical guidelines developed within a specific culture may be better suited to addressing those issues. On the other hand, global standards are often more useful when handling universal human rights concerns or working in multicultural settings where different ethical perspectives must be balanced.

Creating a global ethical framework that respects cultural differences while maintaining core principles is both a challenge and an opportunity for the counseling field. One possible solution is a tiered ethical system, where universal ethical values are upheld alongside culturally specific guidelines. This approach would require collaboration among international organizations, local counseling associations, and cultural experts to ensure that ethical standards remain relevant and inclusive.

Another way to integrate diverse perspectives is through case-based ethical reasoning. By examining real-world ethical dilemmas from multiple cultural viewpoints, counselors can gain a deeper understanding of how ethical principles apply in different contexts. This method helps bridge the gap between general ethical guidelines and their practical use in diverse cultural settings.

The globalization of counseling ethics also highlights the importance of continued cross-cultural dialogue and research. Comparing how ethical decisions are made in different cultures can provide valuable insights into both shared values and culturally specific approaches to counseling. Such research can also improve ethical training programs, helping counselors navigate the complexities of multicultural or international practice.

FUTURE DIRECTIONS IN ETHICS

Over the next twenty years, counseling ethics are expected to undergo significant changes as new challenges and societal shifts emerge. As mental health care evolves, ethical guidelines will need to adapt to address fresh concerns, all while keeping the core values of doing good (beneficence) and avoiding harm (non-maleficence).

One major area of change is the integration of advanced technologies into counseling. Breakthroughs in artificial intelligence, virtual reality, and brain-computer interfaces offer exciting opportunities to enhance therapy. For instance, AI-driven therapy platforms could increase access to mental health care and standardize treatment protocols (Luxton, 2014). However, these tools also raise tough questions. They might change the nature of the counselor-client relationship since AI lacks the deep understanding of human emotions and the genuine empathy that human counselors provide (Robin et al., 2024).

As these technologies collect and analyze vast amounts of personal data, ensuring data privacy becomes even more critical. Counselors will need to be clear about what clients can expect in terms of confidentiality and how their information is protected (Barnett & Scheetz, 2003).In short, while advanced technologies promise to transform counseling in exciting ways, ethical guidelines must keep pace. Future frameworks will have to balance innovation with the timeless human elements of empathy and trust, ensuring that technology supports rather than replaces the personal connection between counselor and client.

Another important trend in counseling ethics is the move toward greater cultural relativism. As our world becomes more interconnected, it's clear that one-size-fits-all, Western-centered ethical models might not work everywhere. In the future, ethical guidelines may need to be more flexible and sensitive to local customs, values, and healing traditions (Pedersen, 2003). After all, what works in one culture might not be the best fit in another, and trying to enforce one universal standard can sometimes be both impractical and unfair.

That said, there are challenges with this approach. Some worry that too much cultural relativism could lead to inconsistencies and even undermine essential ethical principles. Striking the right balance between honoring cultural diversity and upholding core values like human rights and dignity will be a key challenge as ethical guidelines continue to evolve (Sue & Sue, 2016).

In addition, there's a growing push to integrate social justice into counseling ethics. This means recognizing that counselors do more than just help individual clients, they also have a role in addressing larger systemic inequalities. With increased awareness of mental health disparities and the broader impact of social conditions on well-being, future ethical guidelines might explicitly include social justice advocacy as part of a counselor's responsibilities (Toporek et al., 2009). This would expand the idea of doing good from focusing solely on individual care to making a positive impact on society as a whole.

Supporters of this approach argue that counselors are in a unique position to recognize and address systemic barriers to mental health. They believe ethical practice shouldn't stop at the therapy room but should also engage with larger social issues that impact clients' well-being. However, this perspective raises important questions: Where should the boundaries of a counselor's role be drawn? And how can counselors balance their responsibility to individual clients with broader social justice efforts?

Different professionals have different views on where counseling ethics should go next. Some welcome new technology as a way to improve therapy, while others worry it could make counseling feel less personal.

Similarly, while some believe that incorporating social justice into ethical guidelines is necessary, others wonder whether it might complicate the counselor's primary role, helping the individual sitting across from them.

Policy makers also have their own challenges to consider. If ethical guidelines become more culturally flexible, how do we make sure client safety and professional accountability still come first? If social justice becomes a formal part of counseling ethics, will licensing requirements and professional codes need to change? As society evolves, so too must counseling ethics, but figuring out how to do that effectively is an ongoing and complex discussion.

The impact of these evolving ethical directions will be significant. As counseling ethics continue to develop, they will shape everything from how therapy is practiced to how future counselors are trained. Counseling and psychology programs may need to update their curricula, adding courses on technology ethics, cultural competence, and social justice advocacy to prepare students for the changing landscape.

These shifts could also affect how the public views the counseling profession. A stronger focus on technology in ethical guidelines might make counseling feel more relevant in today's digital world. At the same time, an emphasis on cultural diversity and social justice could position counselors as key voices in broader societal discussions and policy-making. As the field evolves, so too will its role in shaping the future of mental health care.

3

SELF-CARE: AN ETHICAL

IMPERATIVE

THE ETHICAL FOUNDATION OF SELF-CARE

Self-care in counseling is not just a personal choice, it's an ethical responsibility. Professional organizations like the American Counseling Association (ACA), the American Mental Health Counselors Association (AMHCA), and the American School Counselor Association (ASCA) all emphasize its importance in their codes of ethics. These guidelines recognize that a counselor's well-being directly affects their ability to provide effective care.

Self-care refers to intentional practices that support physical, mental, and emotional health. Given the emotional demands of counseling, maintaining personal well-being is crucial for avoiding burnout and ensuring high-quality support for clients.

Two core ethical principles highlight why self-care is essential:

- Beneficence (promoting the well-being of others): Counselors must be at their best to effectively help their clients.
- Non-maleficence (avoiding harm): If a counselor is overwhelmed or emotionally exhausted, it could negatively affect their clients.

Research supports this connection. A study by Lawson and Myers (2011) found that counselors with higher wellness levels experienced greater job satisfaction and reported better client outcomes. This reinforces the idea that self-care isn't a luxury, it's a professional obligation.

The COVID-19 pandemic further emphasized the critical role of self-care in counseling. Mental health providers faced numerous stressors, including the abrupt transition to telehealth, increased client acuity, and the blurring of personal and professional boundaries. A study by Mittal et al. (2023) found that counselors reported heightened emotional exhaustion, disrupted work-life balance, and diminished capacity for empathy, underscoring the risk of burnout and compassion fatigue during the pandemic

These findings highlight the urgent need for sustainable self-care practices to support counselors' well-being in crisis conditions.

Neglecting self-care doesn't just affect individual counselors, it impacts clients and the profession as a whole. Burned-out counselors may struggle with empathy, provide less effective therapy, and face a higher risk of ethical violations. This can lead to subpar client care, potential harm, and even a decline in public trust in the counseling field. Additionally, widespread burnout contributes to high turnover rates, further straining an already understaffed mental health workforce.

A common misconception is that prioritizing self-care is selfish or unnecessary. In reality, counselor well-being is directly linked to ethical and effective practice. Taking care of oneself enhances resilience, cognitive functioning, and emotional availability. A study by Dorociak et al. (2017) found that counselors who regularly practiced self-care experienced lower burnout and higher job satisfaction, which directly improved their client interactions and outcomes.

Self-care isn't an indulgence, it's a professional responsibility that benefits both counselors and the people they serve.

The ethical codes of the ACA, AMHCA, and ASCA emphasize that self-care is not optional, it is a professional responsibility. For instance, the ACA Code of Ethics (2014), Section C.2.g, states:

"Counselors monitor themselves for signs of impairment from their own physical, mental, or emotional problems and refrain from offering or providing professional services when impaired."

This directive makes it clear that maintaining well-being is an ethical duty, ensuring that counselors can provide safe, effective care.

Beyond individual responsibility, self-care is also embedded in professional development and supervision. Ethical supervisors are expected to model and encourage self-care practices among their supervisees, helping them build sustainable habits early in their careers and is discussed further in supervision contexts in Chapter 6. This aligns with the ethical principle of justice, as it ensures counselors remain capable of providing high-quality care consistently over time.

Recognizing self-care as an ethical imperative protects both counselors and clients. It enhances professional effectiveness, prevents burnout, and strengthens the integrity of counseling services. The challenges of the COVID-19 pandemic have only reinforced its importance, making self-care more essential than ever.

As the field of counseling continues to evolve, self-care will remain an obligation of ethical practice, not as a luxury but as a necessity.

PHYSICAL WELL-BEING FOR COUNSELORS

Taking care of your physical health is just as important as supporting your clients' mental well-being. However, many counselors overlook this aspect of self-care. The job often involves long hours of sitting, deep emotional engagement, and high levels of stress, all of which can take a toll on the body.

Many counselors experience issues like muscle pain, poor posture, headaches, and even heart-related concerns. Sitting for long periods during client sessions, paperwork, and administrative tasks can lead to stiffness, weak muscles, and a higher risk of conditions like obesity and diabetes. On top of that, the emotional intensity of counseling can show up in physical ways, tension headaches, stomach problems, and trouble sleeping (Figley, 2002; Skovholt & Trotter-Mathison, 2016).

The demands of counseling don't just affect mental well-being, they can take a serious toll on physical health, too. Managing client caseloads, meeting productivity expectations, and upholding ethical standards all contribute to chronic stress. Over time, this constant pressure can lead to high cortisol levels, a weakened immune system, and a greater risk of illness (Norcross & Guy, 2007). On top of that, the emotional weight of counseling, especially exposure to clients' trauma, can lead to compassion fatigue, making physical health problems even worse (Figley, 2002).

When counselors are physically unwell, their ability to provide quality care can suffer. Fatigue, discomfort, or stress can make it harder to stay fully present in sessions, which may impact a client's experience. Additionally, poor physical health can impair cognitive function, making it more difficult to navigate ethical dilemmas or make sound decisions in emotionally charged situations.

Some organizations have tried to address these challenges through workplace wellness programs, offering gym memberships or on-site fitness classes. Others have focused on ergonomic solutions, such as standing desks or supportive chairs. While these initiatives acknowledge the importance of physical health, they don't always fully address the unique demands of the counseling profession (Baker, 2003).

Improving physical health among counselors requires intentional strategies that fit within the demands of the profession. Several potential solutions could help address this issue:

1. **Incorporating Movement into Counseling Sessions**

Encouraging movement throughout the workday can be a game-changer. Simple practices like stretching between sessions or offering walking therapy when appropriate can increase physical activity and even enhance client engagement. However, challenges may include maintaining professional boundaries and ensuring clients feel comfortable with a non-traditional session format.

2. **Scheduled Self-Care Time**

Allocating specific time for physical activity, meditation, or other wellness practices during the workday can promote better health and job satisfaction. This approach signals strong organizational support for well-being. However, some workplaces may resist, fearing productivity losses, and it may be difficult to implement consistently across different counseling settings.

3. **Integrating Physical Well-being into Counselor Education**

Teaching future counselors about physical health, stress management, and the physiological impact of counseling could create long-term change. Adding this content to counselor training programs would provide early intervention and encourage lasting healthy habits. However, challenges include revising curricula, ensuring faculty expertise, and balancing this material with existing educational requirements.

Successfully implementing these solutions requires overcoming key challenges, especially gaining organizational support. Many of these strategies involve changes to established work routines, making leadership buy-in essential. Long-term success depends on fostering a workplace culture where physical well-being is seen as a fundamental part of professional competence. Reframing physical health as an ethical responsibility, rather than just a personal choice, can help reinforce its importance.

Practical Tips for Everyday Well-being

Counselors can take simple steps to improve their physical health, even within a demanding work schedule:

- **Move More:** Set reminders to take short breaks for movement, such as stretching at your desk, taking a brief walk between sessions, or using a stability ball instead of a traditional chair.
- **Eat Well:** Prepare nutrient-dense meals that support cognitive function and energy levels, avoiding the temptation of quick but unhealthy options.
- **Prioritize Sleep:** Stick to a consistent sleep schedule and create a relaxing nighttime routine, such as reducing screen time before bed, to improve rest and recovery.

By integrating small, sustainable habits into their daily routines, counselors can enhance their physical well-being, ultimately improving both their personal health and professional effectiveness.

EMOTIONAL RESILIENCE IN PRACTICE

Emotional resilience is essential for counselors, helping them manage the challenges that come with their work. Developing this resilience is a step-by-step process that requires self-awareness, stress management, and consistent practice.

Step 1: Strengthening Self-Awareness
Self-awareness is the foundation of emotional resilience. Understanding personal triggers and emotional responses allows

counselors to navigate difficult situations more effectively. Mindfulness practices and emotion-tracking apps can be useful tools for developing this skill. While facing uncomfortable emotions can be challenging, starting with brief daily reflection periods can make the process more manageable.

Step 2: Practicing Stress Management Techniques

Once self-awareness is established, counselors can build resilience by incorporating stress management strategies. Techniques like meditation, deep breathing, and progressive muscle relaxation are easily accessible through apps and online resources. The biggest challenge is often finding time to practice these skills consistently. One solution is to integrate them into daily routines, such as during commutes, between sessions, or before bedtime, making them easier to maintain.

Step 3: Establishing Emotional Boundaries

Maintaining a healthy separation between professional and personal emotions is essential for resilience. Counselors can develop this skill through boundary-setting worksheets, professional development workshops, and intentional transitional rituals, such as a short walk or meditation, between work and personal time. The challenge lies in balancing empathy with self-protection, but small, consistent practices can help reinforce these boundaries.

Step 4: Building a Support Network

Having a strong support system is crucial. Connecting with colleagues, mentors, or peer support groups provides emotional support and professional guidance. However, seeking help can feel vulnerable. A manageable starting point is establishing trust with one colleague or supervisor before expanding to a broader network. Professional associations also offer valuable resources for support.

Step 5: Practicing Ongoing Self-Reflection

Regular self-reflection helps counselors assess their emotional state and the effectiveness of their resilience strategies. Journaling and self-assessments are useful tools, but consistency can be challenging. Scheduling regular check-ins, whether weekly or monthly, can turn self-reflection into a habit that strengthens long-term resilience.

Each of these resilience-building steps works together to create a strong foundation for emotional well-being:

- **Self-awareness** helps counselors recognize areas that need attention and growth.
- **Stress management techniques** provide practical tools for handling emotional challenges.
- **Emotional boundaries** prevent burnout by distinguishing professional empathy from personal emotional involvement.
- **A strong support network** offers outside perspectives and emotional reinforcement.
- **Continuous self-reflection** ensures that resilience strategies evolve over time.

Developing emotional resilience is not just beneficial for personal well-being, it also strengthens ethical counseling practice. Resilient counselors can maintain professional objectivity, even in emotionally charged situations, allowing them to make sound ethical decisions based on judgment rather than emotional reactions. Additionally, resilience helps sustain long-term empathy and compassion, reducing the risk of compassion fatigue and ensuring high-quality care for clients (Skovholt & Trotter-Mathison, 2016).

Counselors who cultivate emotional resilience create a more stable and supportive therapeutic environment, which is essential for client progress. They can effectively manage countertransference, preventing their own emotions from interfering with the therapeutic process. Furthermore, by demonstrating healthy emotional regulation and coping strategies, resilient counselors serve as positive role models for clients, indirectly helping them build their own emotional resilience. This, in turn, enhances the overall effectiveness of therapy.

PROFESSIONAL BOUNDARIES AND SELF-CARE

Take Dr. Smith (fictional), a counselor who gives everything to clients but does not practice her own self-care. Dr. Smith works at a busy community mental health clinic. Known for being dedicated, Dr. Smith often stays late to accommodate extra sessions, responds to client emails after hours, and skips breaks to finish documentation. Over time, signs of emotional exhaustion begin to appear. Dr. Smith forgets to follow up on a client's safety plan and becomes noticeably irritable in supervision. Eventually, a client files a complaint after a crisis session is canceled due to illness, but no notification was provided in time.

The fictional example of Dr. Smith illustrates how poor boundaries and lack of self-care can result in ethical risk. These issues are explored in greater depth in Chapters 5 and 15. While dedication to clients is admirable, taking it to extremes, such as working long hours, being constantly available, and neglecting personal needs, can ultimately harm both the counselor and the quality of care provided.

At first, the erosion of professional boundaries may seem minor, answering emails late at night, skipping lunch breaks, or taking on extra sessions. However, over time, these small concessions can lead to significant burnout and an unhealthy work-life balance. Dr. Smith's experience underscores the importance of setting clear boundaries, not only for personal well-being but also as a model for clients, demonstrating the value of maintaining a healthy separation between work and personal life.

Dr. Smith's fatigue and irritability are clear signs of burnout, a condition marked by emotional exhaustion, depersonalization, and a diminished sense of personal accomplishment. When counselors experience burnout, it can negatively impact client care, leading to decreased empathy, reduced therapeutic effectiveness, and even ethical lapses in judgment.

To prevent burnout and uphold ethical standards, counselors should integrate the following principles into their professional routines:

1. **Establish Clear Boundaries** – Define and communicate specific limits on availability, including office hours, response times for emails, and policies for after-hours contact. These boundaries create a sustainable therapeutic relationship for both counselor and client.

2. **Prioritize Self-Care** – Engaging in self-care is a professional necessity, not a luxury. Maintaining a work-life balance, participating in personal therapy, pursuing hobbies, and ensuring proper rest and nutrition are essential.

3. **Recognize Burnout Signs Early** – Counselors should stay attuned to symptoms of stress and burnout, both in themselves and colleagues, to intervene before serious consequences arise.

4. **Implement Time Management Strategies** – Scheduling buffer time between sessions and setting aside designated periods for administrative tasks can reduce stress and reinforce professional boundaries.

5. **Utilize Supervision and Peer Support** – Regular consultation with supervisors and colleagues offers valuable reflection, problem-solving, and emotional support.

6. **Engage in Ethical Decision-Making** – When faced with boundary dilemmas, counselors should follow a structured ethical decision-making process, considering both client well-being and personal health.

7. **Develop Professional Resilience** – Coping strategies, such as mindfulness, stress reduction techniques, and ongoing professional development, help counselors navigate the emotional demands of their work.

8. **Advocate for Systemic Change** – Addressing workplace issues like excessive caseloads and inadequate resources can help create healthier work environments for counselors.

These strategies require ongoing reflection and adjustment. For example, Dr. Smith could reassess her work schedule and set designated times for checking client emails instead of responding throughout the day. By maintaining this boundary, she protects her personal time while also managing client expectations more effectively.

Another valuable strategy is the delegation of responsibilities. By sharing her workload, Dr. Smith could alleviate stress while enhancing overall client care through a collaborative approach. This aligns with the ethical principle of beneficence, ensuring that clients receive support from a counselor who is not overextended or fatigued.

Dr. Smith's case highlights the risks of neglecting professional boundaries and self-care. It serves as a reminder that counselor well-being and ethical practice are deeply interconnected. By maintaining clear boundaries, prioritizing self-care, and embracing strategies like delegation, counselors can continue to provide effective, ethical care to their clients while protecting their own mental and emotional health.

PREVENTING AND ADDRESSING BURNOUT

Burnout is a serious challenge in the mental health profession, affecting both counselors and their clients. It develops as a result of prolonged occupational stress, often stemming from the emotionally demanding nature of therapeutic work. Counselors frequently engage with clients facing trauma, crisis, or severe mental health issues, making them particularly vulnerable to emotional and physical exhaustion (Maslach & Leiter, 2016).

The symptoms of burnout are wide-ranging and impactful. Physically, counselors may experience chronic fatigue, insomnia, and a weakened immune system. Emotionally, burnout can lead to feelings of cynicism, detachment, and a diminished sense of personal accomplishment. Cognitively, counselors may struggle with focus, decision-making, and creative problem-solving, essential skills for effective therapy (Skovholt & Trotter-Mathison, 2016).

Beyond personal well-being, burnout has serious ethical and professional consequences. A counselor experiencing exhaustion or detachment may struggle to provide the level of care their clients need. Recognizing and addressing burnout is not only vital for the counselor's health but also for maintaining ethical, effective therapeutic practice (Barnett et al., 2007).

Burnout in counseling arises from a combination of individual and systemic factors. Counselors regularly engage with clients facing trauma, grief, and complex psychological challenges, requiring a high level of emotional investment. Without adequate self-care and professional support, this emotional labor can lead to compassion fatigue and emotional exhaustion (Figley, 2002).

Chronic workplace stress further exacerbates burnout. Heavy caseloads, administrative burdens, and limited resources create an ongoing strain that can leave counselors feeling overwhelmed and depleted (Leiter & Maslach, 2009).

The ethical implications of burnout are particularly concerning. Emotionally exhausted counselors may struggle to maintain appropriate boundaries, increasing the risk of ethical violations or diminished client care. Cognitive impairments associated with burnout, such as difficulty concentrating or making sound clinical decisions, can result in suboptimal treatment or overlooked client needs. Additionally, burnout can erode a counselor's empathy and therapeutic presence, both of which are essential for effective and ethical counseling (Norcross & Guy, 2007).

Efforts to prevent and address counselor burnout have yielded mixed results. Individual-focused strategies, such as mindfulness training and cognitive-behavioral techniques, can enhance resilience and stress management. However, these approaches often place the burden solely on the counselor, overlooking systemic issues that contribute to burnout. Organizational interventions, such as workload management and enhanced supervision, tackle these broader challenges but can be difficult to implement consistently across

A more effective approach requires a combination of individual and systemic solutions:

- **Peer Support Groups**: Regular, structured peer support groups within counseling organizations could provide a space for counselors to share experiences, strategies, and emotional support. This fosters a sense of community, reduces professional isolation, and promotes resilience through collective problem-solving. However, challenges may include ensuring consistent participation and maintaining confidentiality, especially in smaller practice settings.
- **Comprehensive Wellness Programs**: Organization-wide wellness initiatives tailored to the unique needs of counselors could integrate stress reduction techniques, professional development, and regular burnout screenings. A holistic approach like this allows for early intervention and ongoing support. However, securing adequate resources and ensuring participation without adding to counselors' workloads can be significant hurdles.

A third approach to combating burnout involves redesigning counseling work environments to prioritize counselor well-being. This could include:

- **Restorative Spaces** – Quiet areas within the workplace where counselors can decompress between sessions.
- **Flexible Scheduling** – Allowing for adjustments that accommodate personal and professional needs.
- **Technology Integration** – Streamlining administrative tasks to reduce paperwork and free up time for direct client care.

These changes address systemic contributors to burnout, but implementation may require financial investment and organizational shifts, challenges that may be difficult for resource-constrained settings.

Early detection of burnout symptoms is equally important. Regular, confidential assessments using validated burnout measures could be integrated into supervision practices. For counselors showing signs of burnout, interventions might include:

- Temporary caseload reductions
- Increased supervision and peer support
- Mandatory restorative leave to prevent long-term exhaustion

Though potentially disruptive in the short term, these strategies are essential for maintaining both professional sustainability and ethical practice.

Burnout prevention isn't just an individual effort, it's a shared responsibility among counselors, organizations, and the broader professional community. Organizations have an ethical duty to foster supportive work environments by:

- Reassessing caseload expectations
- Providing resources for professional development
- Encouraging a culture where seeking support is normalized rather than stigmatized

Professional associations and regulatory bodies also play a crucial role. Incorporating burnout prevention into ethical guidelines and continuing education requirements can help establish counselor well-being as a professional standard. Additionally, advocacy for improved funding and recognition of the emotional demands of counseling is key to creating lasting, systemic change.

ETHICAL CONSIDERATIONS IN PERSONAL THERAPY

Should counselors participate in personal therapy? This question has sparked ongoing debate in the mental health field. It involves key considerations such as professional growth, ethical responsibilities, and personal well-being.

In the past, some believed that personal therapy might interfere with a counselor's objectivity. However, modern perspectives increasingly recognize its benefits.

Supporters argue that personal therapy enhances self-awareness, an essential skill for effective counseling. By working through their own emotions, biases, and challenges, counselors gain valuable insights that help them connect with clients more deeply. For example, a counselor who has addressed personal attachment issues may better understand and support clients facing similar struggles (Orlinsky et al., 2011).

Should counselors be required to engage in personal therapy? This debate raises important issues about privacy, autonomy, and professional development.

Opponents of mandatory therapy argue that counselors should have the freedom to decide based on their individual needs. They also highlight practical concerns, such as financial costs and time commitments, which could create unnecessary barriers to entering the profession.

On the other hand, personal therapy can help counselors manage countertransference, the emotional reactions they have toward clients. Research suggests that those who undergo therapy themselves are often better equipped to recognize and regulate their emotional responses, maintaining clear professional boundaries. For example, a counselor who has processed personal grief in therapy may be less likely to project unresolved emotions onto a grieving client (Hayes, Gelso, & Hummel, 2011).

As understanding of the counseling profession evolves, more training programs encourage or even require personal therapy for trainees. This reflects a growing recognition of its role in professional competence (Rønnestad & Skovholt, 2003). However, its effectiveness depends on factors like the quality of the therapist, the issues being addressed, and the counselor's willingness to engage in the process.

A major benefit of personal therapy is that it allows counselors to experience therapy from a client's perspective. This firsthand understanding can enhance empathy and provide insight into the challenges clients face. Additionally, it offers an opportunity to observe effective therapeutic techniques in action (Orlinsky et al, 2011).

Despite these benefits, mandating therapy for all counselors has drawbacks. A universal requirement may not suit everyone's needs, and some may view it as a bureaucratic obligation rather than a meaningful growth opportunity. This could reduce its overall effectiveness (Norcross, 2005).

In some cases, personal therapy can be especially valuable for counselors. Those working with trauma survivors or in high-stress environments may rely on therapy to process vicarious trauma and maintain their own mental well-being. Likewise, counselors facing personal challenges or major life transitions may benefit from professional support (Figley, 2002).

Ethical concerns arise when counselors seek therapy within their professional community. Dual relationships, where the therapist and client have additional connections outside of therapy, must be carefully managed. To avoid conflicts, counselors may need to seek therapists from outside their immediate professional circles or in different geographic areas (Zur, 2007).

Despite increasing acceptance of personal therapy, stigma still lingers. Some professionals may worry that seeking therapy will be seen as a sign of weakness or incompetence. To combat this, professional organizations and training programs can work to normalize therapy, emphasizing its role in ongoing professional development rather than framing it as a deficiency (Guy et al., 1989).

Considering what was just discussed, personal therapy could become more formally integrated into professional development for counselors. This might include incorporating reflective practices and personal growth components into continuing education or ethical guidelines. However, such initiatives must strike a balance, promoting the benefits of therapy while respecting individual autonomy and diverse professional needs.

SUPERVISION AS A SELF-CARE TOOL

Supervision can be a powerful self-care tool for counselors, combining professional development with personal well-being. This process begins with recognizing the need for supervision, not just for clinical guidance but also for managing stress and maintaining mental health. Self-assessment tools like reflection journals and questionnaires can help counselors identify areas where supervision can provide support. However, some may hesitate to share vulnerabilities, making it important to view supervision as a proactive and strength-based approach to growth.

Choosing the right supervisor is a key step. An effective supervisor offers both professional insight and support for self-care. Counselors can explore professional networks and supervisor profiles to find a good match, but the real challenge lies in selecting someone whose approach and personality align with their needs. An initial meeting to discuss expectations and supervisory styles can help ensure a productive working relationship.

To make the most of supervision, counselors should identify specific self-care concerns and goals beforehand. Tools like supervision preparation worksheets and case conceptualization forms can help clarify priorities. A common challenge is balancing discussions about client cases with personal well-being. To address this, counselors can set aside time in each session specifically for self-care topics, ensuring their own needs are not overlooked.

Reflective practice during supervision allows counselors to explore their personal reactions and self-care needs in depth. Tools like Gibbs' Reflective Cycle and mindfulness exercises can facilitate this process (Gibbs, 1988; Germer, 2009). However, a common challenge is distinguishing between personal struggles and professional development needs. Practicing self-compassion in these discussions helps create a non-judgmental space for exploring experiences and identifying areas for growth (Neff, 2003).

However, a common challenge is distinguishing between personal struggles and professional development needs. Practicing self-compassion in these discussions helps create a non-judgmental space for exploring experiences and identifying areas for growth.

Applying feedback and strategies from supervision is key to strengthening self-care practices. Action plans and goal-setting frameworks can help translate insights into concrete steps. However, maintaining consistency with new self-care strategies can be difficult. Setting small, realistic goals and tracking progress in subsequent supervision sessions can improve follow-through. This approach also fosters accountability while allowing supervisors to provide ongoing guidance and adjustments.

Regularly assessing the impact of supervision on well-being and professional effectiveness ensures its continued value. Well-being scales and professional quality of life measures offer quantitative data, while reflective journaling provides deeper, qualitative insights. Since subtle improvements can be hard to measure, combining both approaches can give a well-rounded understanding of how supervision supports self-care and professional growth.

A structured approach to supervision as a self-care tool plays a crucial role in maintaining ethical standards and preventing burnout in counseling. By integrating personal well-being with professional growth, supervision helps counselors manage the complex demands of their work. Reflective practice within supervision enhances self-awareness, allowing counselors to recognize early signs of stress or ethical dilemmas. With the support and guidance of a supervisor, they can navigate these challenges more effectively.

Implementing concrete self-care strategies from supervision sessions fosters resilience and long-term sustainability in practice. As counselors refine their self-care routines, they build a strong foundation for maintaining their well-being over time. This proactive approach is essential for preventing burnout, a significant concern in the counseling profession.

Supervision also reinforces the ethical dimensions of counseling. Regularly examining personal reactions and professional challenges in a supportive setting helps counselors maintain clear boundaries, manage countertransference, and ensure their well-being does not interfere with client care (Bernard & Goodyear, 2019; Ladany et al., 2005). Ongoing evaluation of supervision's impact further strengthens ethical practice, encouraging continuous self-improvement and adherence to professional standards (Borders et al., 2014).

DEVELOPING A PERSONALIZED SELF-CARE PLAN

Creating a personalized self-care plan is essential for counselors, serving as a proactive strategy to maintain both professional competence and personal well-being. The process begins with a thorough self-assessment, requiring honest reflection on current self-care practices. Counselors must evaluate different aspects of their lives to identify strengths and areas needing improvement. For example, a counselor might recognize regular exercise as a strength while acknowledging difficulties in maintaining a healthy work-life balance.

Alongside self-evaluation, it is important to assess personal and professional stressors. These may include high caseloads, challenging clients, administrative pressures, or personal life events that impact professional functioning. Identifying these stressors helps lay the groundwork for targeted self-care strategies.

After the self-assessment, setting SMART (Specific, Measurable, Achievable, Relevant, Time-bound) self-care goals ensures a structured approach. Instead of a vague goal like "improve work-life balance," a SMART goal would be "leave the office by 6 PM at least four days a week for the next month." This level of specificity allows for clear tracking and progress evaluation. Prioritizing goals based on urgency and importance ensures that the most critical aspects of self-care receive immediate attention.

Choosing the right self-care strategies is a crucial step in developing a personalized plan. Effective self-care should address multiple areas of well-being, including physical, emotional, professional, social, and spiritual health.

- **Physical self-care** might involve regular exercise, balanced nutrition, and maintaining good sleep habits.
- **Emotional self-care** could include mindfulness meditation, journaling, or engaging in therapy.
- **Professional self-care** may focus on time management, setting boundaries, or pursuing continuing education.
- **Social self-care** involves maintaining healthy relationships while setting clear boundaries with clients and colleagues.
- **Spiritual self-care** doesn't have to be religious, it can include meditation, spending time in nature, or engaging in activities that foster a sense of connection and purpose.

For a self-care plan to be effective, it must be realistic and sustainable. Counselors should create a manageable schedule that integrates self-care into their daily routine, such as setting aside specific times for exercise, reflection, or social activities. Identifying potential barriers, like time constraints or lack of motivation, is also key. If time is a challenge, brief self-care activities, such as short mindfulness exercises between client sessions, can be helpful alternatives.

Having a strong support system increases the likelihood of maintaining self-care habits. Colleagues, supervisors, friends, and family can offer encouragement and accountability. Joining or forming a self-care accountability group provides a structured space to share challenges, successes, and strategies, fostering motivation and collective problem-solving.

Regular monitoring and evaluation are essential for ensuring a self-care plan remains effective. Using tools like mobile apps or journals to track progress can provide concrete insights into adherence and impact. Regular check-ins, whether self-reflective or. with a supervisor or peer, offer valuable opportunities to assess what's working, identify challenges, and make necessary adjustments.

For a self-care plan to remain viable long-term, flexibility is key. As professional responsibilities and personal circumstances shift, self-care strategies should evolve accordingly. Adjusting the plan as needed ensures it stays relevant and continues to support ethical practice and professional well-being.

Counselors may face obstacles when implementing a self-care plan, such as resistance to change, difficulty maintaining consistency, or feelings of guilt about prioritizing self-care. Overcoming these challenges often requires a mindset shift, recognizing that self-care is not a luxury but a professional and ethical necessity. Strategies to stay on track include:

- **Starting small** – Implementing gradual changes makes new habits more sustainable.
- **Seeking support** – Colleagues, supervisors, or accountability partners can provide encouragement.
- **Reframing self-care** – Viewing self-care as essential to ethical and effective counseling helps reduce guilt and reinforces its importance.

Take the time to integrate self-care into your daily practice and adapting as needed. Doing so can help maintain both your well-being and professional effectiveness over time.

4

--------------------◦(つ⌒◡⌒つ)◦--------------------

CULTURAL VALUES AND
ETHICAL DECISION-MAKING

Cultural values play a crucial role in shaping ethical decision-making in counseling. The intersection of cultural norms, personal beliefs, and professional standards requires a thoughtful, adaptable approach to ethical practice. Cultural competence, the ability to work effectively with individuals from diverse backgrounds, is essential for navigating these complexities.

Derald Wing Sue's tripartite model of cultural competence highlights three key components (Sue, Arredondo, & McDavis, 1992):

- **Awareness** – Recognizing one's own cultural biases and assumptions and understanding how they may influence therapeutic interactions.

- **Knowledge** – Developing an informed understanding of different cultural worldviews, historical contexts, and the sociopolitical factors affecting various groups.
- **Skills** – Applying cultural awareness and knowledge in practice, including using effective communication and culturally responsive interventions.

Cultural values significantly impact ethical decision-making in counseling. Moral reasoning, or the process of determining right from wrong, is shaped by cultural norms and societal expectations. For example, in individualistic cultures, ethical decisions may prioritize personal autonomy and self-determination. In contrast, collectivistic cultures often emphasize group harmony and interdependence, which may lead to different ethical considerations in therapy.

By integrating cultural competence into ethical decision-making, counselors can provide more inclusive, respectful, and effective care.

Cultural differences significantly shape ethical choices in counseling, particularly when navigating the balance between individual and collective values.

In individualistic cultures (common in many Western societies), ethical principles often emphasize client confidentiality and personal autonomy. In contrast, collectivistic cultures prioritize family and community well-being, which can create ethical dilemmas. For example, a counselor working with an adolescent from a collectivistic background may struggle to balance the client's right to privacy with cultural expectations of parental involvement in decision-making. As discussed cultural ethics can differ sharply between individualistic and collectivist worldviews. These dynamics are revisited in the context of diagnosis in Chapter 16.

Religious and spiritual beliefs also influence ethical considerations in counseling, often serving as moral guides for clients. Counselors must carefully navigate the intersection of religious values and professional ethics, especially when beliefs conflict with evidence-based therapeutic approaches. Ethical concerns may arise when religious or spiritual practices impact client welfare, requiring counselors to balance cultural respect with adherence to professional standards.

NAVIGATING CONFLICTS BETWEEN CULTURE AND ETHICS

Conflicts between cultural norms and ethical guidelines are common in counseling. Examples include:

- **Gender roles and sexual orientation** – Some cultural beliefs may conflict with ethical standards promoting equality and non-discrimination.
- **Parenting practices** – Cultural traditions involving corporal punishment or strict parenting may clash with child protection guidelines.

To address these challenges, counselors must develop cultural self-awareness through ongoing reflection and self-examination. This includes recognizing personal biases, privileges, and limitations. Continuous cultural learning, through professional development, immersion experiences, and engagement with diverse communities, further enhances counselors' ability to navigate ethical complexities effectively.

By integrating cultural competence into ethical decision-making, counselors can provide respectful, informed, and ethical care across diverse client populations.

Applying ethical principles flexibly while maintaining professional integrity requires a careful balance. Counselors must adapt to cultural differences without compromising core ethical values. Strategies for achieving this balance include:

- **Reframing ethical dilemmas** within the client's cultural context
- **Consulting culturally informed colleagues** for guidance
- **Utilizing culturally appropriate decision-making models**

Consider a counselor working with a client from a culture where arranged marriages are the norm. The client feels distressed about an impending marriage but believes refusing is not an option due to family expectations. This presents an ethical dilemma: respecting cultural values while supporting the client's autonomy and well-being.

A thoughtful approach may involve:

- Exploring the client's emotions and concerns within their cultural framework
- Facilitating family discussions if appropriate and welcomed by the client
- Helping the client develop coping strategies that honor both their cultural background and personal needs

Another case example involves a counselor who works with a refugee client who has experienced significant trauma. However, the client's cultural beliefs about mental health stigma prevent them from fully engaging in trauma-focused therapy. The counselor faces an ethical challenge: how to provide effective treatment while respecting the client's cultural perspective.

A culturally sensitive approach might include:

- **Incorporating traditional healing practices** alongside evidence-based interventions
- **Framing mental health discussions** within a culturally relevant and acceptable framework
- **Involving trusted community leaders or cultural brokers** to bridge understanding and reduce stigma

These examples highlight the complexity of ethical decision-making in multicultural counseling. By developing cultural competence, maintaining ethical integrity, and applying flexible problem-solving strategies, counselors can navigate these challenges effectively, ensuring both ethical and culturally responsive practice.

ETHICAL STANDARDS ACROSS CULTURES

Ethical standards in counseling are built on universal principles like doing good (beneficence) and avoiding harm (non-maleficence). However, the way these principles are applied can vary widely across cultures. In Western countries, ethical codes from organizations like the American Mental Health Counselors Association (AMHCA), American School Counselor Association (ASCA), and American Counseling Association (ACA) emphasize individual autonomy, confidentiality, and informed consent. These values align with the individualistic mindset common in Western societies. In contrast, many non-Western cultures place greater importance on collective harmony and social responsibility, shaping ethical practices in different ways.

Take the concept of autonomy, for example. Western counseling ethics prioritize a client's right to make independent decisions. However, in cultures that emphasize interdependence, such as those in Asia, Africa, and parts of Latin America, decision-making is often a family or community matter. In Japan, the idea of *amae* (which reflects a sense of trust and dependence in relationships) can challenge the Western focus on self-determination (Doi, 1973). A counselor working with a client from such a background might need to consider involving family members in discussions rather than focusing solely on individual choice.

Confidentiality, another key pillar of Western counseling, can also be complicated in collectivist cultures. In many Middle Eastern and African societies, personal matters are often seen as family concerns rather than private issues. A counselor working within these cultural contexts may face ethical dilemmas when a client's well-being is at stake, but family involvement is expected. For example, in collectivist cultures, it is common for decision-making and disclosure to involve extended family networks, which can conflict with Western confidentiality norms (Al-Krenawi & Graham, 2000; Bhugra & Bhui, 1997). Striking the right balance between respecting cultural norms and upholding professional ethics requires flexibility and cultural awareness.

Understanding these cultural differences is essential for ethical counseling. Counselors must navigate the complexities of diverse worldviews while maintaining professional integrity. This means being open to alternative ways of supporting clients, whether that involves adapting confidentiality practices, incorporating family into the counseling process, or reframing autonomy in a culturally relevant way (Fernando, 2010; Moodley & Palmer, 2006).

Attitudes toward mental health and help-seeking behaviors differ widely across cultures, shaping the ethical landscape of counseling. In many Western societies, seeking professional psychological help has become more accepted, with stigma gradually decreasing. In contrast, mental health issues in many non-Western cultures remain taboo and are often interpreted through religious or spiritual beliefs. These cultural differences require counselors to adapt their ethical approaches when engaging clients and discussing treatment options (Sue & Sue, 2016).

The evolution of counseling ethics also reflects cultural history and societal values. In the United States, modern counseling ethics emerged in the mid-20th century, influenced by figures like Carl Rogers, who emphasized client-centered therapy and individual autonomy (Rogers, 1957). Meanwhile, in China, counseling ethics developed alongside political and social reforms, leading to a more state-guided approach (Zhao et al., 2011). In India, the blending of ancient philosophical traditions with contemporary psychological principles has created a unique ethical framework that integrates spiritual and holistic elements (Chadda & Deb, 2013).

Each cultural perspective on counseling ethics has its strengths and challenges. Western models prioritize individual rights and self-actualization, making them effective for empowering clients. However, they may fall short in addressing collective needs, which are central to many non-Western cultures. Collectivist ethical frameworks, on the other hand, excel in fostering social harmony and community support but can sometimes overlook individual autonomy. Counselors working in multicultural environments must be able to navigate these differing ethical expectations with sensitivity and flexibility (Pedersen, 2003).

In certain situations, one ethical approach may be more effective than another. For example, in crisis interventions or disaster-stricken communities, a collectivist approach that emphasizes community support may be more beneficial. However, when dealing with cases of abuse or human rights violations, Western ethical principles that prioritize individual protection and advocacy may be more appropriate. Understanding these cultural nuances allows counselors to provide ethical, client-centered care while respecting diverse worldviews.

Creating a more culturally inclusive ethical framework is both a challenge and an opportunity in the counseling field. It requires balancing cultural relativism with universal ethical principles, ensuring that ethical decision-making remains both culturally sensitive and professionally sound. One promising approach involves developing ethical models that incorporate cultural values while maintaining core professional standards. Additionally, integrating indigenous healing practices into ethical guidelines can create a more holistic and inclusive approach to counseling.

While fundamental ethical principles, such as respect for human dignity and professional competence, are widely recognized across cultures, their interpretation and application can vary significantly. Western counseling ethics tend to emphasize individual autonomy, while many Eastern and African traditions prioritize social harmony and collective well-being. This difference requires counselors to adopt a flexible, culturally informed approach to ethical decision-making, especially in multicultural settings (Sue, Arredondo, & McDavis, 1992; Moodley, 2007).

Confidentiality, as aforementioned, remains a cornerstone of ethical practice, is a prime example of these cultural variations. In many Western contexts, confidentiality is considered absolute, with only a few legal exceptions. However, in many non-Western cultures, information sharing within family or community networks is expected, making strict confidentiality more complex. Counselors working across cultural boundaries must navigate these differences thoughtfully, finding ethical solutions that honor both professional standards and cultural expectations (Fernando, 2010; Ekmekci & Arda, 2017).

The counseling profession can move toward a more inclusive framework that respects diverse values while maintaining professional integrity when counselors embrace cultural competence and ethical adaptability. This ongoing evolution in ethical practice is essential for providing effective, culturally responsive care in an increasingly interconnected world (Pedersen, 2003; Ratts et al,, 2016).

LANGUAGE BARRIERS AND ETHICAL PRACTICE

Language barriers in counseling create ethical challenges that can significantly impact the therapeutic process and client outcomes. These challenges go beyond simple linguistic differences, extending to cultural nuances, communication styles, and power dynamics that may hinder effective counseling. In multicultural settings, navigating these complexities requires a thoughtful and ethical approach (Tribe & Thompson, 2009; Sue & Sue, 2016).

One common solution is working with interpreters, but this introduces its own ethical considerations. The presence of a third party can affect confidentiality, alter the therapeutic dynamic, and influence the client's willingness to share sensitive information. To minimize these risks, interpreters must be carefully selected and trained to maintain neutrality, accurately convey emotional content, and uphold confidentiality (ACA, 2014; Tribe, 2007). Still, even with a skilled interpreter, subtle misinterpretations or cultural differences in expression can impact the counselor's understanding of the client's experiences.

Bilingual counselors provide a more direct alternative, allowing for communication in the client's native language without the need for an intermediary. This can foster a stronger therapeutic alliance and reduce the likelihood of miscommunication. However, bilingual counselors must navigate the complexities of working between two linguistic and cultural frameworks, ensuring they accurately interpret cultural nuances that shape mental health perceptions and treatment approaches (Perez Foster, 1998).

Language and communication styles present some of the most subtle yet pervasive challenges in multicultural counseling. These nuances go beyond vocabulary, encompassing nonverbal cues, idiomatic expressions, and culturally specific understandings of mental health and well-being. Misinterpreting these elements can lead to misdiagnosis, inappropriate treatment plans, or a weakened therapeutic relationship (Hall, 1976; Comas-Díaz, 2012).

The ethical issues arising from language differences have multiple root causes. Miscommunication is a primary concern, as translating psychological concepts across languages and cultures is inherently complex. This can create misunderstandings about the client's concerns, therapy goals, or treatment approaches. Additionally, power imbalances may arise when clients struggle to express themselves or fully understand their counselor, potentially leading to feelings of disempowerment or reluctance to engage in therapy (Tribe & Thompson, 2009).

Language barriers also complicate fundamental ethical responsibilities such as obtaining informed consent. Clients who do not fully grasp the counseling process, their rights, or the potential risks and benefits of treatment may be unable to provide truly informed consent. Confidentiality becomes another concern, especially when interpreters are involved or when cultural norms around privacy differ from Western counseling models (ACA, 2014; Pugh & Vetere, 2009).

A strong therapeutic alliance is essential for effective counseling, but language barriers can weaken this bond. Clients may feel less understood or disconnected from a counselor who does not share their language or cultural perspective. This can lead to reduced engagement in therapy, premature termination, or less favorable outcomes (Norcross & Wampold, 2011).

Existing strategies to address these challenges include professional interpreters, cultural competence training for counselors, and multilingual counseling resources. While helpful, these approaches have limitations. Interpreters, for instance, may not always be available or affordable. Cultural competence training is valuable but cannot provide in-depth familiarity with every cultural and linguistic background a counselor may encounter (Sue, Arredondo, & McDavis, 1992).

Several solutions warrant consideration to strengthen ethical practice in the face of language barriers. One promising approach is the development of technology-assisted translation tools tailored for counseling settings. These tools could provide real-time, accurate translation of both verbal and nonverbal communication. While they offer immediacy and potentially greater accuracy than human interpreters, they also raise concerns about data privacy and the loss of human nuance in communication (Luxton, 2014).

Another potential solution is implementing comprehensive language and cultural immersion programs for counselors. These programs would combine intensive language training with extended cultural immersion experiences, equipping counselors with a deeper understanding of their clients' linguistic and cultural contexts. While highly effective, such programs require significant resources and may be difficult to implement on a large scale (Pedersen, 2003).

A third potential solution is the establishment of peer support networks that match clients with culturally and linguistically aligned groups. Facilitated by trained bilingual and bicultural professionals, these groups could offer culturally relevant support and complement traditional counseling services.

As counselors leverage community resources, this approach could help bridge language and cultural gaps while reinforcing the effectiveness of counseling interventions. However, ensuring quality control and seamless integration with professional counseling services may present challenges.

Implementing these solutions comes with obstacles. Technology-assisted translation tools require significant investment in development, testing, and ongoing refinement. Language immersion programs for counselors demand time and financial resources, making large-scale implementation difficult. Peer support networks require careful coordination and oversight to maintain ethical standards and professional integrity.

Ultimately, addressing language barriers in counseling is not just about translation, it is an ethical imperative. Counselors have a responsibility to ensure effective communication and cultural understanding in their practice. This includes actively seeking solutions, advocating for resources to support multilingual and multicultural counseling, and continuously refining their ability to provide ethically sound services (ACA, 2014; Comas-Díaz, 2012).

Counselors can uphold their ethical obligations and improve the quality of care for all clients, regardless of linguistic or cultural background by acknowledging the profound impact of language on the counseling process and working to eliminate barriers.

RECOGNIZING AND CHALLENGING CULTURAL BIAS

Cultural biases can be one of the biggest challenges in ethical counseling, often influencing decisions in ways we may not even realize. To provide fair and effective care, counselors need to make a conscious effort to recognize and address their own biases. This requires ongoing self-reflection, education, and a willingness to challenge long-held assumptions. Later chapters discuss how unchecked bias can shape diagnosis (Ch. 16) and affect ethical decision-making (Ch. 5).

One of the most important tools in this process is **self-reflection**. Counselors who take the time to examine their own beliefs and experiences are better equipped to recognize how those factors shape their perceptions of clients. For example, someone raised in a middle-class household might not fully understand the daily struggles of a client facing extreme financial hardship. Without awareness, it's easy to make assumptions that could affect the counseling process. Research shows that when counselors actively work on cultural awareness, clients feel more understood and engaged in therapy (Owen et al., 2011).

That said, self-reflection has its limits. It's easy to get stuck in our own heads, overanalyzing every thought and action instead of focusing on what the client needs at the moment. Some biases are so deeply ingrained that we may not even recognize them on our own. That's where education and training come in.

Workshops, seminars, and training on cultural competence can help counselors recognize unconscious biases and improve their ability to work with diverse clients. Learning about microaggressions, for instance, can help counselors become more mindful of subtle, unintentional forms of discrimination. Studies show that counselors who engage in ongoing multicultural training are better equipped to navigate cultural differences and avoid missteps that could harm the therapeutic relationship.

However, education alone isn't a cure-all. Just knowing about different cultures doesn't automatically erase bias. It takes real effort to apply that knowledge in meaningful ways. Some of the most effective learning happens outside of structured training, through conversations with colleagues, engagement with diverse communities, and real-world experiences that challenge our perspectives.

Ultimately, recognizing and addressing cultural bias is an ongoing process. It's not about achieving perfection but about staying open, reflective, and willing to grow. The best counselors aren't those who claim to be free of bias but those who actively work to challenge it every day.

One of the most powerful ways to challenge cultural biases is through direct, real-world experiences. Immersing oneself in different cultural settings can foster empathy in ways that books and lectures simply can't. A counselor who participates in a cultural exchange program, for example, doesn't just learn about another culture, they experience it firsthand. Seeing the world through someone else's eyes can break down stereotypes and deepen understanding in a way that theoretical learning often fails to do. Research on empathy development backs this up, showing that real-world exposure to different cultures can improve cross-cultural communication and lead to more meaningful therapeutic relationships.

However, just like reflection, experiential learning also has its limitations. A single trip abroad or a short-term cultural immersion program doesn't guarantee a well-rounded perspective. There's always the risk of overgeneralizing, assuming that one experience with a particular culture applies universally. Some critics also point out that counselors who rely too much on personal experiences may miss the bigger picture of cultural diversity, systemic issues, and historical contexts that shape client experiences.

Different counselors may approach bias in different ways, depending on their own backgrounds. Those from dominant cultural groups often focus on learning about other cultures developing skills to work effectively with diverse populations. Meanwhile, counselors from marginalized backgrounds might emphasize systemic change, advocating for greater awareness of historical trauma, discrimination, and power imbalances. For example, a white counselor may focus on understanding cultural customs, while a counselor from an underrepresented group may stress the importance of addressing racial disparities in mental health care.

Ultimately, there's no single solution to overcoming cultural bias, it requires a mix of self-reflection, education, and direct engagement. Counselors can integrate different approaches by regularly reflecting on their own biases, pursuing ongoing multicultural training, and actively engaging with diverse communities. This could mean keeping a journal to track personal biases, attending cultural workshops, and participating in local events that offer a deeper understanding of different traditions and perspectives.

The key takeaway? Cultural competence isn't a one-time achievement, it's an ongoing process. One could argue that best counselors are those who remain curious, open-minded, and committed to challenging their own assumptions every step of the way.

Working with a refugee family from a war-torn country presents unique ethical challenges that require sensitivity, flexibility, and cultural awareness. Counselors must navigate issues related to trauma, cultural adjustment, and differing beliefs about mental health, all while ensuring ethical and effective care.

One key challenge is the difference between individualistic and collectivistic values. Western counseling often focuses on individual autonomy, helping clients make independent choices and express personal emotions. However, many cultures prioritize family unity and group harmony over individual needs. If a counselor only applies a Western approach, they risk overlooking the family's values and potentially harming the therapeutic relationship. Instead, they might need to adapt trauma interventions to include family members or integrate traditional healing practices that align with the client's worldview (Chung & Bemak, 2002).

Language barriers also create ethical concerns, especially when using an interpreter. While interpreters are essential for communication, they can impact confidentiality and alter the nuances of what the client shares. To address this, counselors must explain confidentiality rules clearly, use trained interpreters when possible, and find culturally relevant ways to discuss mental health so clients feel understood and respected. These considerations are addressed further in Chapters 13 and 17, where interpreter use, informed consent, and group dynamics are explored.

A counselor's decision to seek guidance from a cultural expert reflects a strong commitment to ethical practice and cultural humility. It acknowledges that no counselor can fully understand every cultural background and that consulting experts help bridge knowledge gaps. This aligns with the ethical principle of beneficence, ensuring clients receive the most informed and culturally responsive care. However, it also raises confidentiality concerns, as bringing in an outside expert requires careful handling of client information.

Another challenge is countertransference, particularly when hearing trauma stories from refugees. The counselor must be aware of their own emotional reactions to the family's experiences of war and displacement. Without proper self-reflection and supervision, personal biases or distress could unintentionally affect the therapeutic process.

One possible alternative is referring the family to a counselor from a similar cultural background. This could enhance understanding and trust, aligning with the principle of nonmaleficence, avoiding harm. However, this solution isn't always practical. Specialists may not be available, and cultural matching alone doesn't guarantee a good fit. Instead, all counselors should strive to build strong cross-cultural competencies rather than assuming a shared background is enough.

Another approach is providing extensive psychoeducation about Western counseling methods to help the family understand the process. While this might improve communication, it also risks imposing Western values on clients whose cultural perspectives on mental health and healing may differ. Finding a balance between informed consent and cultural sensitivity is key.

This case highlights two essential lessons:

1. Cultural humility is an ongoing process. Instead of aiming for perfect cultural competence, counselors should remain open to learning from clients and adapting their approach as needed.
2. Ethical guidelines must be applied flexibly. For example, the Western principle of individual autonomy may need to be reinterpreted when working with collectivist cultures that emphasize family or community decision-making. Similarly, confidentiality expectations may differ when family involvement in treatment is the norm.

More broadly, this case highlights why true cultural competence goes beyond simply knowing about different cultures. It's not just about understanding customs or traditions, it's about developing real skills in cultural assessment, adapting interventions, and handling ethical dilemmas that arise in diverse counseling settings. Counselors need to be flexible and open, engaging in ongoing conversations with clients about their values, expectations, and experiences. Culture doesn't just shape how mental health concerns appear, it also influences how clients view therapy, their relationships with counselors, and what they expect from the process.

CULTURAL SENSITIVITY IN ETHICAL STANDARDS

Applying ethical standards with cultural sensitivity starts with a thoughtful cultural assessment. This means taking the time to understand a client's background, values, and beliefs, but doing so in a way that avoids assumptions or stereotypes. Tools like cultural genograms, interviews, or structured assessments can help, but the key is asking open-ended questions and actively involving clients in the conversation. This approach ensures counselors get an authentic picture of the client's cultural perspective.

Next, counselors need to review ethical standards through a cultural lens. This means critically examining professional codes and cultural competence guidelines to recognize any potential biases. Because many ethical frameworks are shaped by Western perspectives, it's important to consult colleagues from diverse backgrounds and stay informed about multicultural ethics research.

Finally, cultural contextualization is essential, meaning ethical principles should be interpreted within the client's cultural framework rather than applied rigidly. This step often involves seeking guidance from cultural consultants or referencing scholarly work on cross-cultural ethics. The challenge is finding a balance between universal ethical principles (like respect and autonomy) and cultural relativism, understanding that what's ethical in one culture might look different in another.

Ethical decision-making, the fourth step, involves applying culturally aware reasoning to real-world counseling situations. Many counselors use ethical decision-making models adapted for multicultural contexts to navigate this process. A key challenge here is managing personal biases and cultural countertransference, the counselor's emotional reactions are influenced by cultural differences. Taking a structured approach and carefully documenting the reasoning behind decisions can help ensure clarity and transparency.

The fifth step is implementing ethical decisions through culturally appropriate interventions. This might mean adapting evidence-based practices to better fit a client's cultural background. Challenges can arise when clients or colleagues resist culturally adapted approaches or when resources tailored to specific cultural groups are limited. The best way to navigate this is through collaboration with the client and maintaining flexibility in approach, ensuring interventions align with both ethical guidelines and cultural considerations.

The final step is reflection and evaluation. Counselors need to assess how well their interventions are working and refine their approach as needed. This process is supported by supervision, peer consultation, and client feedback. One challenge in this phase is recognizing subtle cultural missteps, which can be difficult to detect. Additionally, counselors may experience guilt or defensiveness when realizing they've made an error. A growth mindset is essential, seeing these moments as opportunities for learning and improvement rather than failures.

ALTERNATIVE APPROACHES TO CULTURAL CONTEXTUALIZATION

Different approaches can enhance how counselors contextualize ethical standards within diverse cultural frameworks. Some practitioners advocate for a dialectical approach, where counselors and clients actively discuss the intersection of ethical standards and cultural values rather than relying solely on pre-existing ethical models (Herlihy & Watson, 2006).

Another strategy involves working with cultural brokers, individuals who serve as intermediaries between the counselor's ethical framework and the client's cultural perspective. Cultural brokers can help bridge misunderstandings and ensure interventions remain both effective and respectful (VanLandingham et al., 2023).

A narrative approach can also be useful. By encouraging clients to share personal stories that illustrate their cultural values and ethical dilemmas, counselors gain a deeper, more contextualized understanding of the client's worldview (White & Epston, 1990).

Technology is increasingly playing a role in culturally informed counseling. Virtual reality simulations **and** interactive case studies provide immersive experiences that help counselors develop cultural sensitivity in ethical decision-making. Additionally, AI-driven cultural competence tools are emerging and designed to help counselors identify potential cultural conflicts and suggest culturally appropriate ethical responses (Zhang & Wang, 2024). While promising, these tools must be used carefully to complement, not replace, human judgment and cultural humility (Warrier et al., 2023).

THE EVOLUTION OF ETHICAL STANDARDS IN DIVERSE SOCIETIES

The ethical standards in counseling have evolved significantly and have been shaped by the growing diversity of societies worldwide. A major turning point came during the Civil Rights Movement of the 1960s, which brought attention to the need for cultural competence in mental health services. One of the most influential figures in this movement was Derald Wing Sue, whose work in multicultural counseling helped redefine ethical standards and practices to better serve diverse populations (Sue et al., 1982).

In the 1980s, the counseling profession took its first major steps toward formalizing multicultural counseling competencies. These competencies provided a structured framework for counselors to work more effectively with clients from different cultural backgrounds (Sue, Arredondo, & McDavis, 1992). At the same time, there was a growing emphasis on increasing diversity within the profession itself, recognizing that a more representative workforce could lead to better, more ethical care.

By the late 20th and early 21st centuries, globalization further transformed counseling ethics. One of the most notable shifts was the recognition of indigenous healing practices, challenging the long-standing dominance of Western psychological models. Ethical counseling now requires cultural humility, acknowledging and respecting non-Western healing traditions. For example, in working with Native American clients, some counselors began incorporating traditional healing ceremonies or collaborating with tribal healers when appropriate (Gone, 2010).

Another critical development was the adaptation of Western counseling models to better fit diverse cultural perspectives. Many of the traditional therapeutic frameworks were rooted in individualism, a concept that doesn't always align with collectivist cultures. Ethical counselors needed to rethink and modify their approaches, ensuring their techniques were both culturally relevant and effective for each client's unique background (Chung & Bemak, 2002).

Counseling across borders brings unique ethical challenges, requiring counselors to navigate complex cross-cultural dynamics. Differences in cultural norms, language barriers, and legal frameworks can complicate ethical decision-making. For instance, the principle of confidentiality, a key value in Western counseling ethics, may not align with collectivist cultures, where family involvement in decision-making is prioritized. Ethical counselors must carefully balance respecting cultural traditions while maintaining professional integrity (Tribe & Thompson, 2009).

In recent years, the field has placed greater emphasis on intersectionality and social justice advocacy. Originating from critical race theory, intersectionality highlights how different aspects of identity, such as race, class, gender, and disability, interact to shape a person's experiences (Crenshaw, 1991). This perspective has pushed counselors to consider how overlapping identities influence their clients' challenges and their own ethical responsibilities.

At the same time, social justice advocacy has become a central part of ethical counseling. Counselors are increasingly recognizing that systemic inequalities, such as racism, poverty, and discrimination, have profound effects on mental health. As a result, the counselor's role has expanded beyond one-on-one therapy to include community involvement, activism, and policy advocacy (Toporek et al., 2009).

Today, the conversation around cultural competence acknowledges that it is not a one-time achievement but an ongoing journey. Ethical counselors commit to continuous self-assessment, education, and engagement with diverse perspectives to ensure their practice remains inclusive and culturally informed. This evolving approach recognizes that learning about culture and ethics is never finished, it requires humility, adaptability, and a commitment to growth (Hook, Davis, Owen, Worthington, & Utsey, 2013).

As artificial intelligence (AI) continues to reshape counseling, new ethical dilemmas are emerging, especially across different cultures. AI-driven therapeutic tools bring concerns about data privacy, algorithmic bias, and the risk of reinforcing cultural stereotypes. To ensure that AI benefits all clients equitably, ethical guidelines must evolve to address these challenges while maintaining cultural sensitivity and fairness (Luxton, 2014). The ethical use of AI in assessment ties into broader digital practice issues discussed in Chapters 7 and 17.

Meanwhile, closing global mental health gaps remains an urgent ethical priority. Expanding access to care in underserved regions is only part of the solution, mental health services must also be culturally appropriate and respectful of traditional healing practices. Achieving this requires collaboration between mental health professionals, policymakers, and community leaders to create sustainable, locally relevant interventions (Patel et al., 2018).

While a universal ethical framework could promote consistency and accountability, it must also respect cultural diversity and adapt to different social contexts. This will require ongoing dialogue between counseling professionals worldwide, along with insights from fields like anthropology, sociology, and global health (Fernando, 2010).

5

ETHICAL COMPLAINTS:

PREVENTION AND RESPONSE

WHERE ETHICAL COMPLAINTS COME FROM

Ethical complaints in counseling can arise from a range of factors, including client dissatisfaction, professional misconduct, and legal-ethical conflicts. Common issues include breaches of confidentiality, boundary violations, and conflicts of interest.

One major challenge comes from the tension between legal and ethical obligations. For example, in cases where following the law contradicts ethical best practices (Herlihy & Corey, 2015), counselors may struggle to balance compliance with doing what is right for the client (ACA, 2014, A.1.b.; AMHCA, 2020, 1.5). Counselors must navigate these situations carefully, considering both legal requirements and ethical principles such as beneficence (acting in the client's best interest) and non-maleficence (avoiding harm) (ACA, 2014, B.1.d.; ASCA, 2022, A.3). This tension between legal requirements and ethical responsibilities are discussed in more detail in Chapter 9.

Miscommunication is another frequent cause of complaints. When treatment expectations, therapy goals, or professional boundaries aren't clearly explained, clients may feel misled or even betrayed. Inadequate informed consent can also leave clients unaware of their rights, leading to ethical disputes.

Boundary violations, from inappropriate self-disclosure to more serious misconduct, are among the most serious ethical issues (ACA, 2014, A.5.a.; AMHCA, 2020, 2.3). Even well-intentioned actions, like getting too personally involved, can compromise the therapeutic relationship and trigger complaints (ACA, 2014, A.5.b.; ASCA, 2022, A.8).

When ethical violations become public, they damage trust in the counseling profession. High-profile cases can discourage people from seeking mental health support while also prompting stricter regulations and increased oversight, which may create additional challenges for ethical practitioners.

Many existing strategies for preventing ethical complaints have varying levels of success:

- Ongoing ethics training keeps professionals aware of key issues, but it may not fully prepare them for real-world ethical dilemmas.
- Peer supervision and consultation provide valuable guidance, but their effectiveness depends on how consistently they are used.
- Professional ethics committees offer oversight and advice, but they often lack enforcement power.

While no single approach is foolproof, a combination of education, supervision, and professional accountability is essential to reducing ethical complaints and maintaining trust in the counseling profession.

Several practical strategies can help tackle these challenges.

First, expanding ethics training beyond traditional lectures could make a big difference. A more hands-on approach, such as case-based learning, role-playing, and ethics mock trials, would allow counselors to practice handling real-world ethical dilemmas. This method reinforces ethical principles through experience rather than just theory. The downside? It takes time, resources, and careful planning to ensure consistency across different work settings.

Another useful strategy is creating a clear, structured, ethical decision-making framework designed specifically for counselors as discussed in previous chapters. This would provide a step-by-step way to navigate ethical conflicts, especially when legal and ethical responsibilities seem to clash. A major benefit is that it could bring consistency to ethical decision-making across the profession. However, there's a risk that it might oversimplify complex issues or be applied too rigidly in situations that require flexibility.

Finally, setting up a proactive client feedback system could help catch ethical concerns early. Regular, anonymous surveys focusing on ethical aspects of care would give clients a voice and allow counselors to address issues before they escalate into formal complaints. This approach promotes transparency and continuous improvement, but it also comes with challenges. Ensuring client privacy, preventing misuse of feedback, and maintaining trust in the therapeutic relationship are all factors to consider.

Of course, implementing these strategies isn't without obstacles. Many counselors are accustomed to existing practices and may resist change.

Smaller counseling practices might struggle with limited resources. And getting professional organizations and regulatory bodies on board is crucial for widespread adoption. Also, ethical challenges in counseling are always evolving, so these approaches need ongoing evaluation and adaptation to stay effective.

RISK MANAGEMENT STRATEGIES

Counselors use both proactive and reactive risk management strategies to handle ethical concerns. While proactive strategies focus on preventing ethical issues before they arise, reactive strategies help address problems as they occur. Each approach has its own strengths: proactive strategies emphasize preparation and prevention, while reactive strategies prioritize quick thinking and adaptability.

Proactive risk management is generally more effective in preventing ethical complaints. By identifying potential risks in advance, counselors can put policies, procedures, and training programs in place to minimize ethical dilemmas. For example, regular ethics workshops, clear documentation guidelines, and structured decision-making frameworks can help reduce the chances of ethical violations. These preventive measures create a stronger ethical foundation and lower the risk of future complaints.

On the other hand, reactive strategies are essential for handling unexpected ethical challenges. Since not every situation can be anticipated, counselors must be able to respond effectively when issues arise. This might involve consulting with colleagues or ethics boards, taking immediate corrective action, or adapting policies based on new situations. While reactive strategies don't prevent ethical missteps, they help manage consequences and prevent similar problems from happening again.

Implementing these strategies requires different levels of time and resources. Proactive approaches often demand a significant upfront investment, such as creating detailed ethical guidelines, conducting ongoing training, and setting up supervision systems. While these efforts take time and resources, they can lead to long-term benefits, including fewer ethical risks and better overall practice quality.

Conversely, reactive strategies require less upfront investment but can be more resource-intensive when ethical issues arise. Since they are used on an as-needed basis, they may be unpredictable and sometimes disruptive to daily practice. However, their flexibility allows counselors to allocate resources only when specific ethical challenges emerge.

Both approaches offer unique benefits in terms of legal protection and professional development. Proactive strategies provide stronger legal protection by demonstrating a counselor's commitment to ethical practice and due diligence in preventing issues. This can be especially helpful in legal disputes, as it shows a consistent effort to uphold ethical standards. Additionally, proactive approaches promote ongoing professional development by encouraging continuous learning and reflection on ethical matters.

While reactive strategies may not offer the same level of legal protection, they highlight a counselor's ability to respond effectively to ethical dilemmas. They also contribute to professional growth by providing hands-on experience in real-world ethical decision-making. This practical experience enhances adaptability and strengthens a counselor's ethical competence.

The choice between proactive and reactive strategies often depends on the specific counseling setting. Proactive strategies work best in environments with predictable ethical challenges, such as large counseling centers or educational institutions. In these settings, standardized protocols and systemic safeguards can significantly reduce ethical risks. They are also ideal for high-stakes ethical concerns, where prevention is crucial to avoid serious consequences.

Reactive strategies may be more suitable for dynamic or unpredictable counseling environments, such as crisis intervention services or community outreach programs. In these settings, flexibility and adaptability are essential, allowing counselors to respond effectively to unique and unforeseen ethical challenges.

For a well-rounded approach to ethical risk management, counseling practices should integrate both proactive and reactive strategies. This means building a strong foundation of proactive measures, such as ethical guidelines, training programs, and supervision structures, while also maintaining the ability to respond reactively when unexpected situations arise. For example, a counseling practice might hold regular ethics review meetings (proactive) while also having a rapid response protocol in place for addressing urgent ethical dilemmas (reactive).

ADDRESSING ETHICAL VIOLATIONS

Addressing ethical violations in counseling starts with identifying and documenting the issue. Counselors must stay alert to potential breaches of ethical standards, which requires a solid understanding of professional codes of conduct and relevant legal guidelines. When a violation is observed or reported, it's essential to document the incident thoroughly, focusing on facts rather than personal opinions. This documentation should include specific details such as dates, times, individuals involved, and any relevant communications or evidence.

Next comes the assessment phase, where the severity and implications of the violation are carefully evaluated. Ethical decision-making models can help structure this analysis, ensuring a thorough and objective approach. Counselors may also seek guidance from supervisors or colleagues to gain different perspectives and reduce personal bias. The assessment should consider factors like potential harm to clients, the impact on the counseling profession, and any broader societal consequences.

Once the situation has been assessed, the next step is to develop a response plan. This requires a deep understanding of professional guidelines and, in some cases, consultation with legal counsel, especially if legal issues are involved. The response plan should outline specific actions, designate responsible individuals, and set clear timelines for implementation. It's important to address both the immediate needs of affected clients and the long-term implications for professional practice and organizational policies.

The next phase is implementing the response plan with care and precision. This may involve notifying relevant authorities, taking corrective action, or initiating disciplinary procedures. Clear, professional communication is essential at this stage, as it can greatly impact how the situation is resolved and how those involved perceive the process. In some cases, mediation services may be used to help facilitate discussions and resolve conflicts, especially when different perspectives or interests are at play.

The final step is follow-up and reflection, which ensures that the measures taken were effective and help prevent future ethical violations. This phase may include ongoing monitoring, reviewing organizational policies, and participating in professional development activities. Counselors and organizations should view ethical violations as opportunities for growth, using lessons learned to improve future practices and protocols.

Each of these steps works together to create a well-rounded approach to addressing ethical violations. Proper documentation lays the foundation for all subsequent actions, ensuring responses are based on facts. A thorough assessment helps shape an appropriate response plan, which is then carried out with careful execution and communication. Finally, follow-up and reflection help reinforce ethical standards, feeding insights back into the system to strengthen future identification and assessment processes.

The approach to addressing ethical violations may vary depending on the severity of the issue. For minor violations, an informal resolution may be more appropriate, focusing on education and mentorship rather than formal disciplinary action. This could include peer consultations or targeted professional development to reinforce ethical standards.

In contrast, serious ethical breaches may require a more formal response, potentially involving external review boards or legal authorities. In such cases, thorough documentation and assessment are especially critical, as they may serve as key evidence in legal proceedings or licensure reviews.

Ethical decision-making in counseling is complex, requiring a structured yet flexible approach. By following a clear process while adapting to each situation's unique circumstances, counselors and organizations can uphold ethical standards, protect client well-being, and maintain the integrity of the profession.

EMOTIONAL IMPACT ON COUNSELORS

It is well known that facing an ethical complaint can have a profound emotional and professional impact on counselors. It is a complex issue that affects not only the individual but also the broader mental health field. Ethical complaints bring psychological, professional, and systemic challenges, making it essential to understand their full implications.

From a professional crisis perspective, an ethical complaint can disrupt a counselor's sense of identity and competence. Licensing board complaints often trigger significant emotional distress, including anxiety, self-doubt, and fear about the future of one's career. Thomas (2005) noted that even when complaints are unfounded or dismissed, the process itself can be psychologically taxing, with many practitioners reporting a sense of demoralization and hypervigilance in their clinical work. This emotional toll may lead counselors to question their clinical judgment, alter how they document sessions, or become more hesitant in risk-related cases, all of which can impact their confidence and long-term practice.

However, the impact of an ethical complaint is not always negative. Some view these challenges as opportunities for professional growth. The *catalyst for improvement* perspective suggests that facing ethical scrutiny can lead to meaningful changes in practice. A study on social workers' experiences with licensing complaints found that while many professionals reported emotional distress during the investigation, several also described positive outcomes, such as increased attentiveness to documentation, enhanced ethical awareness, and strengthened commitment to professional standards (Barsky, et al., 2021). Many took proactive steps, seeking consultation, revisiting ethical codes, or improving clinical procedures, which ultimately improved their confidence and practice.

Interestingly enough, newly licensed counselors and experienced practitioners often view ethical complaints differently. While early-career counselors may feel particularly vulnerable, data shows that certain violations occur across levels of experience. A national analysis of disciplinary actions revealed that many of the most common ethical violations, such as dual relationships, continuing education noncompliance, and misrepresentation of credentials, often reflect broader systemic challenges within the profession (Wilkinson et al., 2019). The prevalence of these violations underscores the importance of stronger support systems and ethics education for all counselors, but especially for those entering the field, who may face increased risk due to lack of experience or limited supervision.

Experienced counselors are often more resilient and able to place ethical complaints within the broader context of their professional journey. Their accumulated knowledge, experience, and support networks can help mitigate the stress of facing a complaint. However, they may also face different challenges, such as the risk of becoming complacent or struggling to adapt long-standing practices to evolving ethical standards.

Each of these perspectives has important implications for counselor education, supervision, and professional development. The professional crisis viewpoint highlights the need for stronger support systems and resilience training in counselor education programs. It also suggests that supervisors should offer not only technical guidance but also emotional support to counselors navigating ethical challenges.

SUPPORT RESOURCES FOR COUNSELORS

When counselors face ethical complaints, they have several key resources to turn to for guidance and support.

Ethics Consultation: Many professional associations, such as the American Counseling Association, California Association for Professional Clinical Counselors and The American Mental Health Counselors Association, offer confidential ethics consultation. These services provide advice on handling ethical dilemmas and understanding complaint procedures. For example, if a counselor is unsure about professional boundaries in a potential dual relationship, they can contact the association for clarification and guidance.

Legal Consultation Services: Access to legal experts is another crucial support option. Many professional liability insurance policies include legal consultation, giving counselors direct access to attorneys who specialize in counseling ethics and malpractice. This helps professionals understand their legal rights and the potential consequences of ethical complaints. However, involving lawyers can sometimes escalate conflicts rather than resolve them, so this option should be used thoughtfully.

Peer Support Groups: Connecting with other counselors who have faced similar situations can be incredibly reassuring. Whether online or in-person, peer support groups allow professionals to share experiences, exchange coping strategies, and find a sense of community. For instance, a counselor struggling with the stress of an ethical complaint might find comfort and valuable advice in a local mental health professional support group. However, it's important to be mindful of confidentiality and the risk of misinformation in informal settings.

Supervision and Consultation: Regular supervision and consultation with experienced professionals can offer valuable perspective, emotional support, and ethical guidance. Individual or group supervision sessions focused on ethical practice create a structured space for reflection and growth. While this resource combines professional development with support, it's important to recognize that a supervisor's dual role as both mentor and evaluator can sometimes create tensions.

Ethics Continuing Education: Ongoing ethics training is a proactive way for counselors to strengthen their professional practice and prevent ethical complaints. Specialized workshops and courses cover topics such as maintaining professional boundaries, best documentation practices, and handling complex ethical dilemmas. By staying informed about ethical standards and risk management strategies, counselors can enhance their confidence and competence in ethical decision-making.

Professional Ethics Committees: Many licensing boards and professional associations have ethics committees composed of experienced professionals. While they do not provide direct advocacy, these committees help counselors interpret ethical codes, understand complaint procedures, and navigate the complaint process more effectively.

Employee Assistance Programs (EAPs): Many workplaces offer Employee Assistance Programs that provide confidential counseling, legal consultations, and stress management resources. For counselors employed by organizations, EAPs can be a useful avenue for addressing both the personal and professional impact of an ethical complaint.

Risk Management Consultations: Professional liability insurance providers often offer risk management consultations to help counselors identify ethical vulnerabilities in their practice. These consultations provide strategies for minimizing risk and addressing potential ethical concerns before they escalate into formal complaints.

Professional Writing Services: Responding to ethical complaints requires clear and well-structured documentation. Ethics-focused writing services can help counselors organize their responses in a way that aligns with professional standards and ethical codes. While counselors must provide the content, these services can assist with structure, tone, and presentation to ensure clarity and professionalism.

When counselors consider using these resources, they can receive professional guidance, enhance their ethical knowledge, and proactively manage potential ethical concerns.

DOCUMENTATION BEST PRACTICES

Effective documentation is a key part of ethical counseling. A well-organized system ensures accurate record-keeping while maintaining confidentiality.

Establishing a Secure Documentation System: Using electronic health records (EHRs) and secure cloud storage helps counselors manage client records efficiently. However, security and accessibility must be carefully considered. For example, a counselor might use a HIPAA-compliant EHR system with multi-factor authentication to keep sensitive client information protected while ensuring easy access for authorized users.

Initial Client Documentation: The first step in record-keeping involves gathering essential client information through standardized intake forms and informed consent. To make the process smoother and less overwhelming, counselors can use electronic signature software for consent forms and ensure all documentation is written in clear, jargon-free language. For instance, instead of using clinical terms like "symptoms of major depressive disorder," a counselor might describe a client's concerns as "feelings of sadness and loss of interest in activities."

Ongoing Session Documentation: Keeping clear and consistent progress notes is crucial for tracking a client's development. Using structured note templates helps streamline this process. Some counselors also use voice-to-text software to quickly dictate notes right after a session while details are fresh. The goal is to balance efficiency with thoroughness. For example, a well-documented progress note might read: *"The client reported reduced anxiety symptoms this week. Discussed and practiced deep breathing techniques. Client expressed willingness to continue daily mindfulness exercises."*

Thorough documentation of ethical decision-making is essential for both preventing and addressing ethical complaints. When counselors face complex ethical dilemmas, they should carefully record their reasoning, consultations, and final decisions.

Using Ethical Decision-Making Models: Structured frameworks help counselors document their thought processes clearly. For example, a counselor might write: *"Faced with a potential duty-to-warn situation. Applied the ACA ethical decision-making model. Consulted with supervisor (Dr. Jane Smith) on 5/15/2024. Decision: The client does not meet the criteria for imminent threat. Will continue to monitor and reassess in future sessions."*

A quick note – although the ethics might have been applied in this situation – counselors are expected to know and follow all applicable laws which may have required additional steps.

Regular Documentation Review: Reviewing records periodically helps ensure accuracy, completeness, and compliance with ethical standards. This can be done through self-audits or peer reviews. For instance, a counselor might conduct monthly file reviews using a checklist to verify adherence to documentation guidelines. Peer review sessions with colleagues can also provide valuable feedback and help identify areas for improvement.

Adapting Documentation Practices to Different Settings: Counseling environments vary, so documentation approaches should be tailored accordingly. In private practice, a solo practitioner might rely on self-audits and external consultations, while larger institutions often have established peer review processes or dedicated quality assurance staff. Similarly, the choice of documentation tools depends on the setting, small practices might use cloud-based EHR systems, whereas larger organizations may have integrated platforms that combine documentation and practice management.

Simply by maintaining detailed and accurate records of client interactions, ethical considerations, and decision-making processes, counselors create a clear trail of their professional conduct. Strong documentation practices not only uphold ethical standards but also serve as a critical safeguard if complaints arise.

PROFESSIONAL LIABILITY INSURANCE

Having professional liability insurance is an essential safeguard for counselors, protecting them against claims of negligence or malpractice. There are two main types of policies: occurrence-based and claims-made insurance. Each has its own benefits and considerations.

Occurrence-Based Policies: These policies cover incidents that happen while the policy is active, even if a claim is filed years later, long after the policy has expired. This long-term protection makes occurrence-based policies a reliable choice, especially for counselors who may retire or switch careers.

Claims-Made Policies: These policies only provide coverage if both the incident and the claim occur while the policy is active (or within a designated reporting period). While claims-made policies are often more affordable upfront, counselors must ensure continuous coverage and may need to purchase "tail coverage" to extend protection after the policy ends.

Understanding these differences is crucial for choosing the right coverage. While occurrence-based policies offer greater peace of mind, claims-made policies require careful management to avoid gaps in protection. Selecting the appropriate policy ensures counselors remain professionally and financially safeguarded throughout their careers.

When dealing with ethical complaints, occurrence-based policies generally offer more reliable protection. Since they cover incidents that happened while the policy was active, regardless of when a claim is filed, there's no risk of coverage gaps, even if a counselor changes insurers or allows a policy to lapse.

Claims-made policies, on the other hand, require more careful management. While they only cover claims filed during the active policy period, they can be customized with retroactive coverage, which extends protection to incidents that occurred before the policy's start date, so long as the claim is made while the policy is still in effect.

Cost Considerations

The cost structure of these policies also differs:

- **Occurrence-based policies** tend to have higher initial premiums but offer stable, predictable costs over time.
- **Claims-made policies** start with lower premiums, but costs increase annually as the policy matures, a process known as step-rating. Over time, this can make claims-made policies more expensive than occurrence-based ones.

Flexibility and Additional Benefits

Both policy types vary in coverage limits, deductibles, and added benefits:

- **Occurrence-based policies** offer straightforward, consistent coverage.
- **Claims-made policies** provide flexibility to adjust coverage limits and deductibles as a counselor's practice evolves.
- Some insurers offer extra benefits, such as **legal consultation services or coverage for licensing board complaints**, which can be valuable for counselors facing ethical challenges.

The decision between **occurrence-based** and **claims-made** policies depends on a counselor's specific needs and career stage.

- **Early-career professionals** or those in **high-risk specialties** may prefer the long-term security of an occurrence-based policy despite its higher initial cost.
- **Established practitioners** with stable practices might find claims-made policies more cost-effective, particularly if they can secure favorable tail coverage terms when retiring.

Practice Setting Considerations

The work environment also plays a role in policy selection:

- **Private practice counselors** may benefit from the simplicity and long-term protection of an occurrence-based policy.
- **Institutional counselors** might opt for claims-made coverage if it aligns with their employer's risk management strategy.

Enhancing Liability Protection

Counselors can strengthen their coverage by combining policies or adding specialized riders. For example:

- A counselor might hold a claims-made policy for primary coverage while supplementing it with an occurrence-based policy for high-risk activities.
- Adding cyber liability coverage or a teletherapy rider can address emerging risks in modern counseling, such as data breaches or remote client interactions.

LEARNING FROM ETHICAL MISSTEPS

The case of Dr. Smith and Sarah highlights the ethical challenges counselors may face, especially in small communities where personal and professional lives often overlap. This situation underscores the complexities of dual relationships and the potential consequences of overlooking ethical concerns.

At first, Dr. Smith saw no harm in maintaining both a therapeutic relationship with Sarah and a shared involvement in a local acting theater group. However, this decision reflects a common mistake in ethical decision-making, underestimating the risks of seemingly harmless social interactions.

As questions about how they knew each other arose within the theater group, Sarah became uncomfortable in therapy, affecting the counseling process. This outcome illustrates why maintaining clear professional boundaries is essential, not just to protect clients but also to uphold the integrity of therapy. Even well-meaning actions can lead to ethical breaches when boundaries are not carefully managed.

Dr. Smith's delay in seeking supervision further highlights an important lesson in ethical complaint prevention: the value of timely consultation. Seeking guidance from a supervisor early on could have provided an objective perspective, helping to navigate the ethical dilemma before it escalated. This case reinforces the importance of ongoing professional development and a strong support network for ethical decision-making.

The hope is that learning from cases like Dr. Smith's, counselors can better recognize ethical pitfalls and take proactive steps to prevent similar issues in their own practice.

The alternative approaches explored in this case offer valuable lessons in ethical prevention. Choosing immediate disclosure and engaging in collaborative decision-making with the client promotes transparency and client autonomy, aligning with the ethical principle of informed consent. On the other hand, withdrawing from the theater group illustrates the sacrifices professionals sometimes must make to uphold ethical standards.

From this case, several key principles can be applied to similar situations involving dual relationships and boundary concerns:

1. **Proactive Awareness:** Counselors should actively identify potential ethical conflicts, particularly in small communities. Regular self-reflection and environmental awareness help detect risks early.
2. **Transparent Communication:** Openly discussing potential conflicts of interest with clients fosters trust and allows for collaborative problem-solving.
3. **Prioritizing Professional Ethics:** When personal and professional roles conflict, the counseling role must take precedence, sometimes requiring personal sacrifices to maintain ethical integrity.
4. **Regular Consultation:** Seeking supervision and peer input should be a standard practice, especially when facing complex ethical dilemmas.
5. **Thorough Documentation:** Keeping detailed records of ethical decision-making, consultations, and client discussions ensures accountability and can be invaluable in the event of a complaint.
6. **Boundary Reinforcement:** Consistently establishing and maintaining professional boundaries helps prevent ethical breaches and protects the therapeutic relationship.

7. **Ethical Decision-Making Models:** Using structured frameworks for ethical dilemmas ensures that all relevant factors are considered before making a decision.

The case of Dr. Smith and Sarah reflects larger ethical challenges in the counseling profession. It highlights the importance of continuous ethical education, professional support networks, and proactive decision-making. Again, taking note of these ethical missteps is a great way for counselors to develop stronger ethical practices, and improving client care while protecting the integrity of the profession.

6

---◦⌒◡⌒◦---

ETHICS IN SUPERVISION AND CONSULTATION

THE ETHICAL FOUNDATIONS OF SUPERVISION

Ethical supervision in counseling is built on core principles that ensure both supervisees and their clients are treated with fairness, care, and professionalism. These key principles include:

- **Beneficence** – Acting in the best interest of others by supporting the professional growth of supervisees.
- **Non-maleficence** – Avoiding harm by carefully considering the impact of decisions on both supervisees and clients.
- **Justice** – Ensuring fairness by treating all supervisees equally and without bias.

Supervisors have a unique responsibility to guide and support their supervisees while also protecting client welfare. This means creating a learning environment that fosters growth while implementing safeguards to prevent potential harm.

To navigate ethical challenges, supervisors often use decision-making models. These models provide a step-by-step approach to resolving dilemmas, such as:

1. Identifying the ethical issue.
2. Gathering relevant information.
3. Exploring different options.
4. Evaluating the possible outcomes.

By using these models, supervisors help supervisees develop strong ethical reasoning and critical thinking skills, preparing them to handle real-world counseling situations responsibly.

Professional codes of ethics provide a clear framework for supervisors, guiding ethical decision-making and responsible practice. Organizations like the American Counseling Association (ACA) and the Association for Counselor Education and Supervision (ACES) establish these standards, covering key areas such as:

- **Maintaining professional boundaries** – Ensuring ethical and appropriate relationships.
- **Protecting confidentiality** – Safeguarding client and supervisee information.
- **Promoting cultural competence** – Encouraging inclusive and respectful supervision.

Supervisors are responsible not only for following these ethical guidelines but also for instilling their importance in supervisees. This helps build a culture of integrity that extends beyond supervision.

Ethical supervision strengthens the counseling profession by upholding high standards and maintaining public trust. By addressing ethical concerns early, supervisors help prevent potential violations that could negatively impact clients. Their role is essential in shaping supervisees' ethical awareness, ensuring they provide competent and responsible care.

Ethical supervision is more than just following rules or checking off a list of requirements. It involves:

- **Developing ethical awareness** – Recognizing the deeper implications of decisions.
- **Encouraging critical thinking** – Helping supervisees analyze and navigate complex situations.
- **Engaging in open dialogue** – Creating a space for discussion and ethical reflection.

By focusing on thoughtful decision-making rather than rigid rules, supervisors help supervisees develop strong ethical judgment.

Supervisors also play a key role in promoting cultural awareness and social justice. This means:

- Acknowledging personal biases and assumptions.
- Encouraging discussions on diversity, power, and privilege.
- Helping supervisees develop culturally responsive counseling skills.

GATEKEEPING: AN ETHICAL RESPONSIBILITY

Gatekeeping in counseling supervision is a crucial ethical duty that ensures professional standards and protects client welfare. Both the American Counseling Association (ACA) and the American Mental Health Counselors Association (AMHCA) emphasize the importance of this role in their ethical guidelines. At its core, gatekeeping involves assessing supervisees' competence, ensuring that only qualified individuals move forward in their training and enter the profession.

"Counselors have an ethical responsibility to ensure that supervisees meet the necessary standards of competence, and to take appropriate action when supervisees are unable to demonstrate the required competence" (ACA, 2014, F.6.b.).

However, gatekeeping goes beyond academic performance. Supervisors must evaluate a supervisee's clinical skills, ethical judgment, and personal attributes, all of which impact their effectiveness as future counselors. This process is complex, as some essential qualities, like empathy, cultural competence, and ethical decision-making, are difficult to measure objectively.

One of the biggest challenges in gatekeeping is the subjectivity of assessing competence. Many counseling skills, such as building rapport with clients or handling ethical dilemmas, can be interpreted differently by different supervisors. This variation makes it difficult to establish consistent evaluation criteria.

Another challenge is limited observation opportunities. Supervisors may only see small glimpses of a supervisee's work, relying on brief interactions, client feedback, or recorded sessions to make critical decisions about their readiness for independent practice. These limitations can make gatekeeping a difficult and sometimes inconsistent process (Homrich, 2009) .

Despite these challenges, ethical gatekeeping remains essential. By carefully assessing supervisees and addressing concerns early, supervisors help maintain the integrity of the counseling profession and ensure that clients receive competent, ethical care.

The AMHCA (2020) Code of Ethics discusses gatekeeping stating:

" Clinical supervision is an important component of the counseling process. Supervision assists the supervisee to provide the best treatment possible to counseling clients and to provide training to the supervisee, which is an integral part of counselor education. Supervision also serves a gatekeeping process to ensure safety to the client, the profession, and to the supervisee. "

Another major challenge in gatekeeping comes from the emotional and professional conflicts supervisors face when deciding whether to fail or terminate a supervisee. The power dynamics in supervision, combined with the personal investment supervisors make in their trainees' development, can create hesitation in delivering negative feedback or making difficult decisions (Homrich & Henderson, 2018). This reluctance may stem from concerns about the following:

- **Legal repercussions** – Fear of lawsuits or grievances.
- **Professional relationships** – Worrying about conflicts with colleagues or institutions.
- **Personal commitment** – Wanting to support and nurture supervisees, even when concerns arise.

Supervisors often feel torn between protecting clients and maintaining professional standards while also wanting to encourage growth in their supervisees. This inner conflict can sometimes lead to ineffective gatekeeping, allowing underprepared or ethically compromised individuals to enter the profession.

The Consequences of Ineffective Gatekeeping

Failing to uphold high gatekeeping standards can have serious consequences, including:

- **Client harm** – Unqualified counselors may provide poor or even damaging care.
- **Loss of public trust** – Ethical lapses weaken confidence in the counseling profession.
- **Weakened professional standards** – Allowing unprepared individuals to practice can lower the overall quality of mental health services.

Many programs use multi-faceted evaluation systems that assess academic performance, clinical skills, and professional behavior. While this holistic approach provides a well-rounded view of a supervisee's competence, it has challenges:

- **Time and resource demands** – Comprehensive evaluations require significant effort.
- **Lack of consistency** – Different programs use varying assessment methods, leading to inconsistencies.

Improving Gatekeeping Practices

To enhance fairness and effectiveness in gatekeeping, some possible solutions include:

- **Standardized assessment tools** – Using structured observation checklists, validated rubrics, and ethical decision-making scenarios.
- **Evidence-based evaluations** – Implementing research-supported methods to assess competence objectively.

While these strategies could improve consistency and fairness, challenges include resistance to change and the need for extensive validation studies to ensure their reliability across different training environments.

Another promising solution is the creation of collaborative gatekeeping networks among supervisors and training programs. These networks would allow professionals to:

- **Share best practices** – Learning from others' experiences to refine gatekeeping methods.
- **Consult on challenging cases** – Gaining insight and support when making difficult decisions.
- **Develop standardized guidelines** – Promoting consistency across institutions.

By fostering collaboration, these networks could provide supervisors with greater support and help ensure uniform application of ethical and professional standards. However, implementation challenges include confidentiality concerns and the logistical difficulties of coordinating across institutions with different policies and resources.

Improving supervisor training in effective gatekeeping practices could also lead to more consistent and confident decision-making. A strong training program would address the following:

- **Competence assessment** – Using clear and objective evaluation methods.
- **Ethical and legal considerations** – Understanding the responsibilities and potential risks of gatekeeping.
- **Emotional challenges** – Managing the personal and professional difficulties of making tough decisions.

Well-trained supervisors would be better equipped to uphold high standards while feeling more supported in their roles. However, challenges include the time and resources required to develop comprehensive training and ensure widespread participation across the profession.

By implementing these solutions, the counseling field can strengthen gatekeeping practices, protect clients, and maintain the integrity of the profession.

POWER DYNAMICS IN SUPERVISION

This case study highlights a key issue in counseling supervision: how power dynamics affect communication and ethical decision-making. In this scenario, a new counselor struggles to disagree with their supervisor's approach due to fear of negative consequences. This situation demonstrates the delicate balance between authority, experience, and open dialogue in a supervisory relationship.

Power imbalances in supervision are natural. A supervisor with 20 years of experience and a senior role will inevitably hold more influence than a new counselor. However, when this power gap prevents honest discussions, it can lead to ethical concerns and even impact client care. If a supervisee feels unable to question a supervisor's methods, even when they seem inappropriate, it signals a breakdown in the supervision process.

To be effective, supervision must create a safe, supportive space where supervisees feel comfortable sharing their thoughts without fear of judgment or retaliation. In this case, the supervisor is unaware of the problem, making it even harder to correct the imbalance.

The consequences go beyond the immediate supervisor-supervisee dynamic. If problematic methods are left unchallenged, they could negatively affect clients and hinder the supervisee's growth. Ethical concerns also arise regarding the responsibility to provide competent care and address potentially harmful practices.

Regular feedback sessions can be highly effective in addressing these challenges. These structured discussions give both supervisors and supervisees a chance to share their perspectives, voice concerns, and reflect on their experiences. By making feedback a routine part of supervision, supervisors create an atmosphere of openness and mutual learning. This approach supports ethical principles of transparency and continuous professional growth.

In addition, training on managing power dynamics can strengthen the supervisory process. Such training helps both supervisors and supervisees recognize power imbalances and develop strategies to navigate them effectively. Supervisors can learn techniques for fostering a non-threatening environment and actively encouraging feedback. Meanwhile, supervisees can build assertive communication skills and gain a clearer understanding of their rights and responsibilities within supervision.

This case study reflects broader ethical themes in supervision, particularly the balance between authority and autonomy. It underscores the importance of open communication in maintaining ethical standards and highlights the need for supervisors to actively address power differentials.

Key Principles for Ethical Supervision

1. **Transparency:** Supervisors should openly acknowledge power imbalances and discuss their potential effects on the supervisory relationship.
2. **Collaborative Goal-Setting:** Involving supervisees in setting supervision goals increases their sense of ownership and engagement.
3. **Regular Reflection:** Both parties should routinely reflect on their supervisory relationship, power dynamics, and communication patterns.
4. **Clear Expectations:** Establishing guidelines for giving and receiving feedback can normalize constructive disagreement.
5. **Ethical Decision-Making Models:** Using ethical frameworks helps address complex situations in a structured and principled way.

6. **Continuous Education:** Ongoing learning about ethical practices and effective supervision benefits both supervisors and supervisees.
7. **External Support:** Mentorship or peer support groups provide additional spaces for supervisees to discuss concerns and seek guidance.

Supervisors and supervisees can create a more balanced and ethical supervisory relationship by applying these principles. This not only benefits their professional development but also enhances client care and strengthens the counseling profession as a whole.

CONFIDENTIALITY IN SUPERVISION

Maintaining confidentiality in counseling supervision is a complex but essential responsibility. It requires a thoughtful approach to ensure ethical standards are upheld while balancing the needs of supervisors, supervisees, and clients. This process involves several key steps:

1. **Establishing Clear Confidentiality Guidelines:** The first step is setting clear expectations about confidentiality within the supervisory relationship. Supervisors must define their boundaries while adhering to ethical codes and incorporating these terms into a supervision contract. This helps create a shared understanding of privacy limits while ensuring client welfare. To prevent misunderstandings, supervisors should discuss and document confidentiality expectations from the start.
2. **Obtaining Informed Consent:** Informed consent ensures that all parties, supervisors, supervisees, and clients, understand and agree to confidentiality terms. Written consent forms provide clarity, but ethical concepts can sometimes feel abstract. Using real-world case examples can make these principles more relatable, helping supervisees grasp how confidentiality applies in different situations.
3. **Managing Information Sharing:** Careful handling of information between supervisors, supervisees, and clients is crucial. Secure record-

keeping systems and clear reporting protocols help prevent ethical breaches. One of the biggest challenges is deciding what information needs to be shared and what should remain confidential. Regular discussions about information-sharing practices can improve transparency and reinforce ethical standards.

4. **Addressing Confidentiality Breaches**: Even with precautions, breaches can occur. Responding ethically requires a structured approach. Ethical decision-making models and consultation with colleagues can provide valuable guidance. The challenge is balancing accountability with a supportive learning environment. Developing a clear protocol for handling confidentiality breaches can help navigate these situations effectively.

5. **Maintaining Ongoing Ethical Awareness**: The final step in ensuring ethical confidentiality in supervision is continuous reflection and improvement. Staying informed about evolving ethical standards, new technologies, and best practices is essential. Continuing education and peer consultation provide valuable support, though keeping up with these changes can be challenging. Regular reviews and updates of confidentiality policies help ensure that practices remain relevant, effective, and aligned with current ethical guidelines.

Together, these steps create a strong framework for maintaining confidentiality in supervision. Each stage builds upon the previous one: establishing guidelines lays the foundation for informed consent, which then facilitates effective information management. A well-defined protocol for addressing breaches acts as a safeguard, while ongoing ethical awareness ensures long-term accountability and improvement.

Alternative Approaches to Confidentiality in Supervision
In some situations, confidentiality management requires additional considerations.

- **Group Supervision:** When multiple supervisees are involved, confidentiality becomes more complex. Setting clear group norms around confidentiality helps reinforce its importance. Supervisors should also monitor discussions closely to prevent unintended disclosures that could compromise client privacy.

- **Interdisciplinary Teams:** When professionals from different fields collaborate, confidentiality must be managed carefully. Establishing shared confidentiality protocols that respect each profession's ethical guidelines is crucial. Frequent reviews of information-sharing practices can help maintain confidentiality across disciplines.

- **Technology-Enhanced Confidentiality:** Digital tools can improve confidentiality through encrypted communication platforms and secure digital storage systems. However, they also introduce new challenges, such as ensuring data security and managing digital footprints. Supervisors must be proactive in addressing these risks and implementing best practices for secure technology use.

Along with the ethical principles and these strategies, supervisors can adapt confidentiality practices to various settings while upholding ethical standards. This proactive approach not only protects clients but also strengthens the integrity of the supervisory process and the counseling profession as a whole.

EVALUATING SUPERVISEE COMPETENCE

Supervisors use both formative and summative evaluation methods to assess a supervisee's competence in counseling. Each approach has distinct purposes, strengths, and limitations.

- **Formative evaluation** is an ongoing process that provides continuous feedback throughout supervision. It focuses on the supervisee's growth and development, allowing for regular adjustments and skill improvement.

- **Summative evaluation** occurs at set intervals, typically at the end of a supervision period. It serves as a final assessment, measuring overall competence and readiness for independent practice.

These methods impact supervisee development in different ways. Formative evaluation fosters a supportive learning environment where mistakes are seen as opportunities for improvement rather than failures. For example, a supervisor might provide immediate feedback on a supervisee's use of reflective listening during a session, helping refine their skills in real-time. Summative evaluation, while less focused on day-to-day development, provides a crucial benchmark for determining whether a supervisee is prepared for more independent work.

Both approaches also play a key role in ensuring client safety and quality of care. Formative evaluation allows supervisors to intervene quickly if concerns arise. For instance, if a supervisee struggles to recognize signs of suicidal ideation, immediate feedback can help address the issue before it affects the client's well-being. Summative evaluation, meanwhile, serves as a final safeguard, confirming that a supervisee meets the necessary standards for ethical and effective practice.

By balancing both formative and summative evaluation methods, supervisors can support supervisee growth while maintaining high standards of client care and professional competence.

Evaluating supervisees requires careful ethical consideration. Formative evaluation, which happens continuously, can create a more open and collaborative relationship between supervisors and supervisees. However, frequent interactions can introduce bias, so objectivity must be maintained. On the other hand, summative evaluation, conducted at specific points, is often more objective but may oversimplify a supervisee's progress over time.

When it comes to feedback, formative evaluation is highly effective because it offers timely, specific guidance. For example, if a supervisor observes a session and notices an area for improvement, they can immediately suggest alternative strategies for the supervisee to apply in future sessions. Summative evaluation, while less immediate, provides a broader assessment that can help shape long-term professional goals.

In terms of gatekeeping, summative evaluation plays a key role in determining whether a supervisee is ready for independent practice. It provides clear, documented assessments that support decisions regarding licensure or certification. Formative evaluation, though not typically used for final decisions, helps identify and address issues early, potentially preventing negative outcomes later.

Each method has its place. Formative evaluation is especially useful in the early stages of supervision when new counselors need frequent feedback. Summative evaluation becomes more important as they near the end of their training, offering a final assessment of their readiness for professional practice.

A balanced approach, combining both methods, ensures a more ethical and well-rounded assessment. For example, a supervision program might include weekly formative feedback sessions alongside quarterly summative evaluations. This approach provides continuous development while also marking key milestones in a supervisee's progress.

ETHICAL CONSULTATION PRACTICES

Ethical consultation in counseling involves balancing professional responsibilities, interpersonal dynamics, and moral considerations. Unlike supervision, which follows a structured, hierarchical approach, or therapy, which focuses on client treatment, consultation is a collaborative exchange where professionals share expertise to improve client care. Consultants have ethical duties beyond simply giving advice, they must uphold professional standards, maintain confidentiality, and prioritize client well-being.

One major ethical challenge in consultation is maintaining appropriate boundaries. Consultants must provide expert guidance while respecting the consultee's autonomy. This becomes even more complex in multi-party consultations, where professional roles can overlap. For example, a consultant advising a team of therapists might unintentionally influence treatment decisions beyond their intended role. If this happens, it could undermine the authority of the primary therapist and confuse the client about who is responsible for their care.

Confidentiality is another critical issue, especially in settings involving multiple professionals. Consultants must carefully decide what information to share to ensure effective consultation while protecting client privacy. This challenge is particularly evident in interdisciplinary teams, where different professions may have conflicting confidentiality standards. For instance, a mental health consultant working with a medical team may feel pressure to disclose more client information than ethical counseling guidelines allow.

Unethical consultation practices can have serious consequences. Overstepping boundaries or violating confidentiality can damage client trust, weaken treatment effectiveness, and even result in legal repercussions. Additionally, such breaches can harm the consultant's reputation and the counseling profession as a whole, eroding public confidence in mental health services.

Ethical consultation often relies on professional codes of ethics and institutional guidelines. While these provide a solid foundation, they may not fully address the complexities of modern consultation. For example, traditional guidelines may overlook challenges related to digital consultation platforms or the nuances of cross-cultural consultation in an increasingly globalized profession.

To strengthen ethical consultation, several potential improvements could be explored:

1. **Developing a Specialized Ethical Framework**

   A tailored ethical framework for consultation could offer clearer guidance on distinguishing consultation from supervision and therapy. It could also provide specific protocols for managing confidentiality in multi-party settings. While this approach ensures greater clarity, implementing a standardized framework may be difficult due to the diverse nature of consultation across counseling specialties.

2. **Integrating Ethical Decision-Making Models**

   Ethical decision-making models designed specifically for consultation could be incorporated into counselor education and professional development programs. These models would help consultants systematically analyze ethical dilemmas, weigh possible solutions, and make sound ethical choices. However, their effectiveness depends on consistent application and regular updates to address emerging challenges.

3. **Establishing Peer Consultation Networks**

   Creating peer consultation networks focused on ethical practice could provide a collaborative space for professionals to discuss and resolve ethical dilemmas. These networks encourage the sharing of best practices, collective problem-solving, and mutual accountability. While they promote ethical awareness and continuous learning, sustaining them requires ongoing commitment and structured management to ensure discussions remain productive and confidential.

Different consultation settings may require distinct ethical approaches. Peer consultation often emphasizes reciprocity and professional growth while maintaining collegial relationships. In contrast, interdisciplinary collaboration may need more structured protocols for information sharing and decision-making across professional boundaries. Regardless of the context, the ultimate ethical goal remains the same: to enhance client care while upholding professional integrity and ethical principles.

SUPERVISION CONTRACTS

Creating an ethical supervision contract is a crucial step in establishing a productive and professional supervisory relationship. The process begins with identifying the key components of the contract. These typically include the roles and responsibilities of both the supervisor and supervisee, supervision goals, and ethical guidelines that will shape the relationship.

Professional ethical codes and supervision literature offer useful guidance, but the contract should strike a balance between being comprehensive and easy to understand. If it is too complex, it may become overwhelming rather than helpful.

Once the essential elements are defined, the next step is drafting the contract. It should be clear, concise, and written in plain language so that both parties fully understand its terms. Supervisors can use existing templates as a starting point and adjust them to fit the specific needs of their supervision process. In some cases, legal consultation may be necessary to ensure the contract is legally sound and protects both parties. A key challenge at this stage is finding the right balance between specificity and flexibility, the contract must provide clear guidelines while allowing room for the supervisory relationship to evolve.

The final step is reviewing and discussing the contract with the supervisee. This phase requires open communication and collaboration. Supervisors should encourage supervisees to ask questions, express concerns, and offer input. This approach helps address potential power imbalances and ensures that both parties are fully invested in the agreement. While the supervisor typically drafts the initial contract, the final version should reflect a shared understanding and mutual agreement.

Once both parties have negotiated and agreed on the terms, the contract is finalized and signed. This step includes incorporating any revisions, conducting a final review, and ensuring that all aspects of the supervisory relationship are clearly outlined. Using a checklist can help confirm that nothing has been overlooked. After both parties sign the contract, copies should be provided to everyone involved. This formalization process reinforces the professional nature of the agreement and the commitment to ethical supervision.

The contract isn't just a one-time document, it requires ongoing review and implementation. Regular supervision sessions offer opportunities to assess how well the contract is working in practice. Both parties should have a way to provide feedback, raise concerns, or suggest modifications as needed. A common challenge is maintaining adherence to the contract over time, especially as the supervisory relationship evolves. Scheduling periodic contract reviews can help keep expectations clear and ensure the agreement remains relevant and effective.

Adopting steps create a strong ethical foundation for the supervisory relationship by setting clear expectations, encouraging open communication, and providing a structured approach to handling potential challenges. The very process of developing and implementing the contract models professional behavior and ethical practice.

While this structured approach works well in most cases, different supervision settings may require adjustments. For example, in group supervision, contracts must address confidentiality among members and establish ground rules for group interactions. In practicum or internship settings, where supervision is time-limited, contracts may focus more on specific learning objectives and evaluation criteria.

For students in educational programs or those working toward clinical licensure, supervision contracts often include additional requirements. These may involve specific documentation, compliance with program or licensing board standards, and clear links between supervision activities and competency development. Educational institutions and licensing boards typically provide guidelines for these components, which must be carefully integrated into the contract to ensure compliance with regulatory requirements.

TECHNOLOGY IN SUPERVISION

The use of technology in counseling supervision has grown significantly, raising important ethical considerations. An article by Perle et al. (2024) discusses the increase of counseling supervisors found incorporate some form of technology in their practice and trainees receiving telesupervision. These findings highlight both the widespread adoption of technology and the ethical challenges it presents. However, it provides a number of methods that can be used to improve these services to ensure quality.

Comparing face-to-face and online supervision provides further insight into technology's impact. While research generally indicates no significant difference in supervisee competence between the two formats, online supervision showed higher rates of miscommunication and technical difficulties. This suggests that digital supervision introduces unique challenges that require careful ethical consideration. However, due to the study's limited sample size and duration, these findings should be interpreted with caution (Koçyiğit Özyiğit, 2022).

The growing recognition of technology's role in supervision is evident in ethical codes from various counseling organizations. A content analysis of ten counseling organizations found that eight have developed specific guidelines for technology use, focusing on key issues like confidentiality, competence, and informed consent. This widespread inclusion of technology-related ethics reflects an industry-wide effort to address emerging challenges. However, written guidelines do not always translate into consistent practice, highlighting the need for ongoing education and enforcement.

Some argue that existing ethical principles are sufficient to address technology-related concerns, but this view overlooks the unique risks of digital communication and data security. Online supervision poses distinct challenges, including potential data breaches and increased chances of miscommunication, which require more detailed ethical guidelines. A nuanced approach that specifically addresses these risks is essential for maintaining ethical and effective supervision in digital environments.

The increasing use of technology in counseling supervision underscores the need for updated ethical guidelines and training programs tailored to digital supervision. Several key steps can help ensure that supervisors are prepared to navigate the ethical complexities of technology use effectively.

First, there is a clear need for comprehensive, technology-specific ethical guidelines. These guidelines should address confidentiality, data security, informed consent, and competency in using digital platforms. Existing ethical codes provide a foundation, but more detailed guidance is necessary to address the unique risks of online supervision.

Second, training programs for supervisors should include dedicated modules on the ethical use of technology. These should cover not only the technical aspects of various digital platforms but also the ethical challenges they present. Supervisors must be prepared to manage confidentiality in digital spaces, minimize miscommunication risks, and ensure the secure transmission of sensitive information.

Third, ongoing research is essential to track how emerging technologies impact supervision. As digital tools evolve, ethical guidelines and training programs must be regularly updated to remain relevant and effective. Research can help identify new challenges and inform best practices for ethical supervision in online settings.

Fourth, professional organizations should consider developing certification programs focused on the ethical use of technology in supervision. These certifications would help ensure that supervisors possess the necessary skills and knowledge to engage in ethical and effective digital supervision.

Finally, establishing best practices for managing technology-related risks is crucial. These may include secure data transmission protocols, strategies for handling technical difficulties during supervision sessions, and guidelines for fostering clear and effective digital communication.

By implementing these measures, the counseling profession can ensure that technology enhances supervision while maintaining ethical integrity and protecting client confidentiality.

7

TECHNOLOGY AND ETHICAL

PRACTICE

NAVIGATING THE DIGITAL SHIFT IN COUNSELING

Technology has transformed the counseling field, opening up new ways for therapists to connect with clients. Online counseling platforms and teletherapy services have changed how mental health support is delivered, making it more accessible and flexible than ever before. Counselors are no longer limited to in-person sessions, allowing them to reach people who might not have had access to mental health care in the past.

One of the biggest benefits of this shift is accessibility. Online platforms remove geographical barriers, helping people in remote or underserved areas get the support they need. At the same time, digital counseling can be more affordable, making mental health care available to those who might otherwise struggle with costs or lack insurance coverage.

However, these advancements also bring challenges, particularly in building strong therapeutic relationships. Face-to-face conversations allow counselors to pick up on body language and other non-verbal cues, things that can be harder to detect through a screen. As a result, counselors must adapt their approach to ensure meaningful connections with clients in virtual settings. There's also the issue of the digital divide, not everyone has reliable internet access or the technical know-how to navigate online counseling platforms, which can create barriers for some individuals (Feijt et al., 2020).

To address ethical concerns, professional organizations have developed guidelines for online counseling, covering key issues like informed consent, confidentiality in digital spaces, and handling technical difficulties. While these guidelines help establish ethical standards, they sometimes struggle to keep up with the fast pace of technological change. As digital counseling continues to evolve, mental health professionals must stay informed and adaptable to navigate new ethical challenges effectively (Glueckauf et al., 2018).

As technology becomes more integrated into counseling, ensuring ethical practice is crucial. Several potential solutions could help address the unique challenges of digital mental health services. One approach is developing a clear, technology-specific ethical framework tailored to digital counseling. This would provide counselors with specific guidelines for navigating online therapy, covering areas like privacy, security, and professional boundaries. However, because technology evolves so quickly, these guidelines would need constant updates to stay relevant (Schueller et al., 2019).

Another solution is requiring ethics training in counselor education and professional development programs. Teaching counselors how to handle ethical dilemmas in digital counseling helps them stay prepared for real-world challenges. However, it is possible that some institutions and professionals may resist adding more training requirements, seeing them as an extra burden.

A third option is establishing a regulatory body dedicated to digital counseling. This organization could certify online platforms, monitor ethical practices, and investigate potential violations. While this would increase accountability and public trust, setting up such a system would require significant resources and coordination, especially considering the global nature of online counseling (Luxton et al., 2016).

Each of these solutions comes with challenges. A technology-specific ethical framework would require ongoing collaboration between mental health professionals, ethicists, and tech experts. Incorporating technology ethics training into counselor education would mean updating curriculums and developing new learning materials. Creating a regulatory body would involve legal action, funding, and careful oversight.

Ultimately, the key to ethical digital counseling is adaptability. Ethical guidelines, education, and regulations must evolve alongside technological advancements while remaining grounded in core mental health principles. Using a proactive, multifaceted approach, counselors can confidently embrace technology's benefits while maintaining the highest ethical standards.

CONFIDENTIALITY IN THE CLOUD

In digital counseling, maintaining confidentiality means protecting client information stored and shared online. As more counseling practices move to cloud-based systems for record-keeping and communication, safeguarding sensitive data has become more important than ever. Trust between counselors and clients depends on ensuring that personal information stays secure and private.

Protecting client data in the cloud requires multiple layers of security. Encryption is one key safeguard, it converts information into a code that can only be unlocked with a specific key or password. Strong encryption methods, like AES-256, help protect data whether it's being stored or transmitted. Access controls add another layer of security by limiting who can view, edit, or share client information. These controls often include user authentication, role-based permissions, and audit logs that track who accesses the system.

Even with these protections, digital record-keeping comes with risks. Weak passwords, phishing scams, and insider threats from employees with access to sensitive data can all lead to security breaches. Because digital systems are interconnected, a vulnerability in one area can put an entire network at risk. That's why a strong, well-rounded security strategy is essential for maintaining confidentiality in the digital age.

When a data breach occurs in counseling, the consequences go far beyond just losing confidentiality. One of the biggest risks is the loss of client trust. Trust is the foundation of any therapeutic relationship, and if clients fear their personal information isn't secure, they may hesitate to open up. This can seriously hinder the effectiveness of counseling.

Legal consequences can also be severe. Data breaches can lead to hefty fines lawsuits, and even damage a counselor's professional reputation. In some cases, they may put an entire practice at risk.

Many misunderstandings about cloud storage security come from a lack of familiarity with modern digital systems. Some counselors assume that storing records on-site is safer than using the cloud. However, major cloud service providers often have stronger security measures than most private practices can afford to implement.

Another common myth is that cloud data is vulnerable to physical theft. In reality, cloud data centers are highly secure, with multiple layers of both digital and physical protection, making unauthorized access far less likely than with personal computers or office-based servers.

When used correctly, digital security measures can actually enhance confidentiality. Advanced tracking and auditing tools allow counselors to monitor who accesses client information, helping to detect and prevent breaches before they happen.

Secure cloud systems also make it easier and safer to share information when necessary, such as for client referrals or collaborative care. Granular permission settings ensure that only authorized individuals can access specific information, protecting confidentiality while allowing for smooth coordination between professionals.

As counseling integrates more digital tools, understanding encryption is essential. Counselors should be familiar with end-to-end encryption for secure communication and at-rest encryption for stored data. Just as important is encryption key management, without proper protection of these keys, even encrypted data can be compromised. To maintain strong digital confidentiality, counselors need ongoing training and updates on emerging encryption standards and best practices.

Access controls go beyond just using a username and password. Multi-factor authentication (MFA) adds an extra layer of security by requiring a second form of verification, like a fingerprint or a one-time code. Role-based access control (RBAC) ensures that staff members only see the information necessary for their specific roles, reducing the risk of unauthorized access or accidental data leaks.

However, not all security risks come from external threats. Human error, such as sending sensitive information to the wrong person or leaving a device unlocked, can also compromise confidentiality. To prevent this, counseling practices should have clear security policies and provide regular training to ensure all staff members understand best practices.

The consequences of data breaches go beyond individual counseling practices. High-profile breaches can erode public trust in the profession, making people hesitant to seek mental health services. They can also lead to stricter regulations and compliance requirements, affecting the entire field of counseling.

Protecting client confidentiality in digital spaces requires both technological expertise and ethical awareness. By adopting strong security measures and staying informed about emerging digital threats, counselors can use technology to not only protect sensitive information but also improve the quality of care they provide.

INFORMED CONSENT IN THE DIGITAL AGE

Informed consent is a fundamental part of ethical counseling, ensuring that clients understand the nature, risks, and benefits of therapy. While its core principles remain the same, the way informed consent is obtained has evolved with technology-assisted counseling. Traditional in-person counseling typically involves a verbal explanation followed by a signed document, whereas digital counseling often relies on electronic forms and interactive modules to present this information.

The ethical foundations of informed consent, respect for client autonomy and the commitment to beneficence, apply across all counseling settings. However, digital counseling introduces new considerations, such as data security, privacy risks, and potential technical failures. These factors must be clearly addressed in the consent process to ensure clients fully understand the implications of receiving therapy online.

Digital informed consent offers both benefits and challenges. Electronic forms can provide standardized, detailed explanations, sometimes incorporating videos or interactive quizzes to improve client understanding. However, the absence of face-to-face interaction can make it harder for counselors to assess a client's comprehension or answer questions in real-time.

The way informed consent has developed over time reflects the broader shifts in counseling practices. Traditional methods evolved gradually, shaped by ethical guidelines and legal precedents. In contrast, digital consent procedures have changed rapidly, driven by technological advancements and the increasing demand for online therapy. As a result, digital consent protocols require frequent updates to keep pace with emerging ethical and security concerns.

How informed consent is documented and managed differs significantly between traditional and digital counseling. Digital platforms offer secure storage, easy retrieval, and streamlined updates, making ongoing consent management more efficient. They also allow clients to control specific aspects of consent, such as data-sharing preferences. In contrast, traditional methods, while sometimes less efficient, benefit from the personal connection of face-to-face interactions, which can build trust and encourage open communication.

Each approach has its strengths. Traditional consent methods are especially valuable for clients who need personalized explanations or immediate clarification, particularly those unfamiliar with counseling or with limited health literacy. Digital methods, on the other hand, ensure consistency in information delivery, allow clients to review materials at their own pace, and provide more detailed content without time constraints.

The choice between digital and traditional consent methods often depends on the counseling setting and the needs of individual clients. Digital methods work well for tech-savvy clients or those receiving therapy exclusively online. They are particularly useful in situations requiring frequent consent updates, such as research studies or rapidly evolving treatment plans. Traditional methods remain preferable when clients have limited access to technology or require more nuanced, in-depth discussions.

A Hybrid Approach: Combining the Best of Both Worlds

A more client-centered approach to informed consent could integrate the strengths of both methods. For example, counselors might use digital tools to present detailed information with interactive elements, followed by an in-person or video conference session to address questions and ensure understanding.

Adaptive consent processes could further enhance the client experience. Using artificial intelligence, these systems could assess a client's comprehension and adjust the depth and complexity of information accordingly. This approach would ensure that each client receives the right level of detail, making the consent process both thorough and accessible.

BOUNDARIES IN THE DIGITAL AGE

The rise of digital technology and social media has introduced new challenges in maintaining professional boundaries in counseling. A common example is when a counselor receives a friend request from a client on a personal social media account. This situation raises important ethical concerns, as it blurs the line between personal and professional relationships, potentially compromising the integrity of the therapeutic alliance.

How a counselor responds to such a request is critical. Ignoring it may seem like the simplest solution, but it could leave the client feeling rejected or confused. On the other hand, addressing the situation directly in a session offers an opportunity for open communication. Discussing the request allows the counselor to clarify professional boundaries, reinforcing the importance of maintaining a therapeutic relationship that remains ethical and effective.

This then highlights a broader issue: the impact of digital communication on the counselor-client dynamic. A client's decision to send a friend request may stem from a misunderstanding of professional boundaries or a desire for a more personal connection. It underscores the need for counselors to be proactive in setting expectations about digital interactions from the start.

By clearly communicating these boundaries, whether through informed consent, counseling policies, or direct conversations, counselors can help clients understand the professional nature of the relationship, ultimately strengthening trust and ethical practice in the digital era.

Alternative approaches to managing digital boundaries provide valuable insights. One suggestion, accepting a friend request with clear guidelines, might seem appealing to some clients. However, it introduces significant risks, including challenges in maintaining professional distance and potential ethical dilemmas related to dual relationships. This highlights the need for consistent boundaries across all forms of communication, whether in-person or digital.

A more effective strategy is implementing a proactive social media policy. By establishing clear guidelines from the outset, counselors can prevent potential boundary issues before they arise. Such a policy might outline the counselor's stance on social media connections with clients, define acceptable forms of digital communication, and explain how technology will (or won't) be used in therapy.

This case study offers broader lessons for counseling ethics in the digital era. Most importantly, it underscores the value of setting clear digital boundaries at the start of the therapeutic relationship. Proactively communicating policies on digital interactions helps prevent misunderstandings and reduces the likelihood of clients feeling rejected or confused.

Additionally, the ever-changing digital landscape means counselors must remain adaptable. New platforms and communication methods will continue to emerge, presenting novel ethical challenges. Being prepared to navigate these shifts ensures that ethical principles remain intact, even as technology evolves.

The following principles can help counselors maintain ethical digital boundaries in various situations:

1. **Consistency in boundary-setting** – Maintain professional boundaries across all forms of interaction, including in-person meetings, emails, text messages, and social media.
2. **Transparency and clear communication** – Clearly outline digital communication policies at the beginning of the therapeutic relationship to set expectations.
3. **Prioritizing the therapeutic relationship** – Ensure all decisions regarding digital boundaries support and strengthen the counselor-client relationship.
4. **Regular review and adaptation** – Continuously update digital communication policies to reflect changes in technology and ethical considerations.
5. **Education and informed consent** – Educate clients on the risks and benefits of digital communication and obtain informed consent for any online interactions.
6. **Ongoing professional development** – Stay informed about emerging technologies and their potential impact on counseling practice.

COMPETENCE IN THE DIGITAL REALM

Developing and maintaining technological competence in counseling is a dynamic, ongoing process. It requires a structured approach, beginning with an honest self-assessment of digital literacy. Counselors must evaluate their current knowledge and skills related to technology in therapeutic settings. This step establishes a baseline for growth and helps pinpoint areas needing improvement. While self-assessment questionnaires and peer reviews can be helpful, counselors should be mindful of potential biases, overestimating or underestimating their abilities. Seeking constructive feedback from colleagues can provide a more objective perspective.

Once a counselor has a clear understanding of their current competence, the next step is identifying the specific technological skills required for ethical counseling practice. This involves staying informed about professional guidelines and emerging trends in digital counseling. Given the rapid evolution of technology, continuous learning is essential. Instead of focusing on platform-specific skills, which can quickly become outdated, counselors should prioritize foundational skills that apply across multiple digital tools.

Formal training plays a key role in building technological competence. Workshops, webinars, and specialized courses provide structured learning opportunities. Professional development programs and online courses offer valuable resources, though time constraints and financial limitations can be challenges. To maximize the benefits, counselors should prioritize accredited programs that offer Continuing Education Units (CEUs), allowing them to fulfill professional development requirements while expanding their technological expertise.

Acquiring new skills is only the beginning, practical application is essential for true competence. Counselors should implement newly learned technologies in controlled, low-risk environments to build confidence and proficiency. Practice platforms, simulations, and peer training sessions provide safe opportunities to refine skills. However, adapting to new technologies can feel overwhelming. To ease the transition, a gradual approach, introducing one new tool at a time and increasing complexity as comfort grows, can help counselors integrate digital skills into their practice more effectively.

By embracing a structured, step-by-step approach to technological competence, counselors can navigate the digital landscape with confidence, ensuring that they provide ethical, effective, and modern mental health care.

Supervision and feedback play a critical role in refining technological competence in counseling. Engaging in supervision that specifically addresses technology use allows counselors to reflect on their digital skills and receive constructive guidance. Tech-savvy supervisors and peer consultation groups can offer valuable insights and support. However, finding supervisors with relevant technological expertise can be challenging. In such cases, forming a peer group dedicated to technology in counseling provides an effective alternative, fostering collaborative learning and problem-solving.

Maintaining technological competence is an ongoing commitment, requiring counselors to stay current with advancements in the field. Regularly updating knowledge and skills is essential as digital tools and best practices evolve. Professional journals, tech blogs, and conferences serve as valuable resources for staying informed. While the rapid pace of technological change can feel overwhelming, setting aside dedicated time for learning, whether through reading, attending webinars, or engaging in professional discussions, can make this process more manageable.

This all works together in a continuous cycle, with each stage informing and reinforcing the others. The initial self-assessment identifies areas for improvement, guiding the selection of formal training programs. The practical application of new skills generates insights that can be explored in supervision, while staying current with emerging technologies, which may prompt a reassessment of one's competence and restart the cycle of growth.

Recognizing that counselors have diverse learning styles, alternative approaches to developing digital literacy can enhance skill acquisition. For visual learners, video tutorials and interactive demonstrations may be more effective than text-based resources. Kinesthetic learners might benefit from hands-on workshops or immersive technology experiences. Counselors with limited technological backgrounds could find mentor-mentee relationships particularly helpful, allowing for personalized guidance and support. Additionally, collaborative learning environments, such as technology-focused study groups or online forums, offer opportunities for social learners to share experiences and problem-solve together.

By embracing a structured yet flexible approach to technological competence, counselors can navigate the digital landscape with confidence, ensuring ethical and effective integration of technology into their practice.

AI AND VR: ETHICAL HORIZONS IN COUNSELING

The integration of Artificial Intelligence (AI) and Virtual Reality (VR) into counseling presents a landscape rich with both opportunities and ethical challenges. Recent research highlights the promise of these technologies while also underscoring the need for careful ethical consideration.

A 2024 narrative review of artificial intelligence (AI) in positive mental health highlighted a growing body of research exploring AI's role in enhancing psychological well-being, including applications in emotion detection, early identification of mental health concerns, and personalized intervention strategies. These developments suggest that AI holds potential for improving the delivery and effectiveness of mental health support. However, the review also emphasized that most existing studies are still in preliminary phases, with limited empirical validation and a lack of longitudinal data, reinforcing the need for further research and cautious optimism (Thakkar, Gupta, & De Sousa, 2024).

In the realm of VR-based therapy, recent research has explored both the effectiveness and ethical considerations of the technology. Investigating these intervention, Bell et al. (2020) found that VR-based interventions have demonstrated efficacy in treating various mental health conditions, including anxiety disorders and psychosis, particularly by enhancing patient engagement and providing realistic exposure scenarios. However, the study also emphasized the importance of ethical safeguards, noting potential risks such as heightened emotional responses and issues related to data privacy. This duality reflects the delicate balance required when integrating cutting-edge technology into counseling practice, where clinical innovation must be matched with ethical vigilance.

Together, these findings reinforce a key reality: while AI and VR hold the potential to revolutionize mental health care, offering more personalized, efficient, and effective interventions, they also present challenges related to privacy, client autonomy, and the risk of depersonalizing the therapeutic relationship. The future of counseling in the digital age will require an ongoing commitment to ethical vigilance, informed decision-making, and continuous adaptation to new technological landscapes.

A common critique of AI and VR in counseling is the concern that these technologies may depersonalize the therapeutic relationship. While this is a valid consideration, a closer examination reveals that, when implemented thoughtfully, AI and VR can actually enhance human interaction rather than replace it.

For example, AI-driven analytics can provide therapists with deeper insights into client behaviors and emotional patterns, allowing for more targeted, personalized interventions. Rather than diminishing the counselor's role, AI serves as a powerful augmentative tool, enabling therapists to make more informed decisions and tailor their approach to individual client needs.

Similarly, VR environments can create immersive, controlled therapeutic experiences, such as exposure therapy for anxiety disorders, while still requiring the expertise of a trained counselor to guide and interpret the client's responses. The technology functions as a tool, not a substitute, reinforcing the essential role of human judgment in therapy.

Ethical Risks vs. Potential Benefits

Another argument against AI and VR in counseling is that the ethical risks outweigh the potential benefits. However, this concern can be countered by examining successful implementations of these technologies and the ongoing development of ethical guidelines tailored specifically to AI and VR in counseling. As the field evolves, so too will the ethical frameworks designed to address concerns such as:

- **Data privacy and security** in AI-driven analytics
- **Informed consent** in virtual therapy environments
- **Defining the appropriate boundaries** of AI-assisted decision-making in mental health care

Rather than rejecting AI and VR due to ethical concerns, the counseling profession has an opportunity to shape the responsible use of these tools, ensuring they align with core ethical principles while maximizing their benefits.

The rise of AI and VR in counseling necessitates a shift in counselor education and ethical guideline development. Training programs must evolve to include:

- **Technology-focused coursework** covering AI applications and VR-based interventions
- **Hands-on training** to ensure counselors gain practical experience using these tools
- **In-depth discussions** on the ethical considerations of integrating AI and VR into practice

Additionally, professional organizations and regulatory bodies must work proactively to develop and regularly update ethical guidelines for emerging technologies. These guidelines should be informed by empirical research **and** practical experience, providing clear directives on:

- The responsible use of AI-assisted interventions
- Client consent and autonomy in technology-based therapy
- The appropriate integration of VR into different therapeutic contexts

THE EVOLUTION OF ETHICAL POLICIES FOR TECHNOLOGY IN COUNSELING

The development of ethical policies for technology use in counseling has evolved alongside advancements in communication tools, shaping how mental health professionals navigate digital interactions.

1. Early Foundations: Telephone Counseling (1950s–1970s)

The introduction of telephone counseling in the 1950s marked one of the earliest shifts toward remote mental health support (Lester, 1974). Crisis hotlines provided immediate assistance to individuals in distress, prompting the creation of new ethical guidelines to address:

- Confidentiality in telephone-based interactions
- Crisis intervention protocols for remote support
- Limitations of non-visual communication in therapeutic relationships

As telephone counseling gained legitimacy, these foundational ethical considerations paved the way for future discussions on technology's role in mental health care.

2. The Rise of Computer-Based Interventions (1960s–1980s)

By the 1960s and 1970s, the field of counseling saw the emergence of computer-based interventions, primarily used for psychological assessments and basic therapeutic exercises (Butcher, Perry, & Atlis, 2000). While these digital tools introduced new possibilities, they also raised key ethical concerns, such as:

- Data security and client privacy
- The validity of computerized psychological assessments
- The appropriate integration of technology into traditional counseling practices

Recognizing these challenges, the American Psychological Association (APA) developed initial guidelines to regulate the use of computers in psychological practice, laying the groundwork for future **digital ethics policies**.

3. The Internet Age and Online Therapy (1990s–Early 2000s)

The 1990s marked a pivotal shift with the rise of internet-based counseling, leading to the creation of the first comprehensive ethical guidelines for online therapy. Hsiung (2001) writes that organizations such as the International Society for Mental Health Online (ISMHO) introduced policies to address:

- **Informed consent** for digital therapy sessions
- **Therapist competence** in online modalities
- **Managing technological failures** during sessions

This era also sparked intense debate within the counseling profession. Critics raised concerns about:

- The absence of nonverbal cues makes it harder to interpret the client's emotions
- Potential misdiagnosis due to digital communication limitations
- Client confidentiality risks in online spaces

Despite these concerns, online therapy continued to grow, driving the need for ongoing revisions to ethical policies that balance technological innovation with professional standards.

THE IMPACT OF SMARTPHONES AND EMERGING TECHNOLOGIES ON COUNSELING ETHICS

The early 2000s saw the rapid rise of smartphones and mobile apps, transforming the way counseling services were delivered. While these technologies created new opportunities for accessibility, they also introduced ethical challenges that required careful consideration.

The widespread use of mobile devices blurred traditional boundaries between personal and professional communication, raising concerns such as:

- **Client-therapist accessibility:** The expectation of constant availability via text or messaging apps

- **Third-party app usage:** The security and ethical implications of mental health apps collecting sensitive data

- **Social media interactions:** The risks of dual relationships when clients and therapists engage on public platforms

Recognizing these challenges, professional organizations like the American Counseling Association (ACA) revised their ethical codes to provide clearer guidelines on text messaging, social media use, and digital communication in therapy.

The rise of teletherapy and digital mental health platforms defines the modern era of counseling technology. The COVID-19 pandemic accelerated the adoption of video conferencing for remote therapy, sparking new ethical discussions (Smith & Gillon, 2021) around:

- Client privacy in home-based sessions (e.g., ensuring confidentiality in shared living spaces)

- Managing technical disruptions and their impact on therapeutic continuity

- The digital divide, which limits teletherapy access for underprivileged populations

To address these concerns, ethical guidelines now emphasize secure platforms, client education on digital risks, and accessibility considerations in teletherapy practice.

The emergence of Artificial Intelligence (AI) and Virtual Reality (VR) in mental health care introduces exciting possibilities but also serious ethical concerns:

- **AI-powered chatbots and virtual therapists**:
  - Can they supplement human therapy without replacing the human connection?
  - How do we prevent algorithmic bias in AI-driven mental health assessments?
  - What are the ethical implications of AI analyzing sensitive client data?

- **VR-based exposure therapy and immersive counseling**:
  - Ensuring client safety in emotionally intense virtual environments
  - Addressing the risk of dissociation or overstimulation in immersive therapy
  - Establishing ethical guidelines for simulated experiences in treatment

As technology continues to evolve, the counseling profession must prepare for emerging ethical dilemmas in areas such as:

- Brain-computer interfaces and their impact on mental health treatment

- Predictive analytics in therapy, can AI forecast mental health crises ethically?

- Balancing innovation with ethical principles like beneficence, autonomy, and justice

The rapid pace of technological advancement highlights the need for ongoing research, ethical reflection, and professional dialogue. The goal remains to ensure that digital tools enhance therapy without compromising ethical standards or client well-being.

SECURITY PROTOCOLS IN E-COUNSELING

As technology transforms mental health care, e-counseling has become a widely accessible option. However, with the convenience of digital therapy comes the responsibility of protecting client privacy and maintaining trust. Strong security protocols are essential to keeping e-counseling safe, ethical, and confidential.

One of the most important security measures in e-counseling is end-to-end encryption (E2EE). This technology ensures that only the client and counselor can access their conversations, no one else, not even the platform itself.

- **How it works:** Encryption scrambles messages and video calls, making them unreadable to outsiders. Only the sender and receiver can decode them.
- **Why it matters:** Without encryption, sensitive client conversations could be intercepted, leading to serious privacy violations.
- **Real-world use:** Apps like Signal and WhatsApp use E2EE to protect user data. Many e-counseling platforms are adopting the same approach to safeguard client information.

Even the best passwords can be stolen. That's where multi-factor authentication (MFA) comes in. MFA requires users to verify their identity in multiple ways before they can access a platform, making it much harder for hackers to break in.

Common MFA methods:

- **Something you know** – A password or security question
- **Something you have** – A one-time code sent to your phone
- **Something you are** – Biometric authentication like fingerprints or facial recognition

Why it's important:

- Prevents unauthorized access to client records
- Protects against weak or stolen passwords
- Helps counseling platforms meet security standards

Other Essential Security Measures

- To keep e-counseling platforms safe, providers should also:
- Store client data on encrypted servers with limited access
- Conduct regular security audits to catch and fix vulnerabilities.
- Follow privacy regulations like HIPAA and GDPR to ensure legal compliance

Beyond encryption and authentication, additional security measures are essential for protecting client information and ensuring ethical digital counseling practices.

Keeping stored client data safe is just as important as securing live conversations. E-counseling platforms must use advanced encryption for data stored on servers. This ensures that even if a breach occurs, the stolen data remains unreadable without the proper decryption keys.

To further enhance security, platforms should:

- Conduct regular security audits to identify weaknesses
- Perform penetration testing to expose vulnerabilities before hackers can exploit them

Not everyone in an e-counseling system needs access to all information. The principle of least privilege (PoLP) ensures that users, whether counselors, administrators, or IT staff, only have the minimum level of access required to do their job. By restricting access, the potential damage from a security breach is greatly reduced.

E-counseling platforms must follow strict regulations to protect client data. In the U.S., the Health Insurance Portability and Accountability Act (HIPAA) outlines specific guidelines for handling patient health information. Compliance often requires:

- **Detailed access logs** to track who views sensitive data
- **Secure disposal methods** for electronic protected health information (ePHI)
- **Ongoing security training** for staff to stay updated on best practices

Following these regulations helps ensure ethical, legal, and secure digital counseling services.

Even with strong security measures, breaches can still happen. That's why every e-counseling platform needs a clear incident response plan to detect, respond to, and minimize damage from security incidents. A strong plan should include:

- **Quick containment** to stop the breach from spreading
- **Impact assessment** to understand what data was affected
- **Notifying affected parties** when necessary

- **Preventive measures** to reduce the risk of future incidents

Secure video conferencing technology is essential for e-counseling. Platforms must use encrypted video sessions and strict access controls to protect client confidentiality. Features like waiting rooms, where the host approves participants before they join, add an extra layer of security and help prevent unauthorized access.

Keeping e-counseling platforms secure also requires regular software updates. Hackers often exploit software vulnerabilities, so timely updates and patches are crucial. Automated updates can help ensure security fixes are applied quickly, minimizing risks.

User awareness is another key factor in maintaining security. Both clients and counselors should follow best practices, such as using strong passwords, avoiding public Wi-Fi for sessions, and recognizing phishing attempts. Clear guidelines and ongoing education can create a culture of security awareness, helping everyone stay protected.

8

---·◦⌒⌒᷍⌒◦·---

ETHICAL DECISION-MAKING

MODELS

UNDERSTANDING ETHICAL DECISION-MAKING

E thical decision-making is a fundamental part of counseling, guiding professionals through complex client situations and ethical dilemmas. It involves carefully evaluating moral and ethical considerations to ensure decisions uphold the integrity of the profession while prioritizing client well-being. This process is built on three key components: moral awareness, moral judgment, and ethical behavior.

The first step in ethical decision-making is recognizing when an issue has ethical implications. Counselors need to be sensitive to potential concerns, such as boundary violations, conflicts of interest, or breaches of confidentiality. This awareness allows them to address ethical challenges before they escalate.

Once an ethical issue is identified, counselors must evaluate their options using ethical principles, professional guidelines, and legal considerations. This often involves balancing competing values. For example, if a client expresses intent to harm themselves, a counselor must weigh the ethical principles of autonomy and confidentiality against the duty to protect.

Making an ethical decision is only part of the process, following through with appropriate action is just as important. Ethical behavior means applying professional standards in real-life situations, ensuring that decisions align with the counselor's responsibilities and the highest ethical standards.

Ethical decision-making in counseling is rarely straightforward. It is shaped by multiple factors, including personal values, professional ethical codes, and legal requirements. Counselors must navigate these influences carefully to ensure their decisions uphold professional integrity and prioritize client well-being.

Every counselor brings their own personal values shaped by life experiences, cultural background, and belief systems. While these values naturally influence ethical perspectives, counselors must remain aware of potential biases and strive for objectivity. The goal is not to eliminate personal values but to manage them in a way that ensures fair and ethical decision-making.

Ethical codes, such as those established by the American Counseling Association (ACA), American School Counselor Association (ASCA) or the American Mental Health Counselors Association (AMHCA), provide essential guidance for ethical practice. State and federal laws govern the legal boundaries that must be followed in all decision-making processes.

Ethical decisions affect more than just individual clients, they shape public perception of the counseling profession, influence professional standards, and contribute to the evolution of ethical guidelines. Trust is at the heart of the therapeutic relationship, and ethical decision-making plays a crucial role in maintaining that trust. Poor ethical choices can undermine credibility, while well-reasoned decisions reinforce the integrity of the field.

COMMON MISCONCEPTIONS ABOUT ETHICAL DECISION-MAKING

A common myth is that ethical dilemmas always have clear-cut answers. In reality, many ethical situations involve conflicting principles and no perfect solution. Another misconception is that counselors must completely separate personal values from their professional practice.

While objectivity is essential, counselors should instead focus on self-awareness, recognizing how their values influence their decisions and reflecting on them thoughtfully. Structured models have been developed to help counselors navigate complex ethical situations. One widely used model, proposed by Kitchener (1984), offers a step-by-step approach:

1. Identify the ethical issue.
2. Apply relevant ethical codes and legal standards.
3. Consider possible courses of action.
4. Evaluate the potential consequences of each choice.
5. Select and implement the best course of action.

These models provide a systematic way to approach ethical dilemmas, ensuring that all relevant factors are considered. They also promote consistency across different cases and practitioners while reinforcing transparency and accountability in ethical practice.

PRINCIPLE-BASED ETHICS MODELS

Principle-based ethics models provide structured frameworks to help counselors navigate complex moral dilemmas. While these models share common foundations, each has unique characteristics shaped by different philosophical perspectives and developmental influences.

1. **Kitchener's Model**

Developed in the 1980s, Kitchener's model is built on five core ethical principles:

- **Autonomy** – Respecting clients' rights to make their own choices.
- **Nonmaleficence** – Avoiding harm.
- **Beneficence** – Promoting client well-being.
- **Justice** – Ensuring fairness and equality.
- **Fidelity** – Maintaining trust and honesty.

This model has significantly influenced later ethical frameworks in counseling by providing a universal set of principles applicable to various situations.

2. **The ACA Ethical Decision-Making Model**

The American Counseling Association (ACA) takes a more process-oriented approach. Its model outlines specific steps for resolving ethical dilemmas:

1. Identify the problem.
2. Apply the ACA Code of Ethics.
3. Determine the nature and dimensions of the dilemma.
4. Generate possible courses of action.
5. Consider potential consequences.
6. Evaluate and select the best action.
7. Implement the decision.

While this model incorporates ethical principles, it focuses more on the step-by-step process, making it particularly useful for new counselors or complex ethical situations.

THE AMHCA MODEL: INTEGRATING PRINCIPLES AND VIRTUE ETHICS

The American Mental Health Counselors Association (AMHCA) model blends principle-based and virtue-based ethics. In addition to core ethical principles, it emphasizes personal values and character in decision-making. This model encourages counselors to reflect on their own moral compass and professional identity when making ethical choices.

Despite their differences, all three models highlight the importance of systematic analysis and reflection. Kitchener's model provides a broad, principle-driven foundation applicable in diverse settings. The ACA model offers a structured, procedural approach ideal for those needing clear guidance. The AMHCA model integrates personal ethics, making it particularly relevant for counselors who see ethical decision-making as both a professional and personal responsibility.

Each model has strengths, and counselors may find it helpful to draw from multiple approaches when facing ethical dilemmas.

The effectiveness of principle-based ethics models in addressing ethical dilemmas depends on the specific context and nature of the issue. Each model has strengths and limitations that influence its applicability in real-world counseling scenarios.

Kitchener's model, with its clearly defined ethical principles, provides a strong foundation for ethical reasoning. However, it may lack the specificity needed for more nuanced situations. The ACA model offers a structured, step-by-step approach, making it a valuable tool for comprehensive ethical decision-making. However, in urgent situations requiring immediate action, following a detailed process may not always be practical.

One of the greatest strengths of principle-based models is their universality. By providing a consistent set of ethical principles, these models promote ethical clarity and consistency across the profession. They also serve as valuable teaching tools, helping new counselors develop a strong ethical foundation. However, rigidly applying universal principles without considering cultural or contextual factors can sometimes lead to oversimplified ethical judgments.

THE EVOLUTION OF ETHICAL MODELS IN COUNSELING

The development of these models reflects the growing complexity of counseling ethics. Kitchener's model emerged at a time when counseling was establishing itself as a distinct profession, laying the foundation for principle-based approaches.

The ACA model evolved over decades, incorporating insights from real-world practice and new ethical challenges. The AMHCA model represents a more recent effort to integrate multiple ethical perspectives, acknowledging the complexities of decision-making in mental health counseling.

While principle-based models provide essential guidance, integrating other ethical approaches can enhance their effectiveness. For example:

- **Virtue Ethics** emphasizes the counselor's character and personal values, encouraging ethical decision-making that aligns with integrity and moral responsibility.
- **Care Ethics** highlights relational and contextual factors, ensuring that ethical decisions consider the impact on clients and the therapeutic relationship.

By blending principle-based models with other ethical perspectives, counselors can navigate ethical dilemmas with greater depth, flexibility, and awareness of individual circumstances.

THE VIRTUE-BASED ETHICS APPROACH IN COUNSELING

Virtue-based ethics in counseling have their roots in ancient Greek philosophy, particularly Aristotle's concept of *eudaimonia*, human flourishing. Aristotle emphasized the development of virtuous character traits through habitual practice and reflection rather than strict adherence to rules. This idea later became influential in counseling ethics, where the focus shifted from rigid principles to the cultivation of moral excellence.

1. The Modern Revival of Virtue Ethics

Virtue ethics reemerged in contemporary moral philosophy thanks to G.E.M. Anscombe's 1958 essay *Modern Moral Philosophy*, which criticized deontological and consequentialist approaches. This resurgence coincided with growing dissatisfaction among counseling professionals who found principle-based ethical models too rigid to address the complexities of therapeutic relationships.

By the late 20th century, virtue ethics gained traction in counseling as an alternative to dominant principle-based models. The rise of *positive psychology*, led by psychologist Martin Seligman in the 1990s, further emphasized the importance of character strengths and virtues. Research in this field provided empirical support for the role of virtues in psychological well-being, bridging the gap between ancient philosophy and modern counseling practice (Seligman & Csikszentmihalyi, 2000).

2. Key Virtues in Counseling

As virtue ethics became integrated into counseling, several key virtues emerged as essential to ethical practice:

- **Integrity** – Maintaining honesty, trust, and confidentiality in the therapeutic relationship.
- **Compassion** – Cultivating empathy and genuine care for clients.
- **Wisdom** – Combining practical knowledge with moral discernment to navigate complex ethical dilemmas.

3. Application in Modern Counseling

Virtue-based ethics focuses on developing a counselor's overall character rather than merely following ethical codes. This approach encourages ongoing self-reflection, supervision, and professional growth to strengthen ethical decision-making. By prioritizing character development, virtue ethics prepares counselors to respond thoughtfully and ethically to diverse and unpredictable situations, especially those that rigid rule-based models may not fully address.

A key aspect of virtue-based ethics in counseling is the concept of moral exemplars, the idea that counselors should embody the virtues they encourage in their clients. By demonstrating integrity, compassion, and wisdom in their own lives and professional conduct, counselors serve as role models for ethical behavior and personal growth. This approach aligns with the broader therapeutic goal of fostering positive change, as clients benefit from seeing virtues in action (Jordan & Meara, 1990).

Virtue-based ethics have also been shaped by other ethical approaches in counseling. Its emphasis on character development has influenced principle-based models, encouraging a shift from rigid rule-following to deeper moral reasoning. At the same time, virtue ethics has incorporated elements of care ethics, recognizing the significance of relational virtues like empathy and compassion in therapy (MacIntyre, 2007; Slote, 2001).

As the field evolves, virtue ethics is gaining recognition for its ability to address the complexities of real-world counseling practice. Many counseling programs now integrate virtue ethics into their curricula, emphasizing character development alongside technical skills. Professional organizations have also begun acknowledging the importance of virtues, incorporating discussions of moral excellence into ethical guidelines.

The integration of virtue ethics with other ethical models is an emerging focus in counseling ethics. A blended approach could combine the character-based insights of virtue ethics with the structured guidance of principle-based models, offering counselors a more comprehensive framework for ethical decision-making. This integration would provide both the flexibility to navigate complex situations and the clarity needed for ethical consistency, better-equipping counselors to meet the diverse challenges of modern practice.

CULTURAL AND CONTEXTUAL MODELS

Cultural and contextual models in ethical decision-making have become essential frameworks in counseling, addressing the complexities of working with diverse client populations. Unlike traditional ethical models that assume universal principles, these approaches recognize that ethics are deeply influenced by cultural values, social norms, and situational factors. At their core, cultural and contextual models embrace cultural relativism and ethical pluralism, acknowledging that ethical standards vary across cultures and that multiple ethical perspectives can coexist (Frame & Williams, 2005; Houser et al., 2006).

Cultural relativism suggests that moral and ethical beliefs are shaped by cultural context, challenging the idea of universal ethical truths. This perspective encourages counselors to consider a client's cultural background when making ethical decisions rather than rigidly applying a predetermined set of rules. Ethical pluralism takes this concept further by recognizing the legitimacy of multiple ethical frameworks, emphasizing the need for dialogue, flexibility, and negotiation when navigating ethical dilemmas across different cultural contexts (Garcia et al., 2003; Cooper & McLeod, 2011).

169

These models emerged in response to the limitations of traditional ethical frameworks, which have often been rooted in Western philosophy and criticized for lacking cultural sensitivity. As counseling practices expanded globally and client populations became more diverse, it became clear that a one-size-fits-all approach to ethics was insufficient, and potentially harmful. Ethical dilemmas are rarely isolated from cultural realities, and models that fail to account for these complexities risk marginalizing non-Western perspectives or reinforcing biases (Pedersen & Marsella, 1982).

The rise of cultural and contextual models has had a profound impact on counseling ethics. These approaches have increased cultural sensitivity, encouraging counselors to develop a deeper understanding of their clients' worldviews, values, and decision-making processes. They promote recognition of diverse value systems, challenging counselors to examine and move beyond their own cultural biases. Additionally, they allow for flexibility, ensuring that ethical guidelines can be adapted to different cultural settings while maintaining professional integrity (Barnett, 2019).

Different strategies have been developed to integrate cultural and contextual considerations into ethical decision-making. Some of the most prominent include culturally responsive ethical guidelines, which provide flexibility in applying ethical principles across diverse cultural settings; consulting cultural experts or multicultural teams when navigating ethical dilemmas; and encouraging ongoing education and self-reflection to help counselors examine their own cultural biases and expand their understanding of different perspectives (Garcia et al., 2003; Houser et al., 2006).

While these approaches promote inclusivity, they also come with challenges and a risk of oversimplifying complex cultural dynamics or reinforcing stereotypes if culture is treated as a static or monolithic factor rather than a nuanced and evolving influence. To create more effective and inclusive ethical decision-making models, counselors must balance cultural awareness with ethical consistency. This means integrating universal ethical principles with culturally informed perspectives, ensuring ethics remain both adaptable and grounded in professional integrity. The future of counseling ethics lies in models that embrace cultural diversity while upholding the core values of ethical practice, respect, autonomy, and client well-being (Frame & Williams, 2005).

Several strategies can be considered to enhance cultural competence in ethical decision-making. One approach is implementing comprehensive cross-cultural training programs for counselors, which can improve their ability to navigate ethical dilemmas in diverse cultural contexts. While these programs provide valuable knowledge and practical skills, designing training that adequately covers the vast array of cultural perspectives presents a challenge and requires significant time and resources (Houser et al., 2006).

Another strategy involves developing collaborative decision-making models that actively involve clients in the ethical decision-making process. This approach ensures that cultural perspectives are directly incorporated, promoting client autonomy and respect for diverse values. However, conflicts may arise when client values clash with professional ethical standards or legal obligations, requiring careful negotiation and ethical reasoning (Garcia et al., 2003).

A third approach is establishing ongoing cultural competence assessment and feedback mechanisms within counseling practices. Regular evaluation can help identify areas for improvement and support continuous learning. While this approach allows for dynamic adaptation to changing cultural landscapes, it may be resource-intensive and could lead to assessment fatigue among counselors.

Implementing these strategies in multicultural counseling settings presents several challenges. Resistance to change among established practitioners, limited resources for training and assessment, and the complexity of addressing the needs of highly diverse client populations can create obstacles. Ensuring the long-term sustainability of these initiatives requires ongoing commitment from counseling organizations, educational institutions, and individual practitioners (Barnett & Johnson, 2015).

Cultural and contextual models in ethical decision-making represent a crucial evolution in counseling ethics. These approaches recognize the intricate relationship between culture, context, and ethical practice, challenging counselors to develop more nuanced and culturally sensitive approaches to ethical dilemmas. While implementation challenges exist, continued development and refinement of these models are essential to maintaining ethical and effective counseling practices in an increasingly diverse and interconnected world.

APPLYING MODELS TO REAL DILEMMAS

Applying ethical decision-making models in counseling often involves navigating complex challenges. Consider a scenario in which a counselor learns about a romantic relationship between a teacher and a student. This situation requires balancing legal, ethical, and professional considerations.

Using a principle-based ethical decision-making model provides a structured approach to analyzing the ethical dimensions of the case. The counselor must identify the key ethical issues, consider relevant ethical principles, and evaluate potential courses of action. In this instance, confidentiality must be weighed against the duty to report, along with the client's autonomy and the counselor's professional responsibilities.

The legal context adds another layer of complexity. While the student is 18, meaning the relationship is legally permissible, school policies prohibiting teacher-student relationships introduce an institutional ethical standard that may take precedence. This discrepancy between legal and institutional standards highlights the need to consider multiple sources of ethical guidance.

Consulting a supervisor is a crucial step in the ethical decision-making process, allowing the counselor to seek additional perspectives while maintaining client confidentiality. This consultation provides valuable insight and support in navigating ethical dilemmas.

Integrating multiple ethical perspectives can further enhance decision-making. A virtue-based ethics model, for example, encourages the counselor to reflect on personal qualities such as integrity and compassion in determining the best course of action. This approach complements the principle-based model by fostering a more holistic consideration of the counselor's role and responsibilities.

A feminist ethics approach can also provide valuable insights by examining the power dynamics within the teacher-student relationship and considering broader contextual factors. This perspective encourages a more nuanced understanding of the ethical implications and may inform the counselor's decision-making process in ways that principle-based models alone might not.

The complexity of this case highlights the limitations of ethical decision-making models in providing definitive answers to real-world dilemmas. While these models offer structured frameworks for analysis, they often require interpretation and adaptation to specific contexts. Integrating multiple ethical perspectives allows for a more comprehensive analysis, potentially leading to more thoughtful and effective decision-making.

Several key principles emerge from this case that can be applied to similar ethical dilemmas in counseling:

1. **Thorough Ethical Analysis** – Using structured decision-making models provides a systematic way to identify and evaluate ethical concerns, even when no clear-cut solution exists.

2. **Consultation and Collaboration** – Seeking input from supervisors or colleagues enhances ethical reasoning by incorporating additional perspectives and professional support.
3. **Integration of Multiple Ethical Frameworks** – Combining different ethical approaches, such as principle-based, virtue-based, and feminist ethics, fosters a deeper understanding of complex situations.
4. **Balancing Legal, Ethical, and Professional Standards** – Counselors must navigate the intersections of legal requirements, ethical guidelines, and institutional policies, which may not always align.
5. **Considering Contextual Factors** – Ethical decision-making should take into account the specific circumstances and potential consequences of actions within broader social and institutional settings.

Consider how you can develop a more holistic and adaptable approach to ethical dilemmas, ensuring decisions that are both ethically sound and contextually sensitive in your practice.

ENHANCING ETHICAL REASONING SKILLS

Enhancing ethical reasoning skills is an ongoing process that requires continuous learning and self-reflection. The first step in this process is developing ethical sensitivity, the ability to recognize ethical issues within complex professional situations. This skill is essential because it lays the foundation for sound ethical decision-making.

Counselors can strengthen their ethical sensitivity through regular exposure to case studies, thorough examination of ethical codes, and participation in supervision sessions. These activities help practitioners identify ethical nuances they might otherwise overlook. However, recognizing ethical concerns is not always straightforward, as they are often embedded within intricate client situations. To overcome this challenge, counselors should make it a habit to systematically analyze each case for potential ethical dilemmas, even when they are not immediately apparent.

The second step involves mastering ethical frameworks and decision-making models. A strong understanding of ethical approaches, such as utilitarianism, deontology, and virtue ethics, enables counselors to navigate complex dilemmas with confidence (Chapter 1). This knowledge can be gained through academic study, professional workshops, and peer discussions. The real challenge lies in translating these abstract theories into practical applications. To bridge this gap, counselors should actively compare and contrast different ethical models using real-world scenarios from their practice or professional literature. Applying these frameworks in context helps solidify theoretical understanding and improves the ability to select the most appropriate approach for each situation.

The third step is cultivating critical thinking skills, which allow counselors to analyze and evaluate ethical arguments rigorously. These skills can be sharpened through logic courses, structured debate exercises, and reflective practice. A major obstacle in this step is overcoming personal biases that may cloud judgment.

To address this, counselors should consciously consider multiple perspectives on ethical issues, even those that challenge their initial inclinations. Engaging in open discussions with colleagues and supervisors can further enhance objectivity, fostering a more balanced and thoughtful approach to ethical decision-making.

The fourth step, engaging in ethical deliberation, shifts from individual reflection to collaborative problem-solving. Participation in ethics committees or peer consultation groups provides counselors with opportunities to discuss complex dilemmas in a structured environment. These forums expose practitioners to diverse viewpoints, challenging them to articulate and defend their ethical reasoning. A key challenge in this step is balancing conflicting perspectives while staying grounded in ethical principles. Utilizing structured formats like moral case deliberation can help guide discussions, ensuring all relevant aspects of an ethical issue are thoroughly explored.

The final step is a deep reflection on personal values and their influence on ethical judgments. This introspective process helps counselors recognize how their own beliefs and experiences shape decision-making. Tools such as journaling and values clarification exercises can facilitate this self-examination.

However, this step can be particularly challenging, as it often requires confronting uncomfortable truths about oneself. To navigate this effectively, counselors should commit to regular self-reflection and actively seek feedback from colleagues and supervisors for external perspectives on their ethical reasoning.

Each of these steps works together to enhance a counselor's ethical reasoning skills. Ethical sensitivity allows for the recognition of ethical issues, while a strong grasp of ethical frameworks provides structured guidance. Critical thinking strengthens the evaluation of ethical arguments, and ethical deliberation broadens understanding through diverse perspectives. Finally, personal reflection ensures awareness of individual biases and motivations.

Alternative methods for enhancing ethical reasoning include immersive simulations, where counselors practice ethical decision-making in virtual scenarios, an approach particularly effective for visual and experiential learners. Mentorship programs could also provide valuable guidance by pairing less experienced counselors with seasoned practitioners. This approach would be especially beneficial for those who learn best through interpersonal interaction and real-world application.

9

LEGAL ISSUES IN

COUNSELING ETHICS

MALPRACTICE AND NEGLIGENCE

Malpractice and negligence are serious legal and ethical concerns in counseling, with significant consequences for both counselors and their clients. While these terms are often used together, they have distinct meanings.

Malpractice refers to professional misconduct or a failure to meet the expected level of skill, resulting in harm to the client. Negligence, on the other hand, occurs when a counselor fails to provide the standard of care that a competent professional would in a similar situation. Both concepts emphasize the counselor's responsibility to provide ethical, competent, and appropriate care.

Issues related to malpractice and negligence can arise in various ways. Breaching confidentiality, misdiagnosing a client, failing to warn or protect when necessary, engaging in inappropriate relationships, or abandoning a client without proper referrals are all examples. These violations not only harm individual clients but also damage trust in the counseling profession as a whole.

Many malpractice claims stem from common mistakes. Inadequate training or supervision can lead to poor decision-making, especially in complex cases. Poor documentation, such as incomplete or inaccurate client records, can make it difficult to defend against legal claims. Boundary violations, whether intentional or not, are another frequent issue. Additionally, failing to stay updated on evolving professional standards can result in outdated or ineffective treatment.

By maintaining strong ethical awareness, staying informed about legal responsibilities, and engaging in continuous professional development, counselors can reduce the risk of malpractice and uphold the integrity of their work.

Facing a malpractice suit can have serious and far-reaching effects on a counselor's career, finances, and emotional well-being. The cost of legal defense, settlements, or judgments can be overwhelming, sometimes putting financial stability and career prospects at risk. Professionally, a malpractice claim can damage a counselor's reputation, lead to the loss of licensure, and make it difficult to obtain malpractice insurance in the future. On a personal level, the stress and anxiety of a legal battle can take a toll, leading to self-doubt and affecting both personal well-being and professional performance.

To prevent malpractice, many strategies focus on education, supervision, and risk management. Continuing education ensures that counselors stay informed about evolving legal and ethical standards. Clinical supervision provides a space for professional growth and case consultation, helping to navigate complex situations. Risk management practices, such as clear, informed consent procedures and thorough documentation, can reduce legal vulnerabilities. While these approaches are valuable, their effectiveness depends on factors like the quality of education, the availability of experienced supervisors, and the challenges of applying risk management strategies in different practice settings.

Counselors can take proactive steps to minimize malpractice risks. A well-structured informed consent process helps set clear expectations, reducing misunderstandings and potential disputes. While this requires extra time and effort, it promotes transparency and shared decision-making. Regular peer consultations or case reviews can also be invaluable, offering fresh perspectives and identifying ethical or legal concerns early. Though scheduling and confidentiality may present challenges, this collaborative approach can strengthen clinical decision-making and safeguard both clients and counselors.

A third key strategy is maintaining comprehensive documentation protocols that accurately capture clinical details, treatment decisions, and client interactions. Proper documentation not only supports effective client care but also serves as a crucial safeguard against malpractice claims. However, it can be time-consuming and, if not managed efficiently, may take time away from direct client work. Common challenges in implementing strong documentation practices include resistance from experienced practitioners, limited resources in smaller practices or agencies, and the need for continuous training to ensure consistency.

The long-term success of malpractice prevention efforts depends on several factors. Regularly reviewing and updating policies to align with evolving legal and ethical standards is essential. Fostering a culture of ethical awareness and open communication within counseling organizations reinforces the importance of these practices. Additionally, integrating malpractice prevention strategies into counselor education and training ensures that ethical decision-making and risk management become core aspects of a counselor's professional identity from the very start of their career.

LEGAL STANDARDS OF CARE

The legal standard of care in counseling defines the level of competence and professionalism expected from mental health practitioners. It represents the care, skill, and treatment that a reasonably qualified counselor with similar training and experience would provide under similar circumstances. This standard is crucial because it sets the baseline for ethical and effective client care while helping to determine whether malpractice has occurred.

Legal standards of care are shaped by a combination of professional guidelines, state and federal laws, and legal precedents. Organizations such as the American Counseling Association (ACA) play a key role in establishing ethical codes and best practices that often influence legal expectations. These standards evolve through research, expert consultation, and feedback from practitioners. Additionally, court rulings in malpractice cases help refine interpretations of appropriate care, sometimes leading to changes in legal and ethical guidelines.

Several core principles define the legal standard of care in counseling. Competence is essential, counselors must practice within their expertise, stay informed about best practices, and continue their professional development. Confidentiality, again, is another key aspect, requiring counselors to protect client information and only disclose it when legally necessary, such as in cases of imminent harm. Informed consent ensures that clients understand the nature of therapy, potential risks and benefits, and available treatment options before proceeding.

Adhering to legal standards of care does more than guide individual counseling sessions, it plays a vital role in protecting client welfare across the profession. These standards ensure that all counselors meet a baseline level of competence and ethical conduct, providing safeguards for vulnerable populations who might otherwise be at risk of harm or exploitation. Beyond individual client protection, maintaining these standards strengthens the credibility of the counseling profession as a whole. Public trust in mental health services is essential for ensuring widespread access to quality care and fostering a healthier society.

There are several misconceptions about legal standards of care in counseling. One is the belief that these standards impose a rigid, one-size-fits-all approach to therapy, limiting a counselor's ability to provide individualized care. In reality, legal standards are designed to be flexible, allowing for a wide range of therapeutic approaches while still ensuring responsible and ethical practice. Another common misconception is that following these standards is primarily about avoiding malpractice lawsuits. While legal protection is a factor, the primary purpose of these guidelines is to uphold the quality of care and safeguard client interests.

The Connection Between Legal and Ethical Practice

Legal standards of care and ethical practice go hand in hand. Legal requirements provide a clear framework for ethical decision-making, helping counselors translate broad ethical principles into practical applications. For example, the legal obligation to obtain informed consent aligns with the ethical principle of respecting client autonomy. Similarly, confidentiality laws reinforce the ethical responsibility to protect client privacy.

In addition to guiding ethical behavior, legal standards serve as an important mechanism for accountability. They provide a benchmark for evaluating professional conduct, both for self-assessment and for review by peers, supervisors, and regulatory bodies. This ongoing accountability helps maintain the integrity of the counseling profession and encourages counselors to continually reflect on and improve their practice.

ETHICAL CODES VS. STATE LAWS

Ethical codes and state laws both play crucial roles in guiding counselors, but they differ in their foundations, scope, and enforcement. While both aim to protect clients and uphold professional standards, ethical codes originate from professional organizations, whereas state laws are created through legislative processes. These differences influence how they are applied and interpreted within the counseling profession.

The American Counseling Association (ACA) Code of Ethics provides a broad ethical framework focused on client welfare, confidentiality, and professional competence. In contrast, state laws outline specific legal requirements, such as licensing standards and mandatory reporting obligations. Despite these differences, both serve a common purpose: ensuring ethical, responsible, and legally sound counseling practices.

One key area where ethical codes and state laws diverge is in post-termination sexual relationships between counselors and clients. The ACA Code of Ethics requires a five-year waiting period before such a relationship can be considered ethical, while California state law only mandates a two-year gap. This difference highlights the complex relationship between professional ethics and legal regulations, emphasizing the need for counselors to navigate both carefully.

Ethical codes often provide flexibility, allowing for thoughtful decision-making in complex situations. They emphasize guiding principles like beneficence (acting in the client's best interest), non-maleficence (avoiding harm), and respect for autonomy, concepts that can adapt to different counseling contexts. State laws, on the other hand, are typically more rigid and prescriptive, offering clear-cut rules but sometimes lacking nuance for unique circumstances.

Understanding both ethical guidelines and legal requirements is essential for counselors to practice responsibly, ensuring they meet both professional and legal expectations while prioritizing client well-being.

THE EVOLUTION OF ETHICAL CODES AND STATE LAWS

Ethical codes and state laws related to counseling have developed along different paths. Ethical codes evolve through professional consensus, often adapting to new challenges in the field. The ACA Code of Ethics, for example, has undergone multiple revisions to reflect shifting societal norms and professional standards. In contrast, state laws are typically shaped by landmark legal cases and legislative initiatives. Tarasoff v. Regents helped define the duty to protect. This case is introduced in Chapter 2 and referenced here for its legal implications.

Both ethical codes and state laws offer protections for client rights and counselor autonomy, but each has strengths and limitations. Ethical codes take a broad approach to client protection, emphasizing informed consent, confidentiality, and cultural competence while allowing counselors greater autonomy in decision-making. State laws, while often more limited in scope, provide legal enforceability and clear consequences for violations, ensuring that client protections have legal backing.

Navigating Conflicts Between Ethics and Law

Conflicts between ethical guidelines and legal requirements can arise in various situations. For instance:

- **Confidentiality vs. Mandatory Reporting** – Ethical codes emphasize confidentiality as fundamental to trust in counseling. However, state laws may require counselors to break confidentiality in cases of suspected child abuse or harm to others. Note, however, many ethical codes also require reporting harm and neglect.

- **Client Autonomy vs. Involuntary Treatment** – Ethical codes promote client self-determination, yet some state laws allow involuntary treatment under specific conditions, such as when a client poses a risk to themselves or others.

In these cases, counselors must carefully balance ethical obligations with legal mandates, ensuring both compliance and client-centered care.

To reduce conflicts and improve guidance for counselors, several strategies could help align ethical codes and state laws:

1. **Stronger Collaboration Between Professional Organizations and Lawmakers** – By working together, organizations like the ACA and legislative bodies can create more consistent and complementary guidelines.
2. **Integrating Ethical Reasoning into Legal Education** – Training programs can better prepare counselors to navigate complex situations where ethical principles and legal obligations intersect, fostering sound decision-making in real-world practice.

By bridging the gap between ethics and law, counselors can confidently uphold professional standards while ensuring compliance with legal requirements, ultimately protecting both clients and the integrity of the profession.

NAVIGATING LEGAL-ETHICAL CONFLICTS

Imagine a counselor who suspects child abuse but faces threats of legal action from the client. This situation highlights the delicate balance between legal duties and ethical responsibilities in the counseling profession. It's a challenge many practitioners encounter, navigating the gray areas where law and ethics intersect.

At the heart of this dilemma is a conflict between two key obligations: the legal mandate to report suspected child abuse and the ethical duty to maintain client confidentiality, a fundamental part of the therapeutic relationship. While laws clearly require counselors to report abuse, ethical codes stress the importance of trust and privacy. This tension puts the counselor in a difficult position, having to weigh the legal risks of not reporting against the ethical concerns of breaking confidentiality.

The way a counselor approaches this kind of decision is crucial. Seeking guidance from a supervisor or legal expert can provide clarity and support. Ethical best practices encourage collaboration in complex cases, reinforcing that no counselor has to navigate these dilemmas alone. By using available resources and seeking professional input, counselors can make informed, responsible choices that uphold both legal and ethical standards.

The counselor's decision to report suspected child abuse to protective services reflects a fundamental ethical priority: safeguarding a vulnerable child takes precedence over maintaining client confidentiality. This choice reinforces a core principle in counseling ethics, the duty to protect those at risk, particularly minors, can override other ethical concerns. However, it is not without consequences. The counselor may face legal threats from the client or damage the therapeutic relationship, highlighting the difficult trade-offs involved in ethical decision-making. Despite even if backed up by ethical requirements, threats and therapeutic rupture can still happen.

Exploring alternative approaches offers insight into the complexity of these dilemmas. For instance, further discussing concerns with the client before reporting could allow for more information gathering while preserving trust. Encouraging the client to self-report provides another option, balancing respect for autonomy with legal and ethical responsibilities. These alternatives illustrate the importance of considering multiple perspectives and outcomes when facing ethical conflicts.

This case also highlights broader lessons for the counseling profession. Thorough documentation plays a critical role in ethical practice, especially when legal risks are involved. Clear policies on handling legal-ethical conflicts ensure practitioners have institutional guidance and support. Additionally, ongoing training in legal and ethical issues is essential as ethical standards evolve and require continuous professional development.

Ethical decision-making is not a single event but an ongoing process. The counselor's path, from initial suspicion to final action, involves careful deliberation, consultation, and weighing of consequences. This step-by-step approach serves as a model for handling similar conflicts, emphasizing the importance of thoughtful, informed decision-making.

Several key principles emerge from this case. First, prioritizing client welfare should always guide ethical decisions, even when other obligations create tension. Second, seeking guidance from supervisors, colleagues, and legal experts is essential for navigating complex issues. Third, counselors must have a solid grasp of both legal mandates and ethical standards to make informed choices. Finally, maintaining detailed documentation is crucial, particularly in cases with potential legal implications.

The intersection of law and ethics in counseling rarely offers easy answers. Cases like this one provide valuable learning opportunities, helping practitioners develop a deeper understanding of ethical challenges and how to navigate them effectively. By analyzing real-world dilemmas and extracting key principles, counselors can strengthen their ability to balance legal obligations with ethical responsibilities in professional practice.

DOCUMENTATION AND RISK MANAGEMENT

A well-structured documentation system is the backbone of risk management in counseling. Electronic health record (EHR) systems have become the preferred method for maintaining client records due to their security features and ease of use. With built-in encryption, access controls, and audit trails, EHRs help ensure compliance with HIPAA regulations.

However, implementing these systems comes with challenges, such as data migration, staff training, and ongoing maintenance. To ease the transition, it's important to choose an EHR system that fits the practice's specific needs and provides reliable technical support.

Once a documentation system is in place, maintaining consistent and thorough records for each client session is essential. Effective documentation is more than just taking notes, it requires a structured approach that captures relevant clinical details while remaining objective. Using session note templates can help standardize documentation, ensuring that key elements, such as the client's presentation, interventions used, and progress toward treatment goals, are consistently recorded. The challenge lies in finding the right balance: notes should be detailed enough for clinical and legal purposes but not overloaded with unnecessary information. Counselors must develop the skill of writing clear, concise notes that focus on observable behaviors and clinical impressions rather than personal interpretations.

Informed consent is another crucial aspect of documentation, serving both ethical and legal functions. Obtaining a client's signature on a form is just one step; true informed consent involves a meaningful discussion about the treatment process, potential risks, and client rights. This can be particularly challenging when working with clients who have limited English proficiency or cognitive impairments. In such cases, professional interpreters or simplified consent forms may be necessary. Beyond the initial consent, it's equally important to document any follow-up discussions or changes to the treatment plan. This ongoing documentation demonstrates continued client engagement and understanding, reinforcing ethical and legal protections.

Protecting client confidentiality goes beyond initial documentation, it requires safeguards throughout the entire lifecycle of client information. This includes both physical security measures, such as locked filing cabinets for paper records, and digital protections, like encrypted data transmission and secure storage.

One of the biggest challenges in maintaining confidentiality is striking a balance between making information accessible to the treatment team and ensuring client privacy. Regular staff training is crucial, as human error remains one of the leading causes of data breaches. Additionally, counselors must stay informed about emerging technologies, such as telehealth platforms and cloud-based storage, to assess their impact on client confidentiality.

Regular risk assessments are a proactive way to identify and address potential vulnerabilities in counseling practice. These assessments should cover all key areas, including clinical procedures, documentation practices, and office security. Using standardized checklists can help ensure a systematic approach. However, keeping up with evolving legal and ethical standards presents an ongoing challenge. Consulting with legal professionals or risk management experts can provide valuable guidance, helping counselors interpret complex regulations in practical terms.

An effective risk management strategy is multi-layered, with each component reinforcing the others. For instance, thorough documentation of informed consent strengthens confidentiality protections by clearly defining the boundaries of information sharing. Likewise, regular risk assessments can highlight areas for improvement in documentation practices, ensuring compliance with current standards.

In some counseling settings, alternative documentation approaches may be necessary. For example, in crisis intervention or short-term counseling, brief, focused notes may be more appropriate than detailed session documentation.

When working with children or adolescents, age-appropriate assent forms can supplement standard informed consent procedures. In substance abuse treatment settings, counselors must comply with additional confidentiality regulations under 42 CFR Part 2. These variations highlight the importance of adapting documentation practices to the specific counseling context while still upholding ethical and legal requirements.

10

---◦⌒⌒⌒◦---

RESEARCH, HIPAA AND
CONFIDENTIALITY

THE IMPORTANCE OF RESEARCH ETHICS IN
COUNSELING

Research in counseling must balance two critical goals: protecting participants and advancing knowledge. Ethical research ensures that human subjects are treated with care and respect while allowing for meaningful scientific discoveries. Key concerns include informed consent, confidentiality, minimizing harm, and responsibly sharing findings.

One of the biggest ethical challenges in research is the power imbalance between researchers and participants. Because researchers are seen as experts, participants may feel pressured to take part, even if unintentionally. Additionally, the desire for career success or groundbreaking results can sometimes cloud judgment, putting participants at risk.

Unethical research has serious consequences. When ethical breaches occur, they can damage public trust in both the counseling profession and scientific research as a whole. Historical cases, like the Tuskegee Syphilis Study, show how unethical practices can harm individuals and entire communities for generations. Participants who suffer harm in research settings may also experience long-term psychological distress, often worsening the very issues that counseling research seeks to address.

Institutions have safeguards in place to protect research participants, but these systems are not perfect. Institutional Review Boards (IRBs) help ensure that studies meet ethical standards by reviewing research proposals from multiple perspectives. However, IRBs can sometimes be seen as bureaucratic obstacles, delaying important studies or limiting innovative research approaches. Their effectiveness can also vary between institutions, leading to inconsistencies in ethical oversight.

Professional organizations, such as the American Counseling Association (ACA), provide ethical guidelines that help shape responsible research practices. These guidelines establish professional norms and offer a decision-making framework for researchers. However, they may not always keep up with evolving methodologies or emerging ethical dilemmas, especially in the digital age, where data privacy and online research introduce new challenges.

To improve ethical research in counseling, several key strategies could be considered:

1. Enhanced Ethics Education

Providing comprehensive ethics education for researchers and graduate students could strengthen ethical awareness and decision-making. Instead of focusing solely on compliance, these programs would emphasize real-world applications of ethical principles, helping researchers navigate complex situations before issues arise. The success of this approach, however, depends on the quality of instruction and researchers' willingness to actively engage with the material.

2. Stronger Peer Review for Ethics

Strengthening peer review processes by explicitly evaluating the ethical aspects of research proposals and manuscripts could provide an additional layer of accountability. Integrating ethics into the academic publishing process would encourage more thoughtful study designs and reinforce ethical standards. However, this would require training reviewers to assess ethical considerations effectively, as well as additional time and resources.

3. Interdisciplinary Ethics Advisory Boards

Establishing ethics advisory boards within research institutions could offer ongoing guidance throughout the research process. Unlike Institutional Review Boards (IRBs), which focus on approval and oversight, these advisory boards would provide consultation and collaboration, helping researchers address ethical challenges as they arise. The main challenge would be ensuring adequate resources and avoiding excessive bureaucracy.

While implementing these solutions may face obstacles, such as institutional resistance, resource limitations, and the need for widespread adoption, long-term success depends on strong leadership, continuous refinement of ethical practices, and a commitment to integrating ethics into the core values of counseling research.

INFORMED CONSENT IN RESEARCH

Informed consent is a fundamental ethical principle in both counseling and research, but its purpose and application differ between these settings. In clinical practice, informed consent helps build trust and ensures clients have control over their treatment decisions (ACA, 2014, A.2; AMHCA, 2020, I.B.2). In research, however, it serves as a safeguard to protect participants from harm or exploitation while contributing to scientific knowledge. These differing goals shape how informed consent is approached in each context.

At its core, informed consent is about respecting autonomy, but how this is applied varies. In therapy, autonomy is upheld through ongoing conversations and shared decision-making, allowing for adjustments as treatment progresses (ACA, 2014, A.2.a.; AMHCA, 2020, I.B.2). In research, consent is usually a more formal, one-time process at the beginning of a study. This reflects the nature of the relationships involved: the evolving, collaborative bond between therapist and client versus the structured, time-limited interaction between researcher and participant.

The level of detail in informed consent also differs. In clinical settings, it typically covers treatment options, potential risks and benefits, and alternative approaches (ACA, 2014, A.2.b.; AMHCA, 2020, I.B.2). Research consent, however, must go further, explaining the study's purpose, methods, duration, and the participant's role. This ensures participants fully understand their involvement, especially since research may not provide them with direct personal benefits (ACA, 2014, A.2.d.; ASCA, 2022, A.4).

Historical events have played a crucial role in shaping informed consent practices, particularly in research ethics. One of the most infamous ethical violations, the , exposed the dangers of inadequate consent. In this study, treatment was deliberately withheld from African American men with syphilis without their knowledge, leading to severe harm and loss of trust in medical research (Centers for Disease Control and Prevention [CDC], 2022). The public outrage that followed led to the Belmont Report and the establishment of federal regulations for human subjects research (U.S. Department of Health and Human Services, 1979). In contrast, informed consent in clinical practice has evolved more gradually, shaped by legal cases and shifting societal views on patient autonomy.

The effectiveness of informed consent in protecting participants' rights differs between clinical and research settings. Clinical settings benefit from the ongoing nature of the therapeutic relationship, allowing for continuous clarification and reassessment. However, time constraints may sometimes limit in-depth discussions about risks and benefits. In **research**, the initial consent process is often more thorough, but complex study designs and technical language can make it difficult for participants to fully grasp the risks involved. Additionally, incentives or perceived benefits might unintentionally pressure participants into agreeing to take part.

Each approach has its strengths and challenges. Clinical informed **consent** is flexible and responsive to individual client needs but may lack the detailed documentation required in research. Research consent, while standardized and comprehensive, can overwhelm participants with too much information, potentially affecting their ability to make fully informed decisions.

Integrating the best aspects of both approaches could enhance informed consent in counseling research. Adopting the ongoing, conversational nature of clinical consent could improve participant comprehension and engagement. Meanwhile, incorporating the structured, detailed approach of research consent into clinical practice, especially for high-risk or experimental treatments, could provide greater clarity and protection. A tiered consent process in research, similar to the staged disclosure used in therapy, could help balance thoroughness with participant understanding.

These adaptations could be particularly valuable in long-term clinical trials, where periodic reassessment of consent ensures participants remain informed and engaged throughout the study. Likewise, for novel or high-risk treatments in therapy, a more formalized, research-style consent process could enhance transparency and safeguard client autonomy.

CONFIDENTIALITY AND DATA PROTECTION

Ensuring confidentiality and data protection in counseling research starts with a thorough assessment of potential risks. Researchers must carefully evaluate the sensitivity of the data they collect and identify any factors that could compromise participant privacy. One challenge is the risk posed by indirect identifiers, seemingly harmless details that, when combined, could reveal a participant's identity. To prevent this, researchers should consult privacy experts and Institutional Review Boards (IRBs) to identify and mitigate hidden vulnerabilities.

After assessing risks, the next step is designing data collection methods that minimize identifiable information. This often involves anonymization techniques and secure data collection platforms. A key challenge here is balancing privacy protection with the need for useful research data. To address this, researchers commonly use coding systems that separate personal identifiers from the main dataset, preserving analytical value while safeguarding identities.

Once data is collected, it must be securely stored. This requires encrypted databases, access control measures, and regular security updates. While these protections help prevent breaches, researchers must also ensure that authorized team members can access data when needed. To maintain security without hindering access, ongoing staff training and regular updates to security protocols are essential.

By combining thoughtful risk assessment, careful data collection practices, and strong security measures, researchers can uphold ethical standards and protect participant confidentiality in counseling research.

Once data is securely stored, managing data access and sharing becomes a critical step in ensuring confidentiality. This involves setting clear protocols on who can access, use, and share data, typically through data use agreements and secure file transfer methods. One challenge in this phase is balancing the need for collaboration with the necessity of maintaining confidentiality. Strategies such as role-based access control (granting different levels of access based on a researcher's role) and detailed audit trails (tracking who accesses data and when) help maintain security while allowing for necessary data sharing.

Even with strong protections in place, researchers must also prepare for potential breaches of confidentiality. Having a clear response plan in place is essential. This includes incident response templates to guide actions in case of a data breach and access to legal counsel for handling ethical and legal concerns. However, as cyber threats continue to evolve, response plans must be regularly updated and tested through security drills to ensure they remain effective.

These steps, risk assessment, secure data collection, encrypted storage, controlled access, and breach preparedness, work together to create a layered approach to confidentiality protection in counseling research. Each step builds upon the previous one, reinforcing the overall security of the research process.

Alternative Approaches to Data Anonymization

In some research contexts, additional techniques can enhance privacy protection:

- **Differential privacy**: This method adds controlled noise to datasets, allowing researchers to analyze trends without exposing individual participant details.
- **Federated learning**: Instead of sharing raw data, researchers train algorithms locally on different datasets, reducing the need for direct data exchange.

- **Synthetic data generation**: Artificial datasets are created that retain the statistical properties of real data but do not contain actual participant information, further reducing privacy risks.

By integrating these alternative approaches where appropriate, researchers can strengthen confidentiality protections while maintaining the integrity and usefulness of their data.

DUAL ROLES: CLINICIAN-RESEARCHER DILEMMAS

Here is another situation wherein Dr. Smith's case highlights the ethical challenges that arise when counselors take on dual roles as both clinicians and researchers. This situation presents several critical concerns at the intersection of therapy and scientific inquiry, emphasizing the need for clear ethical guidelines in counseling research.

The primary dilemma is the conflict between therapeutic responsibilities and research objectives. As a clinician, Dr. Smith's first duty is to act in the best interests of her clients, providing care tailored to their individual needs. However, as a researcher, she must follow standardized protocols and maintain objectivity. The challenge lies in balancing personalized care with the scientific rigor required for valid research.

A key ethical concern is the risk of coercion or undue influence. Because of the inherent power imbalance in the therapist-client relationship, clients may feel pressured to participate in the study, whether to please their therapist or out of fear that refusal could affect their treatment. This dynamic threatens the voluntary nature of informed consent, which is a fundamental principle of ethical research.

Confidentiality also becomes more complex in this dual role. While therapists must uphold strict confidentiality, research often requires data sharing and publication. Even when data is anonymized, using client

198

information for research may blur the lines between therapy and research, potentially eroding client trust.

Finally, the therapeutic relationship itself may be affected. Participation in a study can shift client expectations and introduce new anxieties or dependencies, which might interfere with treatment. If a client experiences negative effects from the study, it could strain the therapist-client bond and compromise treatment outcomes.

Navigating these dilemmas requires careful ethical planning, including transparent informed consent, clear role boundaries, and safeguards to protect client autonomy and confidentiality.

Dr. Smith's decision to inform her clients about the study without directly recruiting them represents a measured approach to these ethical challenges. By referring interested clients to a colleague for further information and consent, she creates a degree of separation between her roles as therapist and researcher. This strategy helps mitigate the risk of coercion and preserves the integrity of the therapeutic relationship.

Alternative approaches, such as excluding current clients from the study entirely or employing an independent third party for recruitment and consent, offer more stringent safeguards against ethical breaches. These methods provide clearer delineation between clinical and research roles but may limit the pool of potential participants or introduce additional logistical complexities.

The case illuminates broader themes within research ethics in counseling, particularly the tension between advancing scientific knowledge and protecting client welfare. It underscores the importance of maintaining clear boundaries, ensuring voluntary participation, and safeguarding client confidentiality in research contexts. Furthermore, it highlights the need for robust institutional oversight and ethical review processes to navigate the complexities of dual-role scenarios.

Several general principles can be applied to similar situations involving dual roles in counseling research. First, transparency is paramount; all potential conflicts of interest should be disclosed to clients and research participants. Second, the separation of roles should be maintained whenever possible, with clear delineation between clinical and research activities. Third, informed consent processes should be rigorous and ongoing, ensuring that participants fully understand the implications of their involvement.

Additionally, external oversight and consultation play crucial roles in maintaining ethical standards. Institutional Review Boards (IRBs) and ethics committees can provide valuable guidance and serve as impartial arbiters in complex cases. Peer consultation and supervision can also offer important perspectives and help clinician-researchers navigate ethical gray areas.

The principle of beneficence - doing good for others - should guide decision-making in dual-role scenarios. Researchers must carefully weigh the potential benefits of their studies against the risks to participants, always prioritizing client welfare over research objectives. This may involve making difficult decisions, such as excluding vulnerable populations from studies or modifying research designs to minimize risks to participants.

ETHICAL ISSUES IN QUALITATIVE RESEARCH

Qualitative research plays a crucial role in counseling by capturing the nuanced, lived experiences of individuals within therapeutic contexts. Unlike quantitative studies, which focus on numbers and measurable variables, qualitative research explores personal narratives, emotions, and perceptions, offering a deeper understanding of psychological processes and therapeutic outcomes.

Ensuring ethical integrity in qualitative research requires careful attention to participant selection. Researchers must balance the need for a diverse and representative sample with the responsibility to avoid coercion or undue influence during recruitment. This involves clear communication about the study's purpose, potential risks, and benefits, along with ensuring that informed consent is truly voluntary, allowing participants to withdraw at any time without consequences.

Interpreting qualitative data presents another layer of ethical challenges. Researchers must faithfully represent participants' perspectives while remaining aware of their own biases and assumptions. A reflexive approach, where researchers continually examine their influence on the analysis, helps maintain integrity. Member checking, a process where participants review preliminary findings, can further enhance accuracy and authenticity in data interpretation.

One of the most pressing ethical concerns in qualitative research is protecting participant anonymity. Because qualitative studies often include rich, detailed personal accounts, even anonymized data can sometimes reveal identities, especially in small or close-knit communities. To mitigate this risk, researchers can use pseudonyms, alter non-essential details, and aggregate data when appropriate, all while ensuring that these measures do not dilute the depth and meaning of the findings.

Maintaining ethical standards in qualitative research requires ongoing transparency, reflexivity, and participant engagement, ensuring that the research process remains respectful, accurate, and protective of those who share their stories.

The ethical practice of qualitative research extends far beyond individual studies, shaping the broader field of counseling and society at large. By amplifying the voices of marginalized and underrepresented populations, qualitative research can challenge existing power structures and inform policy decisions. For example, studies exploring the experiences of LGBTQ+ clients in therapy have contributed to more inclusive and affirming counseling practices.

Despite these contributions, qualitative research is sometimes criticized for its subjectivity and potential researcher bias. Skeptics argue that interpretive analysis may reflect the researcher's preconceptions rather than participants' true experiences (Grossoehme, 2014). However, rigorous qualitative methods incorporate strategies to enhance trustworthiness and credibility (Nowell, Norris, White, & Moules, 2017):

- **Member Checking**: Involving participants in reviewing and validating findings ensures that their perspectives are accurately represented. This approach not only strengthens credibility but also empowers participants as co-creators of knowledge.
- **Reflexivity**: Researchers actively examine their own biases, assumptions, and positionality throughout the research process. This self-awareness fosters transparency and allows readers to understand the lens through which data is analyzed.
- **Triangulation**: Using multiple data sources, methods, or researchers to corroborate findings enhances depth and reliability. For instance, a study on the therapeutic alliance might integrate client interviews, therapist reflections, and session observations to provide a more comprehensive picture.
- **Audit Trails**: Keeping detailed records of the research process allows others to trace the decision-making and analytical processes, increasing the credibility and replicability of the study.

Ethical considerations in qualitative counseling research are especially critical when exploring sensitive topics. One major concern is the potential for re-traumatization of participants when discussing distressing experiences. To mitigate this risk, researchers must:

- Be trained in trauma-informed approaches
- Have clear protocols for managing participant distress
- Provide appropriate support or referrals when needed

Another key issue is the power dynamic in qualitative research, particularly when participants feel obligated to participate or provide socially desirable responses, especially if there is a pre-existing therapeutic relationship. Strategies to minimize coercion include:

- Using third-party recruiters to invite participants
- Emphasizing the **voluntary** nature of participation
- Clearly defining boundaries between research and therapy

By integrating these ethical safeguards, qualitative research in counseling can uphold the highest standards of integrity, ensuring that findings are credible, respectful, and impactful.

VULNERABLE POPULATIONS IN RESEARCH

The ethical considerations surrounding vulnerable populations in counseling research have evolved significantly over the past century, shaped by historical events, societal changes, and advancements in scientific ethics.

The foundation for protecting these groups in research can be traced back to 1947, with the establishment of the Nuremberg Code following World War II. This code, created in response to the horrific experiments conducted by Nazi physicians, introduced fundamental principles such as voluntary consent and the right to withdraw from research.

Building on these principles, the World Medical Association introduced the Declaration of Helsinki (1964), which expanded ethical guidelines for research involving human subjects. This declaration introduced the need for independent ethical review committees and emphasized special protections for vulnerable populations. Over time, multiple revisions have further strengthened these safeguards to address emerging ethical challenges.

Recognizing Vulnerable Populations

During the mid-20th century, awareness grew regarding the unique vulnerabilities of certain groups, including:

- Children
- Prisoners
- Individuals with cognitive impairments

Again, several unethical studies underscored the urgent need for stronger protections. For example:

- The **Willowbrook Hepatitis Study** (1950s–1970s) deliberately infected institutionalized children with hepatitis to study disease progression.
- The **Tuskegee Syphilis Experiment** (1932–1972) withheld treatment from African American men with syphilis to observe the disease's natural course, violating their autonomy and well-being.

These incidents led to tighter research regulations, culminating in the Belmont Report (1979), which outlined three core ethical principles:

1. **Respect for Persons** – Protecting autonomy and providing special safeguards for vulnerable individuals.
2. **Beneficence** – Ensuring research **maximizes benefits and minimizes harm**.
3. **Justice** – Ensuring **fair selection** of research participants, preventing the exploitation of vulnerable groups.

As briefly discussed earlier, in response to past ethical breaches, the United States established the National Commission for the Protection of Human Subjects of Biomedical and Behavioral Research in 1974. This commission's work led to the Belmont Report (1979), a landmark document that shaped ethical standards for research involving vulnerable populations.

The Belmont Report introduced three core ethical principles:

1. **Respect for Persons** – Ensuring autonomy and providing additional safeguards for those with diminished capacity.
2. **Beneficence** – Maximizing benefits while minimizing potential harm.
3. **Justice** – Promoting fairness in participant selection to prevent the exploitation or exclusion of specific groups.

These principles transformed research ethics, leading to stricter regulations and inspiring global guidelines for protecting human subjects.

A key outcome of the Belmont Report was increased scrutiny of research practices that disproportionately burdened or excluded certain populations. Researchers began emphasizing equitable distribution of risks and benefits, ensuring that vulnerable groups were neither exploited nor unfairly excluded from the potential benefits of research.

In recent years, there has been a shift towards more inclusive and participatory research methods, such as:

- **Community-Based Participatory Research (CBPR):** A collaborative approach where marginalized communities actively participate in all research stages, from problem identification to data collection and analysis. This method ensures research remains relevant and beneficial to the populations being studied.
- **Culturally Responsive Research:** Ethical guidelines now emphasize the need for cultural competence when working with diverse populations. The American Counseling Association's Code of Ethics highlights the importance of respecting cultural contexts in research design and implementation.
- **Global Ethical Standards:** The International Compilation of Human Research Standards, updated annually by the U.S. Department of Health and Human Services, reflects the evolving

nature of global research ethics, ensuring international studies meet ethical requirements across different cultural and regulatory landscapes.

As research evolves, new ethical dilemmas arise, particularly with digital technologies, artificial intelligence, and big data in counseling research. These innovations bring both opportunities and risks for vulnerable populations, requiring ongoing revisions to ethical guidelines.

Key areas demanding attention include:

- **Digital & Remote Research:** As counseling shifts to online platforms, ensuring privacy, informed consent, and data security in virtual settings is crucial.
- **Intersectionality & Vulnerability:** Many individuals belong to multiple vulnerable groups (e.g., a child from a low-income, immigrant background). Ethical guidelines must account for complex, overlapping vulnerabilities.
- **Global Research Collaborations:** Ethical standards vary across cultures and legal systems, raising challenges in maintaining consistent protections for vulnerable populations worldwide.

PUBLICATION ETHICS AND INTEGRITY

Ethical publishing is essential in counseling research, ensuring that knowledge is shared responsibly and with integrity. Upholding these principles builds trust within the academic community and the public. Below are seven key aspects of ethical publishing that every researcher should understand.

Authorship and Credit

Determining who deserves authorship in academic work requires careful consideration. According to the International Committee of

Medical Journal Editors (ICMJE), authorship should be granted to those who:

- Make significant contributions to the study's conception or design
- Help draft or revise the manuscript for intellectual content
- Give final approval before publication
- Take responsibility for the accuracy and integrity of the work

For example, in a graduate student's thesis, the student is typically the primary author, while their advisor may qualify as a co-author if they contributed to the research design, data analysis, or manuscript preparation. Clear authorship guidelines ensure proper credit is given while holding contributors accountable for their work.

Plagiarism and Self-Plagiarism

Plagiarism, using someone else's ideas, words, or research without proper credit, is a serious ethical violation. Self-plagiarism, or reusing one's own previously published work without acknowledgment, is also problematic. In counseling research, where similar methods may be applied across multiple studies, text recycling can blur the lines of originality.

For instance, if a researcher copies sections of a literature review from a previous paper without citing it, that constitutes self-plagiarism. While some overlap in methodology may be unavoidable, it's important to properly cite past work and clearly highlight new contributions.

Maintaining honesty in research is crucial, especially in counseling, where findings can directly influence clinical practice. Ethical publishing requires researchers to report data accurately, disclose conflicts of interest, and present results responsibly.

Data Fabrication and Falsification

Creating false data or manipulating existing data to fit a desired outcome is a serious breach of research integrity. In counseling studies, such misconduct can have real-world consequences, misleading practitioners and potentially harming clients.

For example, a researcher studying therapeutic outcomes might exclude certain data points to make their results appear statistically significant. While this may seem like a small adjustment, it distorts the truth and weakens the credibility of the entire field. Fortunately, modern statistical techniques have made it easier to detect data manipulation by identifying inconsistencies and anomalies in reported results.

Conflict of Interest Disclosure

Transparency is essential in research, and that includes openly acknowledging any potential conflicts of interest. Researchers must disclose financial, personal, or professional relationships that could influence their work.

For instance, if a counseling researcher is studying a therapeutic approach while also consulting for the company that developed it, this relationship should be disclosed. While not necessarily unethical, failing to acknowledge such ties can lead to questions about bias. Non-financial conflicts, such as ideological or theoretical allegiances, can also impact research and remain an ongoing topic of discussion in the field.

Responsible Reporting of Results

Accurate and complete reporting of research findings is fundamental to ethical publishing. Unethical practices such as p-hacking (running multiple analyses until a significant result is found) and HARKing (Hypothesizing After Results are Known) distort scientific conclusions.

In counseling research, misleading reporting can shape clinical decisions in harmful ways. For example, selectively presenting only the significant findings from a study on therapy effectiveness might make an intervention seem more successful than it actually is. To maintain trust in research, it's essential to present all findings, positive, negative, or inconclusive, so that practitioners can make informed decisions based on the full picture.

Maintaining integrity in research requires ethical peer review, responsible data sharing, and clear authorship guidelines. These elements work together to ensure that counseling research remains credible, reliable, and impactful.

Peer Review Ethics

Peer review plays a critical role in maintaining research quality. Reviewers are responsible for providing fair, timely, and constructive feedback while keeping submitted work confidential. However, the system isn't without challenges.

For example, an unethical reviewer might intentionally delay feedback to slow down a competitor's publication, affecting knowledge dissemination and even career progression, especially for early-career researchers. Ongoing debates about blind versus open peer review reflect the field's efforts to balance anonymity with accountability, ensuring that the process remains both rigorous and fair.

Replication and Data Sharing

Recent discussions on research integrity have emphasized the importance of replication and data transparency, partly in response to the replication crisis in psychology. Sharing data and methods allows others to verify findings, strengthening the credibility of research.

In counseling studies, this might involve making analysis code and anonymized data publicly available. However, researchers must also consider confidentiality, as counseling data often involves sensitive personal information. The growing movement toward open science represents a shift in how research is conducted, with long-term benefits for credibility and progress in the field.

The Interconnected Nature of Publication Ethics

Ethical issues in publishing don't exist in isolation, they influence one another in complex ways. For example, disputes over authorship can lead to pressure to manipulate data or findings to satisfy all contributors. Similarly, undisclosed conflicts of interest can compromise the integrity of peer review and the reliability of published results.

By upholding ethical principles across all aspects of publishing, researchers can contribute to a more transparent, trustworthy, and impactful body of knowledge in counseling.

THE FUTURE OF ETHICAL RESEARCH

The future of ethical research in counseling is evolving rapidly, shaped by technological advancements and global collaboration. While these developments open new doors for understanding mental health, they also introduce ethical challenges that researchers must carefully navigate.

Artificial intelligence (AI) and big data analytics are transforming counseling research, offering unprecedented insights into human behavior and mental health. AI can analyze vast amounts of anonymized therapy transcripts, uncovering patterns that may enhance our understanding of therapeutic outcomes. Machine learning algorithms can identify subtle correlations and predictive factors that traditional research methods might overlook.

However, these advancements come with ethical concerns. Data privacy, informed consent, and algorithmic bias must be addressed to ensure the responsible use of AI in mental health research. Who owns the data? How is it stored securely? What are the risks of AI unintentionally reinforcing societal biases? These are critical questions that researchers must consider as they integrate technology into their work.

International research collaborations offer valuable opportunities to study mental health across diverse populations. Cross-cultural studies can lead to more inclusive, culturally sensitive interventions and expand the global knowledge base on counseling practices. Additionally, pooling resources and expertise across borders can accelerate innovation in the field.

However, ethical challenges arise when research spans different cultural and legal landscapes. Privacy laws, consent requirements, and ethical standards vary worldwide, requiring researchers to balance respect for local traditions with the need for consistent ethical practices. Navigating these differences thoughtfully is essential to maintaining the integrity of global research partnerships.

Advancements in virtual reality (VR) and teletherapy are reshaping counseling research, offering exciting new possibilities while introducing unique ethical challenges.

- **VR and Teletherapy in Counseling Research**

VR technology allows researchers to create controlled, immersive environments for studying therapeutic interventions, potentially enhancing the internal validity of research designs. Similarly, teletherapy studies provide opportunities to reach populations that were previously difficult to include, increasing the diversity and representativeness of research samples.

However, these innovations also raise important ethical questions. Can findings from VR-based therapy be applied to traditional face-to-face counseling? How does remote data collection affect confidentiality and informed consent? And how does technology-mediated communication impact the therapeutic alliance? Researchers must carefully examine these issues to ensure that new methodologies maintain both ethical integrity and practical relevance.

- **Adapting Ethical Guidelines for a Changing Landscape**

As research evolves, ethics review boards face the challenge of updating their frameworks to address emerging concerns. Traditional principles, such as respect for persons, beneficence, and justice, must be reinterpreted to apply to AI-driven research, global collaborations, and virtual counseling interventions.

For example, ethics boards may need to establish guidelines to ensure transparency and accountability in AI-based data analysis. Similarly, they must develop protocols for evaluating ethical considerations in international research partnerships and virtual counseling studies, ensuring that these innovations uphold participant rights and data security.

The growing role of technology in counseling research also calls for a shift in training and education. Future counseling professionals will need to develop skills beyond traditional research methods, including:

- **Data Science and AI Ethics** – Understanding how algorithms influence research outcomes and recognizing potential biases in machine learning models.
- **Cross-Cultural Ethics** – Navigating ethical differences in international research collaborations while upholding universal ethical principles.

- **Psychological Impacts of Virtual Environments** – Examining how VR and digital interventions affect client experiences and treatment outcomes.

To uphold ethical standards in this evolving field, researchers must remain committed to protecting participants and preserving the integrity of counseling as a profession. This may involve updating informed consent procedures to clearly explain the complexities of AI-driven data analysis or VR-based therapy. It may also require establishing international ethical standards that balance cultural diversity with core research ethics.

By staying proactive and thoughtful, the counseling research community can embrace innovation while ensuring that ethical principles remain at the heart of scientific progress.

SAFEGUARDING CLIENT CONFIDENTIALITY

Confidentiality is one of the most important ethical responsibilities in counseling. It forms the foundation of trust between counselors and clients, allowing for open, honest communication. Professional organizations such as the American Counseling Association (ACA), American Mental Health Counselors Association (AMHCA), and American School Counselor Association (ASCA) all emphasize the critical role of confidentiality in their ethical guidelines.

Protecting client privacy isn't just an ethical duty, it's also a legal requirement. The Health Insurance Portability and Accountability Act (HIPAA) sets strict guidelines for handling mental health records in clinical settings. Counselors must implement security measures to protect client data, obtain informed consent before sharing information, and only disclose the minimum necessary details for treatment purposes.

In educational settings, the Family Educational Rights and Privacy Act (FERPA) governs student records, including counseling notes. FERPA gives parents access to their child's educational records until the child turns 18 or enters college, at which point those rights are transferred to the student. School counselors must carefully balance protecting student confidentiality with their responsibilities to parents, educators, and the school community.

The ethical foundations of confidentiality rest on three key principles:

- **Autonomy:** Clients have the right to control their personal information and decide how it is shared.
- **Beneficence:** Confidentiality creates a safe space for clients to discuss sensitive issues, ultimately promoting their well-being.
- **Non-maleficence:** Protecting client information helps prevent harm that could arise from unauthorized disclosure.

Maintaining confidentiality is essential to ethical counseling practice, but it often requires careful navigation of legal requirements and situational complexities. By upholding this principle, counselors foster trust and ensure that clients feel secure in seeking support.

Legal protections for client confidentiality have developed through both statutes and case law. Many states recognize counselor-client privilege, similar to attorney-client privilege, shielding counseling records from disclosure in legal proceedings. As discussed in Chapter 2, the landmark case, *Jaffee v. Redmond (1996)*, reinforced this protection at the federal level, affirming that effective therapy relies on trust and confidentiality.

Confidentiality does more than protect individual clients, it plays a crucial role in public health. When people know their privacy is safeguarded, they are more likely to seek mental health care without fear of stigma or discrimination. This is particularly important for vulnerable groups, such as individuals with substance use disorders or survivors of domestic violence, who may otherwise hesitate to reach out for support.

However, a common misconception is that confidentiality in counseling is absolute. While it is a fundamental ethical duty, it does have limits. Ethical codes and legal statutes outline specific situations where confidentiality (also discussed in Chapters 1, 11, and 17) may need to be breached, including:

- **Imminent danger:** If a client poses a serious risk to themselves or others, counselors may be required to intervene.
- **Suspected abuse or neglect:** Laws often mandate reporting suspected abuse of children, elderly individuals, or other vulnerable populations.
- **Legal requirements:** In certain court cases, counselors may be compelled to disclose information under a subpoena, though privilege laws vary by jurisdiction.

Balancing confidentiality with other ethical responsibilities requires professional judgment. The ACA Code of Ethics provides guidance on these complexities. Section B.2.a emphasizes respecting client privacy and avoiding unnecessary disclosures. At the same time, Section B.2.d acknowledges that confidentiality may be broken in cases of clear and imminent danger, illustrating the balance between protecting client information and ensuring safety.

In educational settings, the ASCA Ethical Standards for School Counselors reinforce these principles while addressing the unique challenges of working with students. Standard A.2.g calls for school counselors to protect confidential information as required by federal and state laws. However, Standard A.2.e recognizes the need to balance students' right to privacy with the responsibilities of parents and guardians in guiding their children's well-being.

Navigating confidentiality requires a thoughtful approach, ensuring that client trust is maintained while also upholding legal and ethical obligations. By understanding these nuances, counselors can safeguard both individual rights and broader community well-being.

HIPAA AND COUNSELING: NAVIGATING PRIVACY IN MENTAL HEALTH CARE

HIPAA and traditional counseling confidentiality practices share a common goal: protecting client privacy. However, they differ in their origins, scope, and implementation. Enacted in 1996, HIPAA (Health Insurance Portability and Accountability Act) sets national standards for safeguarding health information, including mental health records. In contrast, counseling confidentiality practices have developed over decades through ethical codes and legal precedents, often emphasizing professional judgment over rigid rules.

Despite their differences, both frameworks prioritize client trust and privacy. HIPAA provides detailed regulations, requiring secure electronic records, access controls, and encryption, to prevent unauthorized access. Counseling ethics, while equally committed to confidentiality, take a broader approach, considering the therapeutic relationship and contextual nuances.

HIPAA has introduced several benefits for mental health professionals:

- **Standardized Privacy Practices:** It ensures uniform confidentiality measures across healthcare settings, including counseling.
- **Stronger Security for Electronic Records:** Requirements like encryption, audit trails, and restricted access reduce the risk of data breaches.
- **Clearer Protocols for Information Sharing:** Counselors working in multidisciplinary teams have defined guidelines on how and when to share client information.

However, HIPAA also presents challenges, particularly for counseling settings:

- **Regulatory Complexity:** Smaller counseling practices may struggle to keep up with HIPAA's detailed compliance requirements.
- **Emphasis on Electronic Records:** While HIPAA strengthens data security, it may not fully account for the nuances of psychotherapy notes and verbal exchanges central to counseling.
- **Potential Gaps in Therapeutic Context:** Standardized privacy rules may not always align with the flexibility needed for client-centered care.

The histories of HIPAA and counseling confidentiality follow distinct yet occasionally overlapping paths. Counseling confidentiality dates back to ancient healing traditions and became formally recognized in professional ethical codes by the mid-20th century. Landmark legal cases, such as Tarasoff v. Regents of the University of California (1976), defined its limits, establishing the duty to warn when clients pose an imminent danger to others.

In contrast, HIPAA (Health Insurance Portability and Accountability Act) was introduced in 1996 primarily to address health insurance portability and electronic record security. Over time, regulatory updates, such as the HITECH Act of 2009, expanded its scope, strengthening enforcement and enhancing patient rights in the digital age.

Strengths and Challenges of HIPAA in Mental Health Care

HIPAA provides valuable protections for mental health records, particularly in the following areas:

- **Comprehensive Data Security:** Requires risk assessments, employee training, and breach notification procedures to safeguard client information.

- **Recognition of Psychotherapy Notes:** Distinguishes psychotherapy notes from general mental health records, granting them **special protections** and requiring separate authorization for disclosure.
- **Legal Framework for Telehealth & Electronic Communication:** Establishes guidelines for protecting virtual therapy sessions and digital records.

However, HIPAA also presents challenges for counseling confidentiality:

- **Blurred Distinctions in Record-Keeping:** Differentiating between psychotherapy notes and general mental health records can be confusing, leading to potential misinterpretation of privacy protections.
- **Limited Coverage in Non-Traditional Settings:** Some counselors, such as those practicing in community-based settings or using innovative therapeutic approaches, may not fall under HIPAA's "covered entity" requirements, leaving privacy concerns unaddressed.
- **Conflicts with Traditional Confidentiality Practices:** In family therapy, group counseling, and working with minors, HIPAA's emphasis on individual privacy can sometimes clash with ethical considerations related to shared confidentiality and family dynamics.

Bridging the Gap Between HIPAA and Counseling Ethics

To integrate HIPAA compliance with counseling ethics, several steps can help align legal and professional standards:

- **Specialized HIPAA Training for Counselors:** Tailored training programs can help mental health professionals navigate HIPAA requirements while preserving ethical confidentiality practices.

- **Collaboration Between Regulators and Professional Organizations:** Counseling associations can work alongside HIPAA regulators to develop clearer guidelines that harmonize legal and ethical principles.
- **Standardized Consent and Confidentiality Frameworks:** Creating templates for informed consent that meet both HIPAA requirements and ethical best practices can simplify compliance while protecting client privacy.

Exceptions to Confidentiality

Confidentiality is a key part of the counseling profession, but there are situations where counselors must break it for ethical and legal reasons. These exceptions exist to protect public safety and follow legal requirements. The most common situations where confidentiality must be breached include:

- Reporting child abuse or neglect
- Reporting elder or dependent adult abuse
- The duty to warn when a client poses a serious threat to someone else

1. Child Abuse Reporting

Counselors are legally required to report suspected child abuse or neglect. The safety of children takes priority over confidentiality, as minors may not be able to protect themselves. For example, if a client shares that they are physically harming their child, the counselor must report it to child protective services to prevent further harm.

2. Elder and Dependent Adult Abuse Reporting

Similarly, if a counselor suspects abuse or neglect of an elderly or dependent adult, they are required to report it. These laws exist to protect vulnerable individuals who may be unable to defend themselves. For instance, if a counselor learns that a caregiver is financially exploiting an elderly client, they must notify the proper authorities to intervene.

3.   The Duty to Warn

The duty to warn comes from the well-known *Tarasoff* case, which established that counselors must break confidentiality if a client poses a serious, identifiable threat to another person. This legal and ethical obligation helps prevent harm. For example, if a client makes a credible threat against their ex-partner, the counselor may need to warn the potential victim and alert law enforcement.

The exceptions to confidentiality exist because of the ongoing balance between individual rights and society's responsibility to protect its members. When vulnerable individuals are at risk, or there's a credible threat to others, intervention becomes necessary. Laws and court decisions help guide counselors through these difficult situations while also minimizing legal risks.

However, breaking confidentiality can affect the therapeutic relationship. Clients may hesitate to share sensitive information if they fear it could be reported. For example, a parent struggling with anger issues might withhold details out of fear that their words could trigger a child abuse report. This hesitation can make it harder for counselors to provide meaningful support.

Managing Confidentiality Exceptions

To handle these challenges, counselors use several approaches:

- **Clear Communication:** At the start of therapy, counselors explain the limits of confidentiality. While this ensures transparency, it may also discourage some clients from seeking help.

- **Ongoing Risk Assessment:** Counselors continuously evaluate potential risks and consult with colleagues or legal experts when necessary. However, risk assessments can be subjective and may not always lead to the right decision.
- **Tiered Disclosure Model:** Instead of overwhelming clients with legal details upfront, counselors can introduce confidentiality limits gradually as trust builds. This method ensures clients are informed while also feeling safe. However, it must be done carefully to avoid appearing deceptive.
- **Decision-Making Frameworks:** Having structured guidelines that incorporate ethics, legal requirements, and best practices can help counselors make informed choices. While helpful, these frameworks must remain flexible to accommodate unique situations.
- **Interdisciplinary Collaboration:** Working with legal experts and policymakers can lead to more refined, context-sensitive confidentiality policies. However, large-scale collaboration requires time, resources, and cooperation across multiple sectors.

As confidentiality challenges evolve, the counseling profession must adapt. Future changes may include shifts in client expectations, new legal and ethical standards, and the need for ongoing training to address emerging issues. By staying informed and adaptable, counselors can uphold ethical standards while maintaining trust with their clients.

CONFIDENTIALITY IN THE DIGITAL AGE

As discussed in Chapter 7, the rapid growth of digital technology has created new challenges for counselors in protecting client confidentiality. As technology becomes more integrated into mental health services, the profession must find a balance between using these advancements and safeguarding sensitive information. The ability to maintain confidentiality in an increasingly digital world is crucial, as it directly affects the trust between counselors and clients.

There are three main perspectives on how to handle this challenge, each with its own ethical and practical implications.

Some believe that fully embracing digital tools, while implementing strong security measures, is the best approach. This perspective highlights the benefits of technology, such as:

- **Increased accessibility** – Teletherapy allows counselors to reach clients in remote areas or those with mobility challenges.
- **Improved record-keeping** – Electronic health records (EHRs) make documentation more efficient and accurate, reducing errors and improving continuity of care.

However, critics warn that no system is completely secure. The healthcare industry is a frequent target for cyberattacks, as seen in the 2015 Anthem data breach, which exposed the records of nearly 79 million individuals. Counselors who adopt this approach must stay vigilant, ensuring their security measures are regularly updated to minimize risks.

Limiting Digital Use and Prioritizing Paper Records

Others advocate for a more cautious approach, limiting the use of digital tools and relying on paper records whenever possible. Supporters argue that this method significantly reduces the risk of large-scale data breaches. Unlike digital records, which can be accessed remotely by hackers, physical records require direct access to be compromised.

While this approach enhances security, it also comes with challenges. Paper records can be lost, damaged, or accessed by unauthorized individuals if not stored properly. Additionally, limiting digital tools may reduce efficiency and accessibility for both counselors and clients.

While limiting digital use may enhance security, critics argue that it's impractical in today's world. Avoiding technology can create barriers to effective mental health care, such as:

222

- **Lack of coordination between providers** – Without easy record-sharing, clients may experience gaps in care.
- **Increased administrative burden** – Managing paper records can take up valuable time that could be spent helping clients.

A Balanced Approach: Combining Digital and Traditional Methods

A third perspective suggests a hybrid approach, using digital tools for convenience while keeping highly sensitive information in more secure, traditional formats. For example, a counselor might:

- Use a secure online platform for scheduling and general communication.
- Keep detailed session notes in a locked physical file rather than an electronic system.

This method offers flexibility, allowing counselors to benefit from technology while minimizing risks. However, some argue that managing multiple systems could create new security challenges rather than solving existing ones.

Attitudes toward technology often vary by generation. Younger counselors who grew up with digital tools may be more comfortable with technology-driven solutions and lean toward fully integrating digital systems. More traditional practitioners, however, may prefer methods that prioritize confidentiality over convenience.

The approach a counselor chooses has broader implications for the profession.

- **A fully digital approach** could make counseling more efficient and accessible but would require ongoing investments in cybersecurity.
- **A paper-based approach** might be seen as more secure but could limit access to care and adaptability.

- **A hybrid approach** would allow for more personalized confidentiality practices but could lead to inconsistencies across the field.

As the profession evolves, striking the right balance between security, accessibility, and trust will remain an ongoing challenge.

CONFIDENTIALITY IN GROUP SETTINGS

A substance abuse support group presents a challenging ethical dilemma, especially when confidentiality is at stake. Counselors must navigate the fine line between protecting individual privacy, fostering trust within the group, and addressing concerns that extend beyond the therapeutic setting.

Confidentiality is a central aspect of group therapy, creating a safe space where participants feel secure sharing personal struggles. In substance abuse treatment, this becomes even more critical, as disclosures can have significant personal and professional consequences. This case highlights how confidentiality can be tested when group members have connections outside the session.

The counselor's immediate reinforcement of the group's confidentiality agreement is a vital first step. This reminder reinforces ethical responsibilities, reassures the group of its commitment to privacy, and may help ease the anxiety of the member who disclosed their relapse. However, a general reminder alone may not fully address the specific concerns of the individuals involved.

One approach is to schedule private follow-up sessions. For the teacher, this provides space to discuss concerns about professional repercussions and explore strategies for maintaining recovery while managing their role as an educator. For the parent, it's an opportunity to emphasize their ethical obligation to confidentiality and address any worries about their child's education.

Another option is addressing the issue in a group discussion. This could promote a deeper understanding of confidentiality among all members but also risks further compromising the teacher's privacy or creating discomfort for others. Alternatively, temporarily placing the two individuals in separate groups might offer a quick resolution, though it could disrupt their therapeutic progress.

Each approach carries benefits and challenges. Ultimately, the counselor must carefully consider how to uphold confidentiality while ensuring the well-being of both the individuals involved and the group as a whole.

This case highlights the importance of proactively addressing confidentiality in group therapy. Counselors should reinforce confidentiality agreements not just at the start but throughout the therapeutic process. Consistently revisiting these guidelines helps maintain awareness and can prevent potential breaches before they arise.

The scenario also underscores the need for clear protocols when group members recognize each other or share pre-existing relationships. Counselors must be prepared to navigate these situations thoughtfully, balancing individual concerns with the integrity of the group. Establishing guidelines for handling dual relationships, whether members know each other from work, school, or the community, can help prevent conflicts and preserve trust.

The principles from this case extend beyond substance abuse support groups. In a grief support group, for example, a participant might recognize another as a colleague of their deceased loved one. In an eating disorder group, a member might identify someone as a well-known figure in the local fitness community. In each situation, the counselor must carefully manage confidentiality while addressing individual concerns and group dynamics.

Key principles for counselors include:

1. **Transparency** – Clearly communicate confidentiality policies and their limitations at the start and reinforce them regularly.
2. **Individualized Approach** – Tailor responds to each situation, considering the unique circumstances of those involved.
3. **Proactive Planning** – Develop protocols in advance for handling confidentiality concerns and dual relationships.
4. **Ethical Decision-Making** – Apply ethical decision-making models to assess the impact on individuals, the group, and the broader community.
5. **Ongoing Education** – Continuously educate group members about confidentiality and the consequences of breaches.
6. **Professional Consultation** – Seek supervision or consultation when faced with complex ethical dilemmas to ensure the best outcomes.

Counselors can create a stronger framework for maintaining confidentiality, ultimately enhancing the therapeutic experience for all participants. This case serves as a reminder of the ethical vigilance required in group counseling, where the intersection of personal relationships and group dynamics presents unique challenges.

CONFIDENTIALITY AND RECORD KEEPING

Maintaining confidentiality in counseling records is a crucial ethical responsibility that requires a structured and thoughtful approach. It starts with establishing a secure record-keeping system to protect client information. This means implementing both physical safeguards, such as locked filing cabinets for paper records, and digital security measures like encrypted storage or secure cloud services. The challenge is finding the right balance between ensuring counselors have easy access to necessary information while preventing unauthorized access. To stay ahead, counselors must regularly update security protocols and stay informed about emerging data protection technologies.

Once a secure system is in place, obtaining informed consent is the next essential step. Clients must clearly understand how their information will be recorded, stored, and protected. Counselors typically use written consent forms and verbal explanations to ensure transparency. The key challenge is making sure clients grasp these procedures without unnecessary anxiety about privacy. Using clear, non-technical language and encouraging questions can help ease concerns while reinforcing trust.

Another important aspect of confidentiality is minimizing sensitive information in records. Counselors should document only what is essential, avoiding unnecessary personal details that aren't directly relevant to the therapeutic process. Standardized templates and ethical guidelines help ensure consistency and appropriate documentation. The challenge is balancing thorough record-keeping with the need to protect client privacy. Regular reviews and updates to documentation practices help maintain ethical standards and align with best practices in the field.

A critical part of maintaining confidentiality in record-keeping is securely storing and transmitting client information. This includes establishing protocols for safeguarding records and ensuring confidentiality when sharing information, such as during referrals or legal disclosures. To protect data in transit, counselors may use secure file transfer methods and encrypted email services. The challenge is maintaining security without disrupting daily workflow. One solution is to develop and consistently use a checklist to verify secure information handling before any data is shared.

The final step in a comprehensive confidentiality approach is regularly reviewing and updating record-keeping practices. This ensures security measures remain effective and compliant with evolving regulations. Counselors can use audit checklists and participate in ongoing professional development focused on confidentiality best practices. Keeping up with changing technology and regulations can be challenging, but scheduling periodic system reviews, perhaps aligning them with license renewal periods, helps maintain compliance and efficiency.

Each of these processes, secure storage, informed consent, minimizing sensitive details, controlled transmission, and regular audits, works together to build a strong confidentiality framework. From data collection to long-term storage and information sharing, this systematic approach helps ensure client privacy remains protected at every stage of the counseling process.

In certain cases, such as working with high-risk clients or within interdisciplinary teams, additional measures may be needed. Some counselors use coded language or abbreviations to obscure sensitive details while still communicating essential information to authorized personnel. Others create separate, more detailed records for high-risk cases with extra layers of security. In interdisciplinary settings, shared electronic health records with tiered access levels allow for necessary collaboration while restricting access to highly sensitive information.

CONFIDENTIALITY ACROSS DIVERSE CULTURES

While this has been discussed throughout the text, it bears repeating that a client's cultural background plays a significant role in shaping their perceptions and expectations of confidentiality in counseling. Research in cross-cultural psychology and counseling ethics highlights how these expectations vary widely. A large-scale survey across ten culturally diverse groups underscores this point, revealing significant differences in attitudes toward information sharing with family members. This finding challenges the assumption that confidentiality is a universally understood or applied principle in counseling.

In some cultures, strict individual confidentiality may conflict with norms that emphasize family involvement in personal matters, including mental health. In collectivist societies, withholding information from family members may be seen as counterproductive, or even disrespectful,

228

to familial bonds. On the other hand, in more individualistic cultures, confidentiality between counselor and client is often considered essential. These differences highlight the challenges of applying standardized confidentiality practices across diverse cultural contexts.

A comparative analysis of psychological ethics codes in 24 countries further illustrates these variations. The study found notable differences in how confidentiality is addressed, particularly regarding minors and family involvement. In several countries, ethical codes reflect cultural norms that prioritize collective decision-making and family consultation, especially in cases involving children or adolescents. In contrast, other countries emphasize the primacy of individual autonomy and privacy, regardless of age. These differences reflect broader cultural values and legal frameworks, reinforcing the importance of culturally sensitive approaches to confidentiality in counseling (Leach & Harbin, 1997).

These findings have significant implications for counseling practice, emphasizing the need for cultural awareness when addressing confidentiality. Counselors who overlook these differences risk misunderstandings, breaches of trust, or ineffective therapeutic relationships. In multicultural settings, it's essential to navigate these complexities with sensitivity, adapting discussions on confidentiality to align with clients' cultural backgrounds and expectations.

While this study highlight the strong influence of cultural background on confidentiality perceptions, it's important to acknowledge their limitations. The cross-cultural survey, though extensive, relies on self-reported data, which may not always reflect actual behaviors in therapy. Likewise, the qualitative study's small sample size offers rich insights but may not be fully representative of broader populations.

Some might argue that core ethical principles, such as confidentiality, are universal. However, this perspective overlooks the nuanced ways in which these principles are interpreted and applied across cultures. While confidentiality is widely recognized as an ethical standard, cultural influences shape expectations around it, reinforcing the need for a flexible, culturally informed approach in counseling practice.

Another counterargument is that individual differences within cultures may outweigh broader cultural influences. While personal experiences certainly shape how individuals perceive confidentiality, the consistent patterns identified in cross-cultural research suggest that cultural background remains a significant factor. The findings from large-scale surveys and ethical code analyses reinforce the idea that cultural norms play a crucial role in shaping expectations around confidentiality.

For counselors working in multicultural settings, these insights have profound implications. Cultural competence must go beyond basic awareness of cultural differences, it requires a deeper understanding of how cultural values influence confidentiality expectations. This means adapting informed consent discussions to be culturally sensitive, negotiating confidentiality boundaries that respect both ethical standards and cultural norms, and developing strategies to navigate potential conflicts between individual privacy and family involvement.

By integrating these culturally informed approaches, counselors can build stronger therapeutic relationships, foster trust, and ensure ethical practices that align with both professional guidelines and clients' cultural perspectives.

CONFIDENTIALITY AND MINORS

Confidentiality in counseling minors presents unique ethical challenges, particularly in educational settings where therapeutic intervention and academic record-keeping often overlap. Counselors must navigate legal, ethical, and developmental considerations while ensuring that young clients understand the limits of confidentiality. A key concern is how information shared in counseling sessions is documented and whether it becomes part of a student's educational record.

In school counseling, this issue is especially complex. The Family Educational Rights and Privacy Act (FERPA) governs the confidentiality of educational records, but its definition of what qualifies as a record can be unclear. If counseling notes are maintained by the school and influence educational decisions, they may be subject to FERPA, making them accessible to parents, guardians, or administrators. This raises concerns about whether sensitive disclosures, intended to remain private, could inadvertently be exposed, potentially damaging trust in the counseling process.

This concern is particularly pressing for minors exploring gender identity and sexuality. If a counselor explicitly documents a student's experiences with gender identity or sexual orientation, that information could become accessible to unintended parties, leading to potential discrimination, familial conflict, or social ostracism. In these cases, the ethical duty to protect confidentiality may come into direct conflict with institutional record-keeping policies and parental rights to access school records.

Counselors must strike a careful balance between maintaining accurate records and protecting client confidentiality. One effective approach is minimalist documentation, recording only essential details necessary for continuity of care and legal compliance. While this reduces the risk of sensitive information being disclosed through educational records, it may also limit a counselor's ability to provide comprehensive care or justify clinical decisions if challenged.

Another strategy is separating clinical notes from educational records. In this model, counselors maintain detailed notes in a secure system while providing only general, non-specific information for school records. However, implementing this approach requires clear institutional policies and may be difficult within existing record-keeping frameworks.

To further protect privacy, counselors can use coded language or neutral terminology in their documentation. For example, instead of explicitly noting a student's exploration of gender identity, they might document "discussing personal identity development" or use predetermined codes understood only by mental health professionals.

Communicating confidentiality limits with minors presents additional challenges. Developmental factors play a major role, as younger clients may struggle to fully understand privacy rights, legal requirements, and ethical boundaries. The abstract nature of confidentiality can be difficult for minors to grasp, particularly given their evolving cognitive abilities.

Power dynamics also influence these conversations. Minors may feel hesitant to ask questions or challenge confidentiality policies, assuming that adults automatically have authority over their personal information. Counselors must create a space where young clients feel safe to discuss concerns, ask questions, and gain a clear understanding of their rights.

Cultural factors also play a role in communication barriers. Different cultural backgrounds shape perspectives on privacy, mental health, and the role of family in personal matters. These nuances can influence how minors perceive and respond to discussions about confidentiality.

The legal landscape adds another layer of complexity. Laws governing minor rights and parental authority vary by jurisdiction, making it difficult to provide clear, consistent guidelines on confidentiality. Counselors must stay informed about local regulations while ensuring their explanations are understandable for young clients.

Institutional factors, particularly in school counseling, further complicate confidentiality boundaries. Counselors often serve as both mental health professionals and school employees, leading to potential confusion about what information remains private and what might be shared within the educational system.

To address these challenges, counselors should use age-appropriate communication strategies that make confidentiality concepts clear and accessible. This may include using concrete examples, visual aids, or interactive discussions to enhance understanding. Regular check-ins throughout the counseling process can reinforce key points and address any evolving concerns, ensuring minors feel informed and empowered in their therapeutic relationships.

ETHICAL FOUNDATIONS IN GROUP COUNSELING

Group counseling as aforementioned presents distinct ethical challenges that require a deep understanding of specialized ethical principles. Unlike individual therapy, group dynamics introduce complexities that demand heightened awareness and sensitivity from counselors.

Confidentiality, a core principle of counseling (yes, another reminder!), becomes more intricate in a group setting. Information shared is not just between the client and counselor but among multiple participants, expanding the responsibility for maintaining privacy. Counselors must set clear expectations from the outset, educating group members on the importance of confidentiality and the potential risks of sharing personal details outside the group.

Another challenge arises from multiple client relationships within the group. Unlike in individual counseling, members interact with one another, creating a complex web of relationships that can influence the therapeutic process. Counselors must carefully navigate these dynamics, balancing individual needs with group cohesion while fostering a safe and supportive environment.

The ethical foundations of group counseling are grounded in key principles that guide professional practice:

- **Beneficence** – Promoting the well-being of all members, not just individuals, ensuring that the group as a whole fosters growth and healing.
- **Non-maleficence** – Preventing harm by monitoring group interactions, addressing conflicts, and intervening when necessary to protect members' emotional safety.
- **Autonomy** – Respecting each participant's right to self-determination while balancing this with the collective needs and structure of the group.
- **Justice** – Ensuring fairness in group participation, decision-making, and access to support while maintaining an equitable and inclusive environment.

Fidelity, the principle of honoring commitments and maintaining trust, is especially critical in group counseling, where the counselor must manage relationships with multiple clients simultaneously. Balancing these relationships requires transparency, consistency, and fairness to ensure that all group members feel equally valued and supported.

Applying ethical principles in group settings demands a heightened level of skill and awareness. Counselors must continually assess and respond to shifting group dynamics while upholding ethical standards. When done effectively, ethical conduct strengthens the foundation of trust and safety, which are essential for meaningful therapeutic work. Group members who perceive their counselor as ethical and impartial are more likely to engage fully, share openly, and support one another, key elements of group cohesion and success.

A common misconception is that strict adherence to ethical guidelines may disrupt the natural flow of group interactions or limit a counselor's ability to intervene effectively. In reality, ethical frameworks enhance rather than hinder the therapeutic process. Clear ethical boundaries provide structure and security, allowing flexibility and creativity to flourish within safe and appropriate limits.

To foster an effective group counseling environment, counselors must:

- **Establish clear boundaries** that protect confidentiality and respect each participant's autonomy.
- **Manage complex relationships with integrity**, ensuring fairness and consistency in interactions.
- **Adapt to evolving group dynamics**, reassessing ethical decisions as new challenges arise.

Ethical decision-making in group counseling is not static, it requires continuous reflection and adjustment. As group needs change, counselors must remain responsive while maintaining the highest standards of professional integrity. By doing so, they create a supportive environment that promotes trust, open communication, and personal growth, the ultimate goal of group therapy.

11

INFORMED CONSENT:

EMPOWERING CLIENTS

FOUNDATIONS OF INFORMED CONSENT

Informed consent is a fundamental ethical principle in counseling, grounded in client autonomy, transparency, and professional responsibility. The American Counseling Association (ACA), American Mental Health Counselors Association (AMHCA), and American School Counselor Association (ASCA) all emphasize its importance in their ethical guidelines. More than just a signed form, informed consent is an ongoing dialogue that empowers clients to make informed decisions about their treatment.

At its core, informed consent fosters a collaborative therapeutic relationship. Clients must receive clear information about the counseling process, including potential risks, benefits, and their rights as participants.

237

This ensures they remain active partners in their care, making choices that align with their personal values and goals.

Three essential components define valid informed consent:

1. **Capacity to Consent** – Clients must be able to understand the information provided and make rational decisions. Factors like age, cognitive ability, or mental state can influence this capacity. When necessary, counselors may need to involve legal guardians or representatives in the consent process.
2. **Voluntariness** – Clients must freely choose to participate in counseling without coercion or undue influence. This is particularly crucial in situations like court-mandated therapy or employee assistance programs, where individuals may feel pressured. Counselors must ensure that clients feel empowered to make their own decisions about engaging in therapy.
3. **Disclosure of Information** – Clients must receive comprehensive details about the counseling process, including goals, potential risks, benefits, confidentiality limits, and available alternatives. Information should be presented in clear, accessible language that matches the client's level of understanding.

One of the key elements of informed consent is disclosure, making sure clients fully understand the counseling process before making any decisions. This means clearly explaining:

- The purpose and process of counseling
- Potential risks and benefits
- Limits of confidentiality and exceptions
- Fees and billing policies
- Available alternative treatments

Counselors should communicate this information in a straightforward, accessible way, avoiding complex jargon that could cause confusion.

ETHICAL AND LEGAL IMPORTANCE OF INFORMED CONSENT

Informed consent isn't just a formality, it's a fundamental ethical obligation. It ensures that clients can make informed choices, reinforcing key ethical principles:

- **Autonomy** – Respecting clients' right to make their own decisions
- **Beneficence** – Acting in their best interest
- **Non-maleficence** – Avoiding harm

Beyond ethics, informed consent also has legal implications. It helps protect both clients and counselors by setting clear expectations and reducing the risk of malpractice claims. When done correctly, it strengthens the therapeutic relationship, creating a collaborative space where clients are active participants in their care.

Many people think informed consent is just a one-time form signed at the start of therapy. In reality, it's an ongoing process. As treatment progresses, new goals, interventions, or concerns may emerge, requiring another conversation about consent. Counselors should regularly check in with clients to make sure they remain informed and comfortable with their treatment.

Integrating informed consent into every stage of counseling not only upholds ethical and legal standards but also empowers clients. It reinforces their right to make decisions about their care and builds trust in the therapeutic relationship.

In the context of school counseling, as addressed by the ASCA Code of Ethics, informed consent takes on additional complexities. School counselors must navigate the dual obligations of respecting student autonomy while also considering the rights and responsibilities of parents or guardians. This often involves obtaining consent from both students and their legal guardians, particularly for minors.

The AMHCA Code of Ethics further emphasizes the importance of cultural competence in the informed consent process. Counselors must be sensitive to cultural differences that may affect a client's understanding of or willingness to engage in counseling. This may involve adapting the informed consent process to accommodate language barriers, cultural beliefs about mental health, or differing concepts of individual autonomy.

COMMUNICATING TREATMENT OPTIONS EFFECTIVELY

Effectively explaining treatment options is a common challenge in counseling and healthcare. Several factors contribute to this difficulty, including client anxiety, complex medical terminology, and time constraints faced by practitioners. At its core, the challenge lies in balancing the complexity of medical and psychological treatments with the emotional state of clients, who may feel overwhelmed by their situation.

One major barrier is the use of technical language that clients may not understand. Counselors and healthcare providers, trained in specialized terminology, might unintentionally use jargon that feels foreign to the average person. This disconnect can lead to confusion and hinder informed decision-making. For example, a counselor discussing cognitive-behavioral therapy might mention terms like "cognitive restructuring" or "behavioral activation" without explaining them in plain language. Without clarification, clients may struggle to grasp the significance of these techniques and how they apply them to their treatment.

Emotional distress can also make it harder for clients to process information. When facing health concerns or mental health challenges, individuals often experience heightened stress, which can lead to selective hearing, focusing on certain details while missing others. A client struggling with severe depression, for instance, may fixate on the possible side effects of medication while overlooking its potential benefits. Anxiety can cloud comprehension, making it essential for practitioners to check in with clients, clarify key points, and offer reassurance throughout the discussion.

Limited time during sessions can further complicate effective communication. Counselors and healthcare providers often have back-to-back appointments, leaving little room for in-depth conversations about treatment options. As a result, explanations may be rushed or incomplete, leaving clients with unanswered questions and uncertainty about their care.

To improve treatment discussions, practitioners should use clear, everyday language instead of technical jargon, check for understanding by asking clients to summarize key points, offer written materials or follow-up resources for further clarity, and encourage questions to ensure clients feel informed and involved. By prioritizing clear, compassionate communication, counselors can empower clients to make well-informed decisions about their treatment, ultimately improving engagement and adherence to care.

Ineffective communication about treatment options can have significant consequences. Misunderstandings may lead to unrealistic expectations, disappointment with outcomes, or even refusal of beneficial interventions. When clients do not fully understand the reasoning behind a treatment plan, they are less likely to follow it, which can undermine its effectiveness. For example, a client who doesn't grasp the importance of regular therapy sessions for managing anxiety might attend sporadically, slowing their progress.

Efforts to improve communication have shown promise but also have limitations. Using plain language and avoiding medical jargon is a common strategy that helps with immediate comprehension. However, oversimplifying complex concepts can sometimes lead to an incomplete understanding of treatment nuances. Providing written materials as a supplement is another widely used method, reinforcing key information.

Yet, this approach assumes a certain level of literacy and may not be accessible to all clients.

Several strategies could be considered to enhance communication. Visual aids and interactive digital tools can help break down complex concepts, making them easier to understand. For instance, a counselor might use an interactive app to illustrate the cognitive-behavioral therapy process, showing how thoughts, feelings, and behaviors are connected. Engaging multiple senses can be particularly helpful for visual learners, though this approach requires investment in technology and practitioner training.

Another effective technique is the use of metaphors and analogies to explain treatment concepts in relatable terms. Connecting unfamiliar ideas to everyday experiences can make them more memorable. For example, exposure therapy for anxiety might be compared to learning to swim, gradually increasing exposure to water until comfort is achieved. While this method can bridge understanding, it requires skill to ensure the analogies remain accurate, culturally appropriate, and do not oversimplify the treatment.

By refining how treatment options are communicated, counselors can improve client understanding, increase adherence, and ultimately enhance the effectiveness of care.

The teach-back method is another powerful tool for improving communication. This approach involves asking clients to explain treatment information in their own words, allowing counselors to identify and correct any misunderstandings immediately (Ha Dinh et al., 2016). For example, after discussing medication options for depression, a counselor might ask the client to summarize their understanding of the potential benefits and side effects. This technique encourages active engagement and reinforces comprehension. However, it does require additional time during consultations, which can be challenging in fast-paced clinical settings.

Implementing these solutions comes with its own challenges. Practitioners may need additional training to effectively use visual aids, craft meaningful metaphors, or apply the teach-back method. Some professionals, especially those accustomed to traditional communication styles, may resist changing established practices. Time constraints can also be a concern, as these strategies may initially seem at odds with the need for efficiency.

For long-term success, systemic changes may be necessary. Adjusting appointment durations to allow for more in-depth discussions, incorporating communication skills training into continuing education, and developing standardized protocols for explaining common treatments could all contribute to more effective communication. By addressing these challenges at both the individual and systemic levels, the counseling field can foster a more informed, engaged, and satisfied client base, ultimately leading to better treatment outcomes.

FULL DISCLOSURE OF RISKS AND BENEFITS

Disclosing the risks and benefits of treatment is a key ethical responsibility in the informed consent process (ACA, 2014, A.2.b.; AMHCA, 2020, I.B.2). This begins with thorough preparation, where the counselor gathers relevant information about potential outcomes (ACA, 2014, A.2.c.; AMHCA, 2020, I.B.2). Reviewing current research, consulting colleagues, and considering the client's unique circumstances help ensure a well-informed discussion.

Creating the right setting for this conversation is equally important. The counselor should allow enough time and choose a private, comfortable environment that encourages open dialogue. Establishing a sense of safety and trust helps clients process potentially sensitive information with greater ease.

When introducing the topic, counselors should emphasize its role in informed decision-making. Framing the discussion in this way helps clients understand its significance. A simple approach might be: *"Understanding the potential outcomes of this treatment is essential for making an informed choice about your care."*

Explaining the benefits of treatment should be clear and specific. The counselor should highlight potential positive outcomes, such as symptom relief, improved functioning, or a better quality of life. For example, in cognitive-behavioral therapy for depression, benefits might include *"decreased feelings of sadness, better sleep, and greater participation in enjoyable activities."*

Equally important is an honest discussion of risks. Counselors must present potential challenges without downplaying their significance. This could include temporary discomfort, increased anxiety during exposure therapy, or the emotional difficulty of processing painful memories. When possible, providing empirical data on the likelihood of these risks can help clients make informed decisions.

By ensuring a balanced, transparent discussion, counselors empower clients to make choices that align with their needs and expectations, ultimately strengthening trust and engagement in the therapeutic process.

A key part of full disclosure is discussing alternative treatment options and their respective risks and benefits. This ensures that clients are aware of different approaches and can make informed comparisons. For example, a counselor might explain the differences between individual therapy, group therapy, and medication management for anxiety, outlining the unique advantages and potential drawbacks of each.

Encouraging client questions throughout the discussion is essential. Counselors should create multiple opportunities for clients to seek clarification or express concerns. This interactive approach not only enhances understanding but also reinforces respect for the client's autonomy and right to information.

Confirming the client's understanding is the final, critical step. The teach-back method, where clients are asked to explain the information in their own words, is a particularly effective way to assess comprehension. This allows counselors to identify any misunderstandings and address them immediately, ensuring that clients have a clear and accurate grasp of their options.

Counselors may face challenges such as client anxiety, resistance to discussing risks, or difficulty processing complex information. To navigate these barriers, they can use plain language, provide written materials as a supplement, and break down information into manageable segments.

For clients with varying levels of health literacy or cognitive abilities, adjustments may be necessary. This might include using visual aids, simplifying language without omitting key details, or involving family members or caregivers in the discussion (with the client's consent).

By providing a comprehensive and transparent disclosure of risks and benefits, counselors uphold the ethical principles of autonomy, beneficence, and non-maleficence. This process empowers clients to make informed decisions, strengthens the therapeutic relationship, and ultimately improves treatment adherence and outcomes.

SPECIAL CONSIDERATIONS: MINORS AND COUPLES

Informed consent for minors and couples presents unique challenges that require careful adaptation of standard counseling practices. While both situations involve multiple stakeholders and complex relational dynamics, the legal and ethical considerations differ significantly.

For minors, the primary challenge is balancing their growing capacity for decision-making with the legal rights of parents or guardians. While young children may not fully understand the implications of counseling, older adolescents may be capable of meaningful participation in the consent process. For example, a 16-year-old seeking therapy for depression may have a greater ability to engage in informed consent than a 7-year-old referred for behavioral concerns.

Couples counseling which we will talk more about in the next chapter, on the other hand, involves navigating the delicate balance between individual and relational needs, as well as potential conflicts of interest. While both partners have full legal capacity to consent, it is essential to ensure that they are equally informed and willing participants in the process.

Confidentiality is another key distinction. In working with minors, counselors must carefully balance the child's right to privacy with the legal rights of parents to be informed about their child's treatment. Setting clear expectations from the start, defining what information will be shared and under what circumstances, helps prevent misunderstandings.

For couples, confidentiality is approached differently, as the focus is on the relationship rather than the individual. Counselors must establish clear protocols for handling private disclosures that may impact the couple's dynamic, such as infidelity or hidden addictions. Addressing these boundaries upfront helps foster trust and prevent ethical dilemmas later in the therapeutic process.

By carefully navigating these complexities, counselors can ensure ethical, transparent, and effective treatment while respecting the rights and needs of all involved.

Conflicts of interest arise differently in counseling minors and couples. With minors, tensions may surface between a child's expressed wishes and a parent's goals for treatment, or between a counselor's clinical judgment and parental expectations. In couples counseling, conflicts can emerge when individual needs clash with relationship goals or when one partner's disclosures put the counselor in an ethically challenging position regarding the other partner.

Parental involvement is a critical factor in counseling minors, with no direct equivalent in couples therapy. The level of parental participation depends on the child's age, the nature of the concerns, and legal requirements. Some cases require active parental engagement, such as family therapy sessions, while others, especially with mature adolescents, may involve minimal parental involvement to protect confidentiality. Counselors must carefully navigate this dynamic, ensuring the minor's best interests remain the priority while also respecting parental rights.

For couples, the challenge lies in balancing individual and relational needs throughout therapy. This begins with the informed consent process, where each partner must fully understand and agree to the terms of therapy. Counselors should clearly outline policies regarding individual sessions within couples counseling, including how private disclosures will be handled. Informed consent should also address scenarios such as one partner choosing to end therapy while the other wishes to continue.

Current informed consent practices for minors often follow a two-tiered approach: securing parental consent while also obtaining the minor's assent when appropriate. This framework acknowledges legal requirements while promoting the child's autonomy. However, it can become complicated when a minor's best interests conflict with parental preferences.

In couples therapy, standard informed consent procedures may not always account for the complexities of relational dynamics, particularly when managing individual disclosures or shifts in the therapeutic alliance.

Addressing these nuances from the outset helps create a more transparent and ethically sound counseling process.

Certain situations require modifications to the informed consent process. In cases involving minors, adjustments may be necessary when parental consent is not appropriate, such as in situations of abuse, or when legal complexities arise, such as obtaining consent from both parents in shared custody arrangements. These scenarios can present logistical and ethical challenges, requiring counselors to navigate legal obligations while prioritizing the minor's well-being.

Couples counseling may also require adaptations, particularly when working with non-traditional relationship structures like polyamorous arrangements or when domestic violence is a concern. In these cases, informed consent must account for unique confidentiality considerations, power dynamics, and safety concerns.

Several strategies could be implemented to enhance informed consent procedures for these special populations. For minors, developing age-appropriate consent materials that explain therapy concepts in accessible language can improve understanding and engagement. Additionally, periodically revisiting the consent process throughout therapy allows for adjustments as the minor's capacity to participate in decision-making evolves.

For couples, a more detailed discussion of confidentiality and its limits within the relationship context can help prevent misunderstandings and ethical dilemmas later in treatment. Establishing clear guidelines from the outset, such as how individual disclosures will be handled, ensures transparency and reinforces trust in the therapeutic process.

CAPACITY ASSESSMENT IN INFORMED CONSENT

Determining a client's capacity to provide informed consent is a nuanced process that involves ethical, legal, and clinical considerations. Capacity refers to an individual's ability to understand relevant information, retain it, weigh their options, and communicate a decision. In counseling, this means assessing whether a client can comprehend the nature of treatment, its potential risks and benefits, and any available alternatives.

There is no single method for evaluating capacity. Instead, counselors may use a combination of formal and informal assessments. Formal tools, such as the MacArthur Competence Assessment Tool for Treatment (MacCAT-T) or the Mini-Mental State Examination (MMSE), provide structured ways to assess cognitive function and decision-making abilities. Informal approaches, including clinical interviews, behavioral observations, and discussions with family members or caregivers, offer additional insights into a client's ability to make informed choices.

However, assessing capacity comes with challenges. Capacity is not always stable, it can fluctuate due to mental health conditions, stress, or external circumstances. A client who struggles to make decisions one day may be fully capable the next, requiring counselors to reassess capacity over time. Additionally, cultural factors influence how individuals approach decision-making and autonomy. Misinterpreting cultural norms as signs of incapacity can lead to ethical missteps, making cultural competence essential in this process.

By integrating thoughtful assessment strategies and maintaining awareness of capacity's fluid nature, counselors can uphold ethical standards while ensuring clients are empowered to make informed decisions about their care.

Assessing a client's capacity for informed consent carries significant legal and ethical implications. Proceeding with treatment when a client lacks capacity can violate their autonomy and may result in legal consequences. Conversely, an overly cautious approach, denying treatment based on an incorrect assumption of incapacity, can prevent clients from accessing beneficial interventions. Striking this balance requires careful documentation and transparent communication with clients and, when necessary, their legal representatives.

Certain populations present unique challenges in capacity assessment. For example, older adults experiencing cognitive decline may still be capable of making informed decisions, depending on the complexity of the choice. Similarly, individuals with cognitive impairments may retain the ability to consent to some forms of counseling while struggling with others. This highlights the need for an individualized, decision-specific approach rather than a one-size-fits-all assessment.

Current capacity assessment practices have strengths and limitations. A major strength is the growing recognition that capacity is not an all-or-nothing concept but varies by decision type. This perspective helps preserve client autonomy by ensuring they are not unnecessarily excluded from making their own choices. However, a key limitation is the lack of standardized assessment protocols across counseling settings, leading to inconsistencies in practice and potential disparities in treatment access.

To improve capacity assessments, several steps could be taken:

- **Develop specialized tools** tailored to specific counseling interventions to enhance accuracy.
- **Integrate capacity assessment training** into counselor education programs to ensure practitioners are well-equipped for these evaluations.
- **Implement peer review or consultation** for complex cases to minimize bias and promote consistency in assessments.

How counselors assess a client's capacity for informed consent can significantly shape the therapeutic relationship. A thoughtful and transparent approach fosters trust, demonstrating respect for the client's autonomy and reinforcing ethical practice. In contrast, a poorly conducted or inadequately explained assessment can damage rapport, making clients feel powerless or stigmatized, especially those from vulnerable populations.

Capacity assessment in counseling is more than a procedural step; it is a fundamental ethical responsibility. It requires a careful balance of clinical judgment, legal awareness, and cultural sensitivity. As the field continues to evolve, so too must our assessment approaches, ensuring they uphold the principles of autonomy, beneficence, and justice in every client interaction.

DOCUMENTING INFORMED CONSENT

The process of documenting informed consent in counseling begins with carefully prepared consent forms. These documents establish a shared understanding between counselor and client regarding the nature of therapy, potential risks and benefits, confidentiality limits, fees, and alternative treatment options. To ensure accessibility, consent forms should be written in clear, straightforward language, avoiding unnecessary jargon that could confuse or overwhelm clients.

Beyond simply providing a document for signature, counselors must actively engage clients in a meaningful review of its contents. This step requires more than reading aloud; it involves explaining key sections in a way that ensures comprehension. Counselors should remain attentive to clients' verbal and nonverbal cues, watching for signs of confusion or hesitation that may indicate the need for further clarification.

Encouraging clients to ask questions is essential. Counselors should create a welcoming environment where clients feel comfortable seeking clarification without fear of judgment. A two-way discussion fosters collaboration and reinforces the client's role in the decision-making process. Patience and clear explanations are key, as the complexities of psychological services may require repeated discussions for full understanding.

To confirm comprehension, counselors can use techniques like the "teach-back" method, where clients summarize key points in their own words. This approach helps identify and correct misunderstandings before finalizing consent. While it may require extra time, it significantly reduces miscommunication and ensures that clients make informed decisions about their care.

Obtaining signatures marks the official documentation of informed consent. Both the client and counselor must sign and date the form, with the counselor's signature confirming that all necessary information has been provided and understood. When working with minors or individuals with diminished capacity, additional signatures from legal guardians or authorized representatives may be required, necessitating a clear understanding of applicable legal requirements.

Providing clients with a copy of the signed consent form is more than a professional courtesy, it is an ethical responsibility. This ensures that clients have a reference for the agreed-upon terms of therapy, reinforcing transparency and informed decision-making. Counselors should emphasize the importance of retaining the document and encourage clients to review it as needed.

Proper storage of the original consent form is crucial for maintaining confidentiality and compliance with legal and ethical standards. Beyond simply filing the document, counselors must adhere to strict security protocols, whether using physical records or electronic storage systems. Digital records should be protected with robust security measures to prevent unauthorized access or data breaches.

Given the evolving nature of counseling, informed consent should not be treated as a one-time event. As therapy progresses, new treatment approaches may emerge, or confidentiality parameters may need to be adjusted. Counselors should periodically revisit and update consent documentation to ensure it accurately reflects the current therapeutic relationship, fostering ongoing client engagement and ethical practice.

In group counseling, informed consent must address unique dynamics, such as confidentiality limitations and the risks of sharing personal information in a collective setting. Clients should be made aware that, while counselors uphold confidentiality, they cannot guarantee that group members will do the same. Clear guidelines on respectful communication and privacy expectations should be outlined in the consent process.

For telehealth services, consent documentation must cover technology-specific issues, including data encryption, platform security, and procedures for handling technical disruptions. Clients should be informed about potential privacy risks associated with online communication and the measures in place to protect their information. Additionally, contingency plans should be established in case of connectivity issues during sessions.

Thorough documentation of informed consent serves as a safeguard for both clients and counselors. For clients, it reinforces their right to autonomy and informed decision-making. For counselors, it provides a legal and ethical safeguard, demonstrating compliance with professional standards and reducing liability in case of disputes.

Technological advancements have introduced digital options for consent, such as electronic signatures and online consent forms. While these methods offer convenience and efficiency, they also pose unique challenges. Counselors must ensure that digital consent complies with legal standards for authenticity and verification. Additionally, the use of electronic platforms requires heightened attention to data security and privacy concerns to prevent unauthorized access or breaches.

CULTURAL CONSIDERATIONS IN INFORMED CONSENT

Obtaining informed consent in counseling involves more than just explaining procedures, it requires an understanding of cultural influences that shape how clients perceive mental health, autonomy, and decision-making. These cultural factors can significantly impact the effectiveness of the consent process and the overall therapeutic relationship.

While language differences are an obvious challenge, the issue goes beyond simple translation. Many cultures have no direct equivalents for psychological concepts commonly used in Western counseling. For example, the term "depression" may not exist in certain languages, and emotional distress may be expressed in physical symptoms rather than psychological terms. This can lead to misunderstandings about treatment goals, risks, and expected outcomes.

Western counseling practices emphasize individual autonomy, assuming that clients make their own decisions about treatment. However, in many collectivist cultures, major decisions, including those about health, are made collectively, often involving family or community elders. If a counselor insists on obtaining consent only from the individual, it may create tension or even alienate the client. A culturally sensitive approach involves recognizing when family participation is essential and adapting the consent process accordingly.

Clients from different cultural backgrounds may have alternative explanations for mental health issues. Some may attribute symptoms to spiritual factors, ancestral influences, or social disharmony rather than biological or psychological causes. If a counselor disregards these beliefs or presents treatment solely through a Western medical lens, the client may feel misunderstood or distrustful. Instead, counselors should explore the client's perspective and, where possible, integrate culturally appropriate interventions into the therapeutic process.

By approaching informed consent with cultural awareness, counselors can foster trust, improve communication, and enhance the overall effectiveness of therapy. Sensitivity to language, decision-making norms, and diverse health beliefs ensures that clients fully understand and feel respected throughout the consent process.

Cultural misunderstandings in the consent process often arise from a lack of cultural awareness among counselors, biases built into consent procedures, and limited institutional support for culturally inclusive practices. As a result, consent discussions may not fully inform or empower clients from diverse backgrounds.

When consent processes fail to account for cultural differences, the consequences can be significant. Clients may lose trust in their counselor and the therapeutic process, leading to poor treatment adherence, early termination of therapy, and negative mental health outcomes. On a larger scale, these issues contribute to health disparities and reinforce systemic barriers that make it harder for marginalized communities to access quality mental health care.

Efforts to address these challenges include using professional interpreters, providing cultural competence training for counselors, and developing consent materials that reflect diverse perspectives. While these strategies help, they don't always fully capture the complex ways culture shapes a person's understanding of mental health and treatment.

To strengthen cultural competence in informed consent, several key improvements should be considered. One effective approach is integrating professional interpreters trained in mental health terminology. More than just translating words, these interpreters help bridge cultural and conceptual gaps between counselors and clients. However, implementing this solution requires significant resources, which may not always be available in every setting.

Second, developing culturally adapted consent materials tailored to specific cultural groups can improve understanding and engagement. These materials should go beyond simple translation, incorporating culturally relevant examples, clear explanations, and visual aids. While this approach makes consent information more accessible, it requires ongoing research and adaptation to remain effective across diverse and evolving cultural contexts.

Third, comprehensive training in cross-cultural communication can help counselors navigate cultural differences more effectively. This training should not only cover cultural knowledge but also emphasize cultural humility and flexibility in applying consent procedures. The challenge lies in designing programs that are both practical and nuanced, ensuring they avoid oversimplification or cultural stereotyping.

Fourth, involving cultural consultants in the consent process can provide valuable insights and mediation. These consultants help interpret cultural nuances, recommend appropriate communication strategies, and bridge gaps in understanding between counselors and clients. However, integrating cultural consultants into the consent process requires careful consideration of confidentiality concerns and may not be feasible in all therapeutic settings.

Implementing these solutions comes with challenges. Limited resources, particularly in underfunded mental health services, can make it difficult to provide interpreter services or develop extensive culturally adapted materials. Additionally, resistance to change within established institutions can slow the adoption of more culturally sensitive consent practices.

For long-term sustainability, cultural competence must be a priority at both individual and institutional levels. This means regularly updating culturally adapted materials, ensuring ongoing professional development in cross-cultural communication, and embedding cultural competence into organizational policies and procedures.

When implemented thoughtfully, these solutions can strengthen ethical practice and empower clients from diverse backgrounds. By addressing the cultural complexities of informed consent, counselors can build trust, improve treatment adherence, and ultimately provide more equitable and effective mental health care.

12

ETHICAL CHALLENGES IN

COUPLES THERAPY

NAVIGATING MULTIPLE CLIENT DYNAMICS

Couples therapy presents unique ethical challenges that differ from those in individual therapy, as outlined by the American Counseling Association (ACA) and the American Mental Health Counselors Association (AMHCA). While both forms of therapy uphold core ethical principles like beneficence and non-maleficence, managing multiple clients within the same session adds layers of complexity.

In individual therapy, the counselor's primary focus is on building a therapeutic alliance with one client, maintaining confidentiality, and working toward their personal goals. The ACA Code of Ethics emphasizes respecting client autonomy and promoting self-determination. In contrast, couples therapy requires balancing the needs and goals of two individuals while addressing the dynamics of their relationship. These parallel challenges in group settings (see Chapter 13) and informed consent scenarios (Chapter 11).

The AMHCA Code of Ethics highlights the importance of obtaining informed consent from both partners and clarifying the nature of the therapeutic relationship (AMHCA, 2020, I.B.2; AMHCA, 2020, III.A). A key distinction in couples therapy is that the couple, as a unit rather than either individual, is considered the client. This fundamental shift in perspective carries significant ethical implications, particularly in areas like confidentiality, decision-making, and potential conflicts of interest.

Balancing individual needs with relationship goals is one of the biggest challenges in couples therapy. Unlike individual therapy, where personal growth is the primary focus, couples therapy requires integrating each person's objectives within the broader context of their relationship. For example, one partner may seek greater independence while the other desires more intimacy. In such cases, the counselor must carefully navigate these differing needs, maintain neutrality, and avoid the perception of taking sides.

Managing power dynamics in therapy differs significantly between individual and couples therapy. In individual therapy, the primary power dynamic exists between the therapist and the client. In couples therapy, however, the therapist must also be attuned to power imbalances between partners, as well as their own influence on the relationship. This requires heightened awareness to prevent unintentional alliances or biases that could affect the therapeutic process.

Conflicting client objectives add another layer of complexity to couples therapy. While individual therapy allows for a clear focus on one person's goals, couples therapy often involves negotiating and reconciling differing objectives. The ACA and AMHCA stress the importance of transparency and informed consent in these situations, encouraging counselors to openly discuss the potential challenges and limitations of therapy when partners have conflicting goals.

Ethical guidelines for individual therapy were established long before those for couples therapy. The foundations of individual therapy ethics trace back to the late 19th century, with Sigmund Freud's development of psychoanalysis emphasizing confidentiality and therapist neutrality (Lynn & Vailiant, 1998). In contrast, couples therapy ethics evolved more recently, with key contributions from pioneers like Virginia Satir and Murray Bowen in the mid-20th century. Their systemic approaches emphasized the importance of relational dynamics in therapeutic work (Nichols & Schwartz, 2004; Titelman, 2014).

Each form of therapy has its strengths when it comes to maintaining therapist neutrality. Individual therapy, with its singular focus, allows for a more straightforward therapeutic relationship. Couples therapy, on the other hand, provides the advantage of observing and addressing relational dynamics in real-time, which can lead to deeper, systemic change. However, ensuring equitable treatment in couples therapy requires ongoing vigilance to avoid inadvertently favoring one partner over the other.

Handling client secrets and disclosures presents a unique ethical challenge in couples therapy. While confidentiality guidelines in individual therapy are straightforward, couples therapy requires careful navigation of shared information and private disclosures. The AMHCA Code of Ethics advises therapists to establish clear policies on handling secrets at the beginning of therapy, ensuring that the client (both partners) understand how confidential information will be managed (AMHCA, 2020, I.B.2; AMHCA, 2020, I.C.2).

In some cases, individual-focused interventions within couples therapy may be necessary, especially when addressing personal traumas or mental health concerns that significantly impact the relationship. On the other hand, couple-focused interventions are essential for working through communication patterns, intimacy issues, or shared goals. Integrating both individual and systemic approaches can enhance ethical practice by providing a more holistic treatment experience. This may involve alternating between joint sessions and individual check-ins, with the explicit agreement of both partners and clear guidelines on how information will be handled.

CONFIDENTIALITY IN FAMILY SYSTEMS

Confidentiality in family therapy presents unique challenges that go beyond those in individual counseling. The complexity of family relationships, power dynamics, and competing interests requires a nuanced approach to maintaining ethical standards while supporting therapeutic progress. Unlike in individual therapy, where confidentiality is more straightforward, family therapy blurs these boundaries since information shared by one member can significantly impact others.

Confidentiality concerns in family therapy typically fall into two key areas: information sharing among family members and the therapist's duty to both individuals and the family unit. Therapists must carefully balance fostering open communication with respecting individual privacy. For example, if a teenager discloses substance use, the therapist must decide whether to keep this information private or share it with the parents. Similarly, conflicts may arise when one family member shares something in confidence that could affect the entire family, such as a spouse revealing plans for divorce.

The root of these dilemmas often lies in conflicting interests within the family and legal or ethical obligations, particularly regarding minors. Family members may have differing goals, secrets, or perspectives that create tension in therapy. Additionally, therapists working with minors must navigate the balance between protecting a child's privacy and honoring parental rights, all while fulfilling legal duties such as reporting potential harm or abuse.

Confidentiality plays a crucial role in family therapy, directly affecting trust and the effectiveness of treatment. A perceived breach of confidentiality can severely damage the therapeutic relationship, making family members less willing to share openly. On the other hand, maintaining strict confidentiality may unintentionally reinforce dysfunctional family dynamics or communication patterns. For instance, keeping a significant secret from other family members might perpetuate cycles of mistrust or enable harmful behaviors to continue unchecked.

Approaches to Managing Confidentiality

Therapists use several strategies to navigate confidentiality in family therapy, including setting clear guidelines at the beginning of treatment, using family-centered confidentiality agreements, and employing selective disclosure techniques. While these approaches have benefits, they also come with limitations.

Clear guidelines help establish expectations but may not anticipate every situation. Family-centered confidentiality agreements promote transparency but may not fully address power imbalances. Selective disclosure allows for nuanced information sharing, but it requires careful clinical judgment and may be misinterpreted as favoritism or manipulation.

To address these challenges, three possible solutions merit consideration:

1. **Tiered Confidentiality Model** – This approach categorizes information into different levels of confidentiality based on its nature and potential impact. It allows therapists to navigate disclosure more flexibly, balancing individual privacy with family system needs. While this model offers adaptability, it can also be

complex to implement and may lead to disagreements about how information should be classified.

2. **Regular Confidentiality Review Sessions** – Integrating periodic discussions about confidentiality throughout therapy can enhance transparency and foster open dialogue about information sharing. These sessions allow family members to express their comfort levels, address concerns, and adjust confidentiality agreements as needed. The benefits include increased family involvement and improved trust and communication. However, challenges may arise in scheduling and managing these sessions, and some family members may feel pressured to disclose information they are not yet ready to share.

3. **Collaborative Confidentiality Plan** – A dynamic, evolving confidentiality plan co-created by the therapist and family members can provide flexibility as therapy progresses. This plan would outline agreed-upon guidelines for information sharing and be revisited at key points to ensure it aligns with the family's evolving needs. The advantages of this approach include its adaptability and its potential to empower family members in decision-making. However, some may resist changes, preferring more rigid boundaries, and reaching a consensus on confidentiality guidelines may be challenging.

ETHICAL DILEMMAS IN CONFLICT OF INTEREST

Consider a therapist treating a couple while also maintaining a significant financial relationship with the spouse's company. This scenario addresses the complex ethical challenges that can arise in couples therapy, where professional responsibilities, financial interests, and therapeutic integrity intersect. The therapist's decision to withhold information about this connection raises key ethical concerns, including transparency, informed consent, and the potential for bias in treatment.

Conflicts of interest in couples therapy can be both subtle and significant. In this case, the therapist's reluctance to challenge Ethan's perspectives illustrates how financial ties can unconsciously influence clinical judgment. Even without intent, such entanglements may compromise the therapist's ability to provide fair and effective treatment to both partners. Ethical guidelines, such as the *American Psychological Association's Ethical Principles of Psychologists and Code of Conduct* (APA, 2017), stress the importance of avoiding relationships that could impair objectivity or effectiveness in therapy.

The failure to disclose this financial connection directly violates ethical standards regarding informed consent. Informed consent is a fundamental principle in psychotherapy, ensuring that clients receive all relevant information to make autonomous decisions about their treatment. In this case, both partners, particularly the spouse Carey, were denied critical information that could have influenced their decision to begin or continue therapy with this clinician.

Addressing conflicts of interest proactively is essential in upholding ethical standards in couples therapy. One immediate solution is full disclosure to both partners, allowing for an open discussion about how the financial relationship might impact therapy. This approach ensures transparency and enables the couple to make an informed decision about whether to continue treatment. It aligns with the ethical principle of *respect for persons*, which emphasizes individuals' right to make autonomous choices based on complete information (Kitchener & Anderson, 2011).

Another ethically sound alternative is referring the couple to another therapist. This option removes the conflict of interest entirely, ensuring that treatment remains unbiased. However, the potential disruption to therapy, especially after three months of progress, must be carefully weighed. The therapist must balance the ethical obligation to maintain professional boundaries with the potential harm of discontinuing an established therapeutic relationship.

This case highlights a broader ethical challenge in couples therapy: navigating professional boundaries while managing complex interpersonal and external influences. It underscores the need for therapists to remain vigilant about potential conflicts of interest, not only at the beginning of treatment but throughout the entire therapeutic process.

The subtle impact of financial entanglements, such as the therapist's hesitation to challenge the husband, demonstrates how such conflicts can unconsciously shape therapy. Ongoing self-reflection, ethical awareness, and clinical supervision are crucial in preventing these issues from undermining therapeutic integrity.

Conflicts of interest can arise in various ways in family and couples counseling, making ethical awareness and proactive management essential. The following principles provide guidance for navigating such situations while maintaining professional integrity:

1. **Transparency and Proactive Disclosure** – When potential conflicts arise, therapists should disclose them as early as possible, ensuring clients have all relevant information to make informed decisions about their care.
2. **Regular Ethical Self-Assessment** – Ethical dilemmas can evolve over time. Clinicians should continually evaluate their professional relationships and potential conflicts to identify and address ethical concerns before they escalate.
3. **Prioritizing Client Welfare** – The well-being and autonomy of clients should always take precedence over any financial, professional, or personal interests of the therapist.
4. **Consultation and Supervision** – When facing ethical dilemmas, seeking guidance from colleagues, supervisors, or ethics

committees can provide valuable perspectives and help ensure ethical decision-making.

5. **Thorough Documentation** – Keeping detailed records of ethical decisions, disclosures, and actions taken helps protect both the therapist and clients by providing a clear rationale for decisions made.

The ethical complexities of couples and family therapy highlight the need for vigilance in recognizing and addressing conflicts of interest. By adhering to these principles, therapists can maintain transparency, uphold ethical guidelines, and prioritize the best interests of their clients, ensuring the integrity of the therapeutic process.

DOMESTIC VIOLENCE: ETHICAL RESPONSES

Domestic violence presents a complex ethical challenge in couples therapy, requiring counselors to remain vigilant and sensitive to subtle and overt signs of abuse. These signs may include one partner dominating conversations, displaying controlling behaviors, or the other partner appearing fearful or hesitant to speak openly.

More obvious indicators range from physical injuries to direct disclosures of threats or violence. Counselors must stay attuned to these warning signs while balancing their ethical obligations, particularly the tension between confidentiality and client safety.

The ethical dilemma of confidentiality versus safety is especially challenging in cases of suspected domestic violence. While professional ethics emphasize protecting client confidentiality, counselors also have a duty to prevent harm.

This balance becomes even more complicated due to varying state laws on mandatory reporting. Some states require counselors to report suspected domestic violence to authorities, while others mandate reporting only when children or vulnerable adults are involved. Additionally, the therapist's duty to warn or protect potential victims may necessitate breaking confidentiality to ensure safety.

When domestic violence is suspected or disclosed, the counselor must carefully determine the best course of action. Continuing joint sessions can put the victim at further risk and reinforce harmful power dynamics. On the other hand, moving to individual sessions may create a safer space for disclosure and intervention, but it could also alert the abusive partner, increasing the risk of retaliation. The decision between immediate intervention and a more gradual approach depends on the severity of the danger and the victim's readiness for change.

Ethical guidelines for managing domestic violence in couples therapy prioritize client safety above all else. The American Counseling Association's Code of Ethics, for example, states that counselors have a responsibility to protect clients from physical, emotional, and psychological harm. However, applying these guidelines in practice can be challenging, especially when faced with ambiguous situations or conflicting client preferences. Clinically, we do not provide therapy to couples at the same time when there is abuse – that is contraindicated.

One approach to addressing domestic violence ethically is a staged assessment process, which involves screening for abuse at the beginning of therapy and at regular intervals throughout treatment. This method creates multiple opportunities for disclosure and allows counselors to continually assess risk. However, it may also introduce tension if one partner perceives the screenings as invasive or accusatory.

Another strategy is the development of a safety protocol, which both partners agree upon at the start of therapy. This protocol outlines the steps to take if domestic violence is suspected or disclosed, such as separating sessions or referring clients to specialized services. While this approach fosters transparency and preparedness, it may also discourage couples from engaging in therapy or lead to early termination if the abusive partner feels threatened.

A third potential strategy **is co-therapy**, where two therapists work collaboratively, each focusing on one partner. This model allows for both individual and joint sessions, offering a structured way to address abuse while maintaining a couples therapy framework. The benefit of this approach is that it provides targeted support without entirely abandoning the relationship-focused aspect of therapy. However, it requires additional resources and strong coordination between therapists to ensure consistency and prevent conflicting interventions.

Each of these strategies presents its own challenges. Staged assessments must be carefully timed and framed to preserve trust. Safety protocols require delicate communication to introduce the topic without alienating either partner. Co-therapy demands seamless collaboration between professionals with potentially different therapeutic styles. While no single approach is perfect, a thoughtful and flexible application of these strategies can help counselors navigate the ethical complexities of domestic violence in couples therapy.

The long-term impact of these strategies varies. Staged assessments can lead to earlier identification and intervention, potentially preventing the escalation of violence. Safety protocols empower victims by outlining clear steps for action, but they may also create a false sense of security if not accompanied by strong support systems. The co-therapy model offers a more comprehensive treatment approach, yet if not carefully managed, it could unintentionally reinforce divisions within the relationship.

Navigating domestic violence in couples therapy requires counselors to balance multiple ethical responsibilities. Ensuring client safety must be weighed against respecting client autonomy and supporting the therapeutic goal of relationship improvement. To manage these complex situations effectively, counselors need rigorous ethical decision-making frameworks, ongoing professional development, and clear institutional policies to guide their practice.

CHILD ABUSE REPORTING IN FAMILY SETTINGS

In family therapy, handling suspicions or disclosures of child abuse requires a structured and ethical approach. The process begins with recognizing the signs of abuse, which can be both obvious and subtle. Therapists must stay attentive to physical marks, behavioral shifts, and indirect disclosures, such as those expressed through play or artwork. The American Professional Society on the Abuse of Children (APSAC) provides valuable guidelines for identifying potential abuse, serving as an essential resource for clinicians.

However, distinguishing abuse from other family issues can be challenging. Therapists must strike a balance between vigilance and avoiding premature conclusions. Understanding family dynamics and cultural contexts is crucial, as what may be seen as abusive in one cultural setting could be considered an accepted form of discipline in another. To navigate this complexity, therapists should approach each case with cultural sensitivity and gather comprehensive information before making any determinations.

When abuse is suspected, the child's safety becomes the top priority. Assessing immediate risk involves evaluating the severity of potential harm, the presence of protective factors within the family, and the child's perceived sense of security. The Structured Decision Making (SDM) model offers a standardized framework to help clinicians assess risk and make informed decisions while considering the complexities of family dynamics.

Balancing urgency with thorough assessment is essential when handling suspected child abuse. In cases where immediate danger is evident, therapists may need to act quickly by involving child protective services or law enforcement. However, when the situation is less clear, a more measured approach can help prevent unnecessary family disruption.

Consulting with colleagues or supervisors is a crucial part of ethical decision-making. Seeking additional perspectives not only improves judgment but also helps mitigate personal biases. Structured case discussion frameworks, such as Kitchener's (1984) ethical decision-making model, provide valuable guidance for these consultations.

Confidentiality during these discussions presents a challenge. Therapists must carefully anonymize case details while ensuring enough context for meaningful input. It's best to consult professionals with expertise in child protection and frame discussions around ethical and legal obligations.

Clearly informing clients about mandatory reporting requirements is a necessary but delicate step. Ideally, this should be addressed at the start of therapy as part of informed consent. However, if abuse concerns arise later, therapists must revisit this topic, ensuring that clients understand the focus is on protecting the child's well-being.

Family resistance or fear is common in these situations. Therapists can help by framing the reporting process as a way to access support and resources rather than a punitive measure. Maintaining a non-judgmental stance and showing empathy for the family's concerns can help preserve trust and the therapeutic relationship during these difficult conversations.

Reporting suspected child abuse to child protective services or law enforcement is a critical moment in the therapeutic process. Therapists must ensure they have all relevant information, including specific observations or disclosures that led to the suspicion. Since reporting requirements vary by jurisdiction, therapists should familiarize themselves with local guidelines to ensure compliance.

As mentioned in a previous chapter, the impact of reporting on the therapeutic relationship can be significant. Some families may feel betrayed or angry, possibly leading to therapy termination, while others may feel relief that the issue is being addressed. Therapists must be prepared for a range of emotional responses and have strategies in place to manage potential ruptures in trust.

Once a report is made, the focus shifts to ongoing care and support for the family. This may include helping them navigate the child protection system, connecting them with additional resources, or adapting the therapeutic approach to address the aftermath of the report. The Child Welfare Information Gateway provides extensive resources that therapists can use to support families through this process.

At this stage, challenges often involve family fragmentation or the discontinuation of therapy. To rebuild trust, therapists may need to increase transparency, validate the family's emotions, and focus on their strengths and resilience. By fostering open communication and emphasizing support, therapists can help families work through this difficult transition while prioritizing the child's safety and well-being.

BALANCING INDIVIDUAL AND FAMILY NEEDS IN THERAPY

Family therapy navigates the delicate balance between individual-focused and family-focused approaches, each with distinct ethical considerations. Individual-focused approaches prioritize personal autonomy and well-being, while family-focused approaches emphasize the interconnected nature of family relationships and collective healing. These perspectives shape ethical guidelines in family therapy, influencing both theory and practice.

Individual-focused therapy, rooted in psychodynamic and humanistic traditions, emphasizes personal growth, self-actualization, and the resolution of internal conflicts. This approach assumes that when individual needs are met, the family as a whole benefits. In contrast, family-focused therapy, based on systems theory, views the family as an interconnected unit, where changes in one member affect the entire system. This perspective prioritizes interventions that address relational patterns and communication dynamics.

The effectiveness of these approaches depends on the therapeutic goals. Individual-focused therapy excels in fostering autonomy and providing space for self-expression and personal decision-making. However, family-focused therapy often leads to more sustainable change by addressing the broader context that shapes behavior. When the goal is strengthening family cohesion, family-focused interventions typically produce more immediate results by directly improving relational dynamics. Meanwhile, individual-focused work can still contribute to family harmony by enhancing each member's ability to engage in healthier relationships.

Intergenerational patterns add another layer of complexity to family therapy. Family-focused approaches are particularly effective in identifying and disrupting dysfunctional patterns passed down through generations. By working with the entire family system, therapists can facilitate lasting change across multiple generations. Individual-focused therapy, while less direct in addressing intergenerational issues, can still break cycles by empowering individuals to make different choices and develop healthier coping strategies.

The historical evolution of ethical guidelines in family therapy reflects the tension between these two approaches. Individual-focused ethics, rooted in the medical model and psychoanalytic traditions, prioritize confidentiality, non-maleficence, and beneficence for the identified client. Influential figures such as Sigmund Freud and Carl Rogers helped shape this perspective. Meanwhile, family-focused ethics emerged from the work of pioneers like Murray Bowen and Salvador Minuchin, who emphasized the importance of treating the family as an interconnected system rather than focusing solely on individual pathology.

Each approach has strengths and limitations in navigating common challenges in family therapy. When family members have conflicting goals, individual-focused therapy allows for a deeper exploration of personal needs and desires. However, this can sometimes intensify conflicts rather than resolve them. Family-focused therapy, while better suited for fostering collective solutions, may risk overlooking individual concerns in pursuit of overall family harmony.

Power imbalances within the family are another key consideration. Family-focused interventions provide a structured framework for recognizing and restructuring unhealthy dynamics, directly addressing disparities in power and control. On the other hand, individual-focused therapy empowers family members to assert themselves and establish healthier boundaries, even if systemic power shifts take longer to emerge.

A key goal of family therapy is fostering long-term family well-being. Family-focused approaches often lead to immediate improvements in communication and relational patterns, while individual-focused interventions create deeper personal growth that can contribute to lasting family stability over time.

The decision between these approaches depends on the specific circumstances and presenting issues. Individual-focused therapy is particularly effective when addressing significant psychopathology, trauma, or situations where family members are unwilling or unable to participate in therapy together. In contrast, family-focused interventions work best when the primary issues involve relationship conflicts, dysfunctional communication, or patterns deeply embedded in family dynamics.

A promising approach is the integration of individual and family-focused therapy, which acknowledges the interconnected nature of personal well-being and family relationships. This flexible model allows therapists to tailor interventions, using individual sessions to address personal struggles and family sessions to navigate relational challenges.

By combining these perspectives, therapists can more effectively assess ethical dilemmas, balancing individual rights with family responsibilities and fostering sustainable therapeutic outcomes.

ETHICAL DECISION-MAKING IN COUPLES THERAPY

The evolution of ethical decision-making in couples therapy has been shaped by advancements in psychotherapy and broader societal changes. Ethical frameworks for couples counseling began developing in the mid-20th century, alongside the rise of family therapy as a distinct field. As systemic thinking gained prominence, the focus shifted from individual pathology to relational dynamics, requiring a reassessment of traditional ethical guidelines.

Pioneers like Murray Bowen, Salvador Minuchin, and Virginia Satir introduced systemic approaches in the 1950s and 1960s, emphasizing the interconnected nature of relationships (Nichols & Schwartz, 2004). This shift raised new ethical challenges, such as managing multiple relationships within a family system and considering the effects of therapy on non-present family members (Goldenberg & Goldenberg, 2012).

By the late 1960s and early 1970s, feminist theory began influencing couples therapy ethics. Scholars like Harriet Lerner and Marianne Walters critiqued traditional power dynamics in relationships, advocating for gender-sensitive therapeutic approaches. Their work introduced ethical principles that addressed power imbalances, gender biases, and the broader sociopolitical context of couples' issues (Carson, 1992).

A major milestone in the ethical development of couples therapy came in 1962 with the establishment of the American Association for Marriage and Family Therapy (AAMFT) Code of Ethics. This code offered a structured framework tailored to the unique challenges of working with couples and families. Over time, the AAMFT Code has undergone multiple revisions, adapting to the evolving complexities of ethical practice in the field.

The recognition of same-sex relationships brought another significant shift in couples therapy ethics. As societal attitudes toward LGBTQ+ relationships evolved in the late 20th century, therapists faced new ethical challenges. These included confronting personal biases, enhancing cultural competence, and addressing legal and social barriers that same-sex couples encountered. In response, the American Psychological Association (APA) released its Guidelines for Psychological Practice with Lesbian, Gay, and Bisexual Clients in 2000, providing ethical guidance for working with this population (American Psychological Association, 2000).

In recent years, ethical decision-making in couples therapy has increasingly emphasized multicultural competence. Scholars such as Kenneth Hardy and Monica McGoldrick have highlighted the importance of cultural context in shaping relationships and ethical dilemmas. This has led to the integration of cultural competence as a core ethical principle, encouraging therapists to consider factors like race, ethnicity, religion, and intersectionality in their ethical decision-making (Hardy & Laszloffy, 1995; McGoldrick, 2005).

The rise of technology in therapy has significantly impacted ethical decision-making in couples counseling. The widespread use of online therapy platforms and social media has introduced new challenges, such as maintaining confidentiality in digital spaces, managing professional boundaries online, and addressing technology's role in relationship dynamics. Recognizing these complexities, the American Counseling Association's 2014 Code of Ethics incorporated guidelines on the ethical use of technology in counseling, emphasizing secure communication and digital privacy.

Modern ethical decision-making models in couples therapy now integrate systemic perspectives, cultural awareness, power dynamics, and technological considerations. However, the field continues to evolve, requiring ongoing ethical reflection to address emerging challenges.

One such challenge is the growing recognition of non-traditional relationship structures, such as polyamorous and consensually non-monogamous relationships. These dynamics introduce unique ethical dilemmas related to confidentiality, consent, and therapist neutrality. Ethical frameworks are expanding to ensure inclusivity and non-judgmental practice, helping therapists navigate these complex relational systems responsibly.

Another emerging frontier is the integration of neuroscience into ethical decision-making. As research on attachment, relationship dynamics, and neurobiology advances, therapists face new ethical questions. These include the implications of using neuroscience-based interventions, such as targeting specific neural pathways or incorporating neurofeedback into couples therapy. Ensuring that these approaches align with ethical principles of informed consent, beneficence, and non-maleficence is essential as the field continues to incorporate scientific advancements.

13

NAVIGATING ETHICS IN
GROUP COUNSELING

SCREENING AND PREPARATION

Ensuring ethical screening and preparation of group members is essential for the success of counseling groups. These processes require a careful balance of professional judgment, ethical considerations, and client well-being. A key part of this is informed consent as previously discussed, which means providing potential members with clear, comprehensive information about the group's purpose, structure, and possible challenges. This transparency allows clients to make informed, autonomous decisions about their participation, aligning with the ethical principle of respect for individuals.

Determining whether a client is a good fit for a group involves evaluating their needs, goals, and interpersonal style in relation to the group's purpose. Counselors must carefully navigate the tension between inclusivity and group effectiveness. On the one hand, everyone deserves access to support; on the other, an unsuitable match can disrupt group dynamics or hinder therapeutic progress.

Ethical dilemmas often arise when balancing diversity and potential harm. Counselors may feel pressure to include individuals from underrepresented backgrounds, even when a different therapeutic approach might better serve their needs. For example, including a client from a marginalized group can promote diversity, but if their concerns require specialized attention, individual therapy may be a better option.

The Consequences of Inadequate Screening

Without proper screening, group counseling can have unintended negative effects. Bringing together individuals with conflicting needs or communication styles can lead to group disruption, making it difficult for members to benefit from the experience. Additionally, client distress can occur if individuals feel unprepared for the emotional challenges of group interactions. In some cases, this can worsen existing mental health concerns or create new stressors.

Counselors use various methods to prepare members for group participation. Pre-group orientation sessions help set expectations, establish ground rules, and address concerns, but they don't always account for individual differences. Some professionals use standardized assessment tools to determine suitability, but while these provide structure, they often lack the nuance needed to fully assess interpersonal compatibility.

To improve these processes, several strategies are worth considering:

1. **Multi-Stage Screening**: A structured, multi-step process, such as an initial questionnaire, an individual interview, and a trial group session, allows for a more thorough evaluation of potential members. This

approach provides valuable insight into how a client may interact within the group. However, it can be time-consuming and may limit access to therapy for those who need immediate support.

2. **Tailored Preparation Programs**: Different types of counseling groups require different levels of preparation. For example, a trauma-focused group may benefit from additional pre-group education to ensure members have the coping skills necessary for emotionally intense discussions. While this approach improves readiness, it requires significant resources to develop and implement specialized programs.

3. **Peer Support and Mentorship**: Pairing new members with experienced group participants for mentorship can reduce anxiety and offer firsthand insights into the group experience. While this strategy draws on the strengths of seasoned members, it must be carefully managed to maintain confidentiality and prevent power imbalances.

Each of these strategies presents practical challenges, from time constraints and resource limitations to the need for ongoing supervision. However, the long-term benefits outweigh these difficulties. A well-prepared group is more cohesive, leading to stronger therapeutic outcomes. Additionally, by reducing negative experiences, ethical screening and preparation foster trust in the counseling process and lower dropout rates.

By prioritizing thoughtful, ethical screening and preparation, counselors can create group environments that are not only inclusive but also safe, effective, and supportive for all participants.

CONFIDENTIALITY IN GROUP SETTINGS

The case of a group member disclosing a relapse in a substance abuse recovery group highlights the complex ethical challenges counselors face in group therapy. This case underscores the delicate balance between maintaining individual confidentiality and fostering group trust, a fundamental ethical dilemma in group counseling. The counselor's decision to uphold confidentiality while encouraging voluntary disclosure reflects a thoughtful approach to navigating these competing obligations.

Unlike one-on-one counseling, group therapy introduces unique confidentiality concerns. Here, the ethical principle of privacy intersects with the need for group cohesion and trust. The American Counseling Association's Code of Ethics stresses the importance of confidentiality while acknowledging that group settings come with limitations and exceptions. This case demonstrates how these ethical guidelines play out in real-world situations, requiring counselors to carefully manage complex interpersonal dynamics.

At the heart of the counselor's approach is a commitment to client autonomy, a core ethical principle. By protecting the member's confidentiality, the counselor respects their right to privacy and self-determination. However, this choice also carries risks for the group. When significant information, such as a relapse, is withheld, it may affect the authenticity of interactions and weaken the trust built over months of therapy.

At the same time, the counselor has an ethical responsibility to the group as a whole. Group therapy depends on creating a safe, trusting space where members feel comfortable sharing openly. By encouraging voluntary disclosure rather than breaching confidentiality, the counselor attempts to balance individual privacy with group well-being. This approach aligns with the ethical principle of beneficence, aiming to support both the individual and the group's collective progress.

In this case, alternative approaches, such as discussing the concept of relapse without identifying the individual or exploring hypothetical scenarios, demonstrate creative ways to address ethical dilemmas. These strategies seek to uphold confidentiality while still providing valuable therapeutic discussions for the group. They highlight the importance of flexibility and creativity in ethical decision-making within group counseling.

This case also sheds light on broader ethical themes in group therapy, particularly the need for clear communication about confidentiality from the outset. Establishing explicit guidelines on how sensitive information will be handled can help prevent conflicts down the line. Additionally, this case illustrates that ethical decision-making is an ongoing process. Counselors must continually assess the impact of their choices on both individual members and the group as a whole.

Key Ethical Principles for Managing Confidentiality in Group Counseling

1. **Prioritizing client safety and well-being** – When confidentiality may pose a risk to a client or others, counselors must carefully evaluate potential consequences before making a decision.
2. **Transparency in the process** – Clearly defining confidentiality boundaries and ethical responsibilities at the start of group therapy helps set expectations and reduce misunderstandings.
3. **Encouraging self-disclosure** – Supporting clients in finding appropriate ways to share sensitive information can strengthen both their personal growth and overall group cohesion.
4. **Utilizing ethical decision-making models** – Applying structured frameworks can help counselors navigate complex situations systematically and defensibly.
5. **Considering cultural context** – The meaning and significance of confidentiality can vary across cultural backgrounds, requiring counselors to adopt culturally sensitive approaches.
6. **Seeking supervision and consultation** – Complex ethical dilemmas benefit from the insights of experienced colleagues or supervisors, ensuring that all perspectives are considered.
7. **Documenting decision-making processes** – Keeping records of ethical decisions and their rationale provides valuable guidance

for future cases and reinforces adherence to professional standards.

MANAGING ETHICAL GROUP DYNAMICS

Ethical group management in counseling starts with establishing clear guidelines. This foundational step involves setting rules for group interaction, informed by professional standards such as the American Counseling Association's Code of Ethics and established group counseling literature. To ensure clarity, counselors should communicate these guidelines in accessible language, using real-world examples to illustrate ethical behavior. However, achieving full understanding and agreement among all group members can be a challenge, requiring ongoing discussion and reinforcement.

Creating a safe and supportive environment is equally critical. Group members must feel secure in sharing their thoughts and experiences without fear of judgment. Counselors foster this atmosphere through active listening and empathy, helping participants feel heard and respected. However, some members may struggle with feelings of discomfort or vulnerability in the group setting. To address this, counselors should routinely check in with participants and adjust the group process as needed to maintain a sense of safety.

Navigating power dynamics within the group is another essential responsibility. Imbalances in influence or status can subtly shape interactions, potentially limiting some members' ability to engage fully. Counselors must stay attuned to these dynamics, ensuring that all voices are heard and that no single member dominates discussions. By encouraging equal participation and validating diverse perspectives, counselors help create a more balanced and inclusive group experience.

Finally, managing conflict in an ethical manner is crucial for maintaining group cohesion. Disagreements are natural in any group setting, but how they are handled can significantly impact group trust and effectiveness. Counselors should use conflict resolution and de-escalation strategies to address tensions in a fair, constructive manner. When emotional reactions run high, maintaining neutrality and focusing on the underlying issues rather than personal differences can guide the group toward a positive resolution.

Upholding professional boundaries is an ongoing process in ethical group management. Counselors must ensure appropriate relationships both with and among group members, following clear boundary-setting guidelines. This can become particularly complex when navigating dual relationships or attraction between members. To maintain the integrity of the group, counselors should regularly review and reinforce boundary expectations, ensuring that all interactions remain professional and therapeutic.

These ethical principles work together to create a structured, safe, and supportive group environment. Clear guidelines provide a framework for interactions, fostering an atmosphere where power dynamics can be addressed openly, and conflicts can be managed constructively. Throughout this process, maintaining professional boundaries safeguards the therapeutic purpose of the group and reinforces trust among members.

In certain cultural contexts or specialized groups, alternative approaches may be necessary to align with the group's unique needs. For example:

- Collectivist cultures may require a more indirect approach to conflict resolution to prioritize group harmony.
- Trauma-focused groups may need additional safeguards to prevent re-traumatization and ensure psychological safety.
- Addiction recovery groups often have specific protocols for relapse management and confidentiality to protect members' privacy and progress.

ETHICAL RESPONSIBILITIES OF GROUP LEADERS

Group counseling leaders carry significant ethical responsibilities to ensure the safety, effectiveness, and integrity of the therapeutic process. These responsibilities include competence, informed consent, and confidentiality management, each playing a vital role in maintaining ethical group dynamics.

A competent group leader must have the necessary skills and knowledge to guide group dynamics effectively. This includes specialized training in group counseling techniques, an understanding of group development stages, and the ability to manage interpersonal conflicts. For example, a dedicated leader might pursue advanced certification in group psychotherapy, demonstrating a commitment to mastering the nuances of this modality. Competence is not just a professional expectation, it is essential for protecting the client's well-being and ensuring positive therapeutic outcomes.

Group leaders must provide clear, comprehensive information about the group's purpose, structure, and potential risks and benefits. Unlike individual counseling, group therapy presents unique confidentiality challenges that clients must understand before participating. A thorough informed consent process might include a written document outlining these confidentiality limitations, such as the inability to guarantee that other group members will keep shared information private. By fostering transparency, group leaders empower participants to make informed decisions about their involvement.

Managing confidentiality in group counseling is both complex and essential. While leaders must maintain professional confidentiality, they also have a duty to educate group members on privacy expectations and limitations. This includes discussing scenarios where confidentiality might be breached, such as when there is a risk of harm to self or others. If a breach occurs, a skilled leader might use it as a teachable moment, reinforcing the group's commitment to trust and exploring the impact of such breaches on group cohesion and individual well-being.

Navigating dual relationships in group settings can be challenging. Leaders must be mindful of maintaining clear professional boundaries to prevent conflicts or ethical concerns. This means avoiding situations where personal relationships, such as social invitations or business dealings, could interfere with the integrity of the therapeutic process. The goal is always to ensure that group members' well-being remains the top priority.

Cultural competence is a crucial ethical responsibility for group leaders. It goes beyond simply respecting diverse backgrounds, it requires actively adapting leadership styles and interventions to meet the cultural needs of participants. For example, a culturally competent leader might integrate healing practices or metaphors that resonate with a particular ethnic or cultural group. By doing so, they create a more inclusive and effective therapeutic space where everyone feels understood and supported.

Ethical decision-making is at the heart of responsible group leadership. Leaders often face complex dilemmas, such as how to address a disruptive member without disrupting the group dynamic. Applying structured ethical decision-making models helps ensure fair, consistent, and thoughtful resolutions that protect the group's cohesion and therapeutic goals.

Finally, professional growth is an ongoing ethical duty. Effective group leaders continuously refine their skills, stay updated on new research, and seek supervision or peer support. For instance, joining a professional consultation group focused on group therapy techniques can provide valuable insights and enhance the quality of care. This commitment to learning not only strengthens the leader's expertise but also sets a powerful example for group members.

These ethical responsibilities are deeply interconnected, each reinforcing the others. For example, cultural competence directly shapes ethical decision-making in group settings. A leader who understands diverse cultural perspectives is better equipped to handle ethical dilemmas in a way that respects and honors the values of all group members. Likewise, a strong grasp of group dynamics helps leaders navigate challenges like confidentiality concerns or dual relationships more effectively.

This interconnectedness highlights the complex and demanding nature of ethical group leadership. Successful group counseling requires more than just clinical expertise, it calls for a deep understanding of interpersonal dynamics, cultural awareness, and ethical reasoning. As the field evolves, new ethical considerations will likely emerge, such as the responsible use of technology in group therapy, the ethical implications of online counseling, and the integration of artificial intelligence in therapeutic settings. Staying attuned to these developments ensures that ethical group leadership remains relevant and effective in an ever-changing landscape.

ETHICAL SELF-DISCLOSURE IN GROUPS

Self-disclosure in group counseling presents a complex ethical challenge. When used thoughtfully, a counselor's personal sharing can be a powerful therapeutic tool. However, in a group setting, where multiple clients with diverse needs are present, self-disclosure must be handled with extra care. The American Counseling Association's Code of Ethics stresses the importance of client welfare and maintaining professional boundaries, both of which are even more critical when addressing a group rather than an individual.

When done appropriately, counselor self-disclosure can foster connection, model healthy sharing, and strengthen the therapeutic alliance. For instance, a counselor might briefly share a personal experience of overcoming anxiety to help normalize similar struggles among group members. However, this kind of disclosure also carries risks. It could unintentionally shift the focus away from clients, blur professional boundaries, or create pressure for members to share personal details they may not be ready to disclose.

Ethical self-disclosure requires careful attention to timing, content, and purpose. Counselors must ask themselves: Does this disclosure serve the therapeutic goals of the group? Factors such as the group's stage of development, members' presenting concerns, and overall group dynamics all play a role. A poorly timed or overly personal disclosure could disrupt the process or overwhelm clients who are not ready to engage with the counselor's experiences.

The content of self-disclosure is just as important as the timing. Any personal revelation should be brief, relevant, and supportive of the group's work, never a distraction or emotional burden. For example, a short anecdote about overcoming a challenge might be beneficial, whereas sharing deeply personal struggles or unresolved issues would cross ethical boundaries. Counselors must always distinguish between therapeutic self-disclosure and personal catharsis, ensuring that their sharing serves the clients, not themselves.

Cultural competence is essential when considering ethical self-disclosure in diverse group settings. What is appropriate in one cultural context may be perceived as intrusive or unprofessional in another. Counselors must be attuned to the cultural backgrounds and values of group members, adjusting their approach accordingly. This sensitivity also extends to power dynamics, factors such as gender, ethnicity, and socioeconomic status can influence how counselor disclosures are received and interpreted within the group.

Ethical self-disclosure also requires ongoing reflection and supervision. Counselors should regularly examine their motivations for sharing personal information, ensuring that disclosures serve the needs of the group rather than fulfilling personal needs. Supervision offers an external perspective, helping counselors identify blind spots or unintended consequences that could impact the therapeutic process. Common violations, such as blurred boundaries or breaches of confidentiality, are explored in greater depth in Chapters 1 and 15.

Documentation is another important ethical consideration. While there is no need for detailed records of every disclosure, noting significant instances and their intended therapeutic purpose can serve as both a reflective tool and a means of maintaining ethical accountability.

Informed consent takes on additional complexity in group counseling. Before engaging in self-disclosure, counselors should establish clear guidelines with the group regarding the purpose and boundaries of personal sharing. This includes discussing both the potential benefits and risks and securing agreement from members to respect confidentiality regarding what is shared in the group setting.

Finally, ethical self-disclosure requires vigilance in maintaining professional boundaries. Personal sharing can sometimes blur the line between professional and personal relationships, particularly in small communities where counselors and group members may interact outside the therapeutic setting. Counselors must proactively address any emerging ethical dilemmas to ensure that their role remains clear and professional.

ESTABLISHING ETHICAL GROUP NORMS

Creating ethical group norms in counseling starts with a clear understanding of their purpose. Group norms, shared expectations that guide behavior, form the foundation of a safe, productive, and ethically sound therapeutic environment. In the first session, counselors introduce these concepts in simple, accessible language, using concrete examples to ensure clarity. Handouts outlining common group norms can serve as helpful reference points for members throughout the process.

After this introduction, counselors guide a collaborative discussion where group members contribute their own ideas about essential norms. This participatory approach fosters a sense of ownership and investment in the group's ethical framework. To ensure everyone has a voice, counselors may use structured techniques like round-robin sharing. Visual aids, such as a whiteboard or flip chart, can help document suggestions and keep the process transparent and inclusive.

Integrating professional, ethical standards is a key step in establishing group norms. Counselors introduce core ethical principles, such as confidentiality and mutual respect, based on established guidelines like the American Counseling Association's Code of Ethics. This step requires balancing professional standards with group preferences, making it important to clearly explain the reasoning behind each ethical norm. When members understand why these principles matter, they are more likely to uphold them, strengthening the overall integrity of the group.

Once group norms have been proposed, the next step is building consensus. Using decision-making techniques such as voting or structured dialogue, group members work together to finalize a set of norms. This process often requires negotiation and compromise, with the counselor guiding discussions to keep the focus on shared goals and the collective benefit of maintaining clear ethical standards.

After reaching an agreement, the finalized norms are documented and prominently displayed. This serves multiple purposes: providing a tangible reference for members, reinforcing their commitment, and establishing a tool for accountability. The language used in this document should be clear and actionable, ensuring that everyone understands expectations easily (Corey et al., 2018).

Implementing and reinforcing these norms is an ongoing process throughout the life of the group. Counselors regularly reference them during sessions, incorporating check-ins and review periods to ensure they remain relevant and effective. Consistently applying these guidelines helps embed them into the group's culture, strengthening the therapeutic environment.

Finally, norms should be periodically reassessed and adjusted as needed. Through structured feedback and open discussions, the group can evaluate whether the norms continue to serve their purpose or if modifications are necessary. This flexible, evolving approach ensures that the ethical framework remains responsive to the group's changing dynamics and therapeutic needs (Corey et al., 2018).

A structured approach to establishing ethical group norms lays a strong foundation for effective therapeutic work. By actively involving members in the norm-setting process, counselors encourage a sense of shared responsibility and commitment to ethical behavior. These norms not only guide individual conduct but also help create a supportive, respectful, and ethically sound group environment.

Different types of groups may require alternative approaches to norm-setting. For example, in addiction recovery support groups, a more structured approach may be necessary, with clear behavioral expectations such as maintaining sobriety during meetings. In contrast, psychoeducational groups might benefit from norms that emphasize learning objectives and active participation in discussions. Tailoring the norm-setting process to the group's specific goals ensures that ethical guidelines are both relevant and effective in supporting the group's overall purpose.

ETHICAL CHALLENGES IN GROUP SETTINGS

Group counseling presents a unique set of ethical challenges that require careful navigation. These challenges arise from the complex interplay of group dynamics, where individual needs intersect with collective goals, and diverse backgrounds converge in a shared therapeutic space.

One of the primary ethical dilemmas in group counseling is balancing individual concerns with group cohesion. For example, when one member dominates discussions, it can hinder the therapeutic progress of others. Counselors must find ways to address individual needs while ensuring that the group as a whole benefits from the process.

The root causes of ethical challenges in group settings are varied. Group members bring diverse values, experiences, and cultural perspectives, which can lead to differences in communication styles, expectations, and comfort levels with self-disclosure. Power dynamics also play a role, as counselors must balance their authority with fostering an environment where all members feel heard and respected (Corey et al., 2018).

If not handled appropriately, these challenges can have serious consequences. Mishandling sensitive situations may cause emotional harm to group members, erode trust, and disrupt the therapeutic process. For instance, a breach of confidentiality by one member can create a ripple effect, making others hesitant to share openly. Additionally, unresolved ethical dilemmas can weaken group cohesion, reducing the effectiveness of the counseling experience. From a professional standpoint, counselors face ethical and legal risks if they fail to manage these issues properly, which could result in complaints, legal action, or damage to their reputation.

Traditionally, ethical challenges in group counseling have been managed by adapting principles from individual counseling. While this approach provides a useful foundation, it often fails to fully account for the complexities of group dynamics. Recognizing this gap, professional organizations have developed specialized ethical guidelines for group therapy. These guidelines emphasize key principles such as informed consent, confidentiality within the group setting, and managing multiple relationships. However, applying these guidelines in practice can be difficult due to the unpredictable and evolving nature of group interactions.

To better address these challenges, several potential solutions should be considered:

1. **Enhanced Ethical Training for Group Counseling** – Standard ethics training often focuses on individual counseling scenarios, which may not fully prepare practitioners for group-specific dilemmas. Training programs should incorporate real-world case studies, role-playing exercises, and interactive simulations. For instance, counselors could practice navigating conflicts between group members or responding to breaches of confidentiality in a way that maintains trust while upholding ethical responsibilities.

2. **Ethical Decision-Making Models for Group Settings** – Developing structured decision-making frameworks tailored to group counseling can help practitioners resolve complex ethical dilemmas more effectively. These models should account for the interconnected nature of group dynamics, considering both immediate ethical concerns and their potential impact on group cohesion and individual well-being. For example, a step-by-step model could guide counselors in handling situations where a group member discloses information that poses a risk to themselves or others, balancing confidentiality with the duty to protect.

A crucial step in addressing ethical challenges in group counseling is establishing regular ethical supervision for group leaders. Ongoing supervision provides a structured space for counselors to discuss emerging dilemmas, receive guidance from experienced professionals, and reflect on their ethical decision-making processes. One effective approach is holding monthly case conferences, where group leaders present anonymized ethical dilemmas, fostering collaborative problem-solving and continuous professional development.

Implementing these solutions comes with challenges. **Enhanced ethical training** requires significant investment in curriculum development and may necessitate updates to counselor education programs. Ethical decision-making models must be both flexible and practical, accommodating diverse scenarios while remaining accessible for real-world application. Regular ethical supervision demands time and resources, which could place additional strain on already busy clinical practices.

Despite these hurdles, the long-term benefits are substantial. Strengthening ethical competence in group counseling can lead to more effective therapy, increased client satisfaction, and reduced risk of harm to group members. Moreover, establishing a robust ethical framework tailored specifically to group settings can enhance the credibility of group therapy, increasing its acceptance and utilization as a valuable therapeutic approach.

14

---◦⌒⌣⌒◦---

ETHICS IN ADVOCACY AND JUSTICE

THE ETHICAL DUTY TO ADVOCATE

A dvocacy is a vital part of counseling, extending beyond the therapy room to address social injustices and systemic barriers that affect clients' well-being. Rooted in the core values of the profession, advocacy is not just encouraged, it's an ethical responsibility. The American Counseling Association (ACA) Code of Ethics explicitly supports this duty. Section A.7.a. states that counselors must advocate at individual, group, institutional, and societal levels to remove obstacles that hinder clients' access to growth and development.

The ethical foundation for advocacy is built on key principles. Beneficence, the commitment to promoting clients' well-being, calls on counselors to address not just personal struggles but also external factors that contribute to them. Justice, another fundamental ethical value, emphasizes fairness and equitable treatment. Advocacy is a direct way to challenge societal imbalances, particularly those that disproportionately affect marginalized communities.

At its core, advocacy aligns with counseling values like empowerment, equity, and human dignity. By advocating for clients, counselors help them navigate complex systems, reinforcing their sense of agency and self-efficacy. Ensuring equity means making sure everyone, regardless of background or circumstances, has access to mental health resources and opportunities for growth. And by challenging discrimination and promoting inclusivity, advocacy upholds the dignity and worth of every individual.

Counselor advocacy has the power to create meaningful change, both in individual lives and across society. On a personal level, advocacy can lead to real improvements for clients, such as better access to mental health care, educational opportunities, or fair workplace conditions. These changes don't just benefit clients' immediate circumstances; they also strengthen the impact of counseling by reducing external stressors that might otherwise hinder progress.

On a larger scale, advocacy drives systemic change. Counselors who engage in advocacy efforts help shape policies, raise public awareness about mental health, and challenge discriminatory practices within institutions. These efforts contribute to a more just and supportive society, making mental health resources more accessible to those who need them.

Despite its significance, advocacy in counseling is sometimes misunderstood. Some worry that it conflicts with a counselor's role or threatens therapeutic neutrality. However, this view overlooks a fundamental truth, counseling doesn't happen in isolation. Clients' mental health is shaped by their social, economic, and cultural environments. The

ACA Code of Ethics recognizes this reality, encouraging counselors to acknowledge and address these external factors when working with clients.

Advocacy doesn't replace therapy, it enhances it. Addressing systemic barriers can make a lasting difference in clients' lives. For example, a counselor supporting a client struggling with depression due to financial stress might advocate for better access to financial literacy programs or fair lending practices. While therapy helps clients build coping skills, advocacy works to remove the obstacles that may be contributing to their distress in the first place.

Beyond helping individuals, advocacy is also a powerful tool for prevention. By tackling systemic issues, counselors help create healthier environments that reduce the risk of mental health challenges, particularly for vulnerable populations. This proactive approach aligns with the counseling profession's core mission, not just treating illness but promoting overall wellness.

BALANCING INDIVIDUAL AND SOCIETAL NEEDS

Advocacy in counseling requires balancing two essential responsibilities: addressing the immediate needs of individual clients and working toward broader societal change. Counselors must navigate this dynamic carefully, ensuring that their efforts promote both personal well-being and social justice.

At the individual level, counselors focus on clients' specific concerns, tailoring interventions to support their psychological, emotional, and behavioral needs. In contrast, societal advocacy seeks to address systemic inequities, challenge oppressive structures, and influence policies that affect larger populations. While these approaches differ in scope, they share a common ethical foundation, both are driven by the principle of beneficence, the commitment to promoting well-being.

However, the way this principle is applied varies. Individual advocacy often involves direct interventions, such as providing therapy, connecting clients with resources, or advocating for their rights in specific settings. Societal advocacy, on the other hand, may take the form of lobbying for policy reform, raising public awareness, or working to dismantle discriminatory practices.

The impact of these approaches depends on context and timeframe. Individual advocacy can bring immediate, tangible benefits, such as securing workplace accommodations for a client with mental health challenges, improving their daily life and well-being. However, its effects may be limited in scope.

Societal advocacy, while often slower to produce visible results, has the potential for lasting, widespread change. Efforts to reform mental health policies or reduce stigma can create healthier environments for entire communities, benefiting many people over time. By addressing root causes, systemic advocacy helps shape a society where mental health support is more accessible and equitable.

Comparing the risks and benefits of prioritizing individual versus societal advocacy reveals deeper ethical complexities. Individual advocacy, while crucial for addressing immediate client needs, can sometimes overlook the broader systemic issues that contribute to those challenges. In some cases, it may even reinforce existing power structures by focusing on helping clients adapt rather than pushing for systemic change.

On the other hand, societal advocacy, while essential for long-term progress, risks neglecting the urgent needs of individual clients in pursuit of broader goals. There is also the ethical concern that counselors may unintentionally impose their own values or political perspectives when advocating for social change, which could blur professional boundaries and objectivity.

Each approach has distinct strengths. Individual advocacy provides immediate relief, offering tailored support that empowers clients and helps them navigate their unique circumstances. However, its impact is often limited in scope and may fail to address the systemic factors that contribute to clients' struggles.

Societal advocacy, by contrast, has the potential for far-reaching, lasting change. By tackling root causes, such as mental health stigma, discriminatory policies, or barriers to care, it helps create a more just and supportive environment for many. Yet, the challenge lies in the time and resources required to achieve meaningful change, as well as the difficulty of measuring its direct impact on individuals.

The best approach depends on the situation. In crisis scenarios, such as when a client is experiencing acute suicidal ideation, individual advocacy takes priority, as immediate intervention is critical. In contrast, when systemic change is both necessary and feasible, societal advocacy can help prevent future harm and promote long-term well-being. Striking the right balance ensures that both immediate client needs and broader social justice goals are addressed effectively.

Systemic advocacy is often the best approach when addressing widespread issues that affect multiple clients or entire communities. For example, school counselors advocating for policies to combat bullying or implement mental health education programs can create lasting benefits for a broad student population.

To provide ethical and effective care, counselors can integrate both individual and societal advocacy into their practice. This requires maintaining a dual focus, supporting clients' immediate needs while also working toward broader systemic change. Strategies for achieving this balance include:

1. **Empowering clients through education** – Helping clients understand the societal factors influencing their mental health encourages self-advocacy and community engagement.
2. **Collaborating with professionals and organizations** – Partnering with other experts allows counselors to address systemic issues while continuing to support individual clients.
3. **Incorporating social justice principles into treatment** – Assisting clients in recognizing and navigating societal barriers can enhance their well-being and resilience.
4. **Engaging in ongoing professional development** – Staying informed about both therapeutic techniques and social issues strengthens a counselor's ability to advocate effectively.
5. **Participating in professional advocacy efforts** – Involvement in organizations that push for policy changes enables counselors to contribute to systemic progress while maintaining their clinical practice.

By balancing individual and societal advocacy, counselors fulfill their ethical responsibilities to clients while promoting meaningful social change. This integrated approach acknowledges the connection between personal well-being and societal conditions, strengthening both counseling practice and community health.

ETHICAL CONSIDERATIONS IN COMMUNITY INTERVENTIONS

Community interventions in counseling advocacy offer a powerful way to address systemic issues and promote social justice on a larger scale. Unlike individual counseling, these efforts focus on entire communities, aiming to create meaningful, collective change. However, the ethical complexities of such interventions require careful reflection and responsible implementation.

At its core, community intervention involves identifying and addressing the social, economic, and environmental factors that influence mental health and well-being. This approach acknowledges that many individual struggles stem from broader societal issues, making it essential to address root causes rather than just symptoms. By working directly with communities, counselors can help foster long-term, sustainable improvements in mental health and overall quality of life.

While community interventions have the potential for widespread positive impact, they also present ethical challenges that must be carefully managed. One major concern is consent and representation. In individual counseling, clients actively seek services, giving them direct control over their participation. In contrast, community interventions may affect individuals who have not explicitly consented, raising ethical questions about imposing change, even with good intentions. Additionally, there is a risk of misrepresenting or oversimplifying a community's needs, leading to solutions that fail to address the true complexities of the situation.

Navigating these ethical challenges requires a thoughtful, inclusive approach that prioritizes collaboration, respect, and cultural sensitivity. By engaging community members in the planning and decision-making process, counselors can ensure interventions are both effective and ethically sound.

Cultural competence is essential in ethical community interventions, as counselors must be mindful of the cultural contexts in which they work. Their own values and perspectives may differ significantly from those of the communities they aim to support. Without this awareness, well-intended interventions can unintentionally impose external values, disrupting local customs, beliefs, or social structures. Misinterpreting community needs due to cultural differences can lead to ineffective or even harmful outcomes, emphasizing the need for thorough cultural assessment and continuous dialogue with community members.

Many ethical community intervention models emphasize participatory approaches, such as Community-Based Participatory Research (CBPR).

These methods engage community members at every stage, from identifying problems to implementing and evaluating solutions, helping to ensure that interventions align with the community's needs and priorities. While participatory approaches improve consent and representation, they also present challenges, such as managing diverse perspectives, navigating power dynamics, and requiring significant time and resources. These factors can sometimes limit their feasibility in certain contexts.

To ensure ethical practice in community interventions, several key strategies can be considered:

1. **Stakeholder Engagement and Representation** – Conducting a thorough stakeholder analysis ensures that key community members and groups are included from the outset. This promotes diverse representation and fosters community buy-in. However, in large or diverse communities, achieving full representation can be challenging. Effectiveness can be assessed by tracking stakeholder diversity and evaluating community participation throughout the intervention.

2. **Establishing a Clear Ethical Framework** – Developing ethical guidelines specifically for community interventions can help counselors navigate cultural competence, consent, and unintended consequences. While this approach promotes consistency and accountability, creating a framework that is both comprehensive and adaptable across different settings can be difficult. Regular ethical audits and team reflection sessions can help evaluate the effectiveness of such frameworks.

3. **Ensuring Ethical Adaptability in Community Interventions -** A third key strategy is implementing a **continuous feedback and adjustment mechanism** throughout the intervention process. This approach allows counselors to address real-time ethical concerns and adapt to changing community needs, recognizing the dynamic nature of community work.

By incorporating ongoing input from community members, counselors can make necessary course corrections to ensure interventions remain ethical and effective. However, this strategy requires significant resources and may introduce instability in the intervention plan. Its effectiveness can be measured by tracking the number and nature of adjustments made in response to ethical concerns, as well as assessing community satisfaction with the responsiveness of the intervention team.

Despite the benefits of these ethical strategies, counselors may encounter challenges, including:

- **Community resistance** – Some members may be skeptical of outside interventions, questioning their necessity or intent.
- **Limited resources** – Comprehensive engagement processes require time, funding, and personnel, which may not always be available.
- **Competing ethical priorities** – Balancing individual needs with broader community goals can create ethical dilemmas.
- **Measuring ethical impact** – Ethical outcomes are often subjective and difficult to quantify, making evaluation complex.

NAVIGATING POLICY ADVOCACY ETHICS

Ethical policy advocacy in counseling begins with the identification of a relevant policy issue. This requires a deep understanding of how existing laws and regulations impact client well-being and mental health equity. Counselors must critically examine policies or proposed legislation that could affect their clients, drawing on policy briefs, client data trends, and the latest research in mental health and counseling.

Once a key issue is identified, the next step is gathering substantive evidence to support the need for policy change. Ethical advocacy relies on empirical data rather than personal opinion or anecdotal experiences. Counselors can strengthen their advocacy by reviewing peer-reviewed studies, consulting professional associations for industry-wide statistics, and, with appropriate consent, incorporating client stories to illustrate the real-world impact of current policies.

A crucial part of ethical policy advocacy is assessing the ethical implications of proposed changes. This step requires a careful review of the *American Counseling Association's (ACA) Code of Ethics or another applicable code* and the application of ethical decision-making models to ensure alignment with core professional values. Counselors must navigate the balance between professional ethics and personal beliefs, ensuring that their advocacy upholds the principles of:

- **Beneficence** – Promoting client well-being.
- **Non-maleficence** – Avoiding harm.
- **Autonomy** – Respecting client self-determination.
- **Justice** – Ensuring fairness and equity

After conducting an ethical assessment, counselors must develop a strategic advocacy plan. This involves identifying key stakeholders, selecting effective communication methods, and outlining concrete actions to influence policy change. A deep understanding of the policy-making process is essential, as well as the ability to tailor advocacy efforts to the specific political and cultural context in which the counselor operates.

With a plan in place, the next step is active implementation. Counselors may engage in advocacy through multiple channels, such as:

- **Raising awareness on social media** to educate the public.
- **Providing expert testimony** to policymakers.
- **Participating in public speaking events** to highlight the issue's importance.

Throughout these efforts, counselors must maintain professionalism, rely on evidence-based arguments, and avoid partisan rhetoric that could compromise their credibility or ethical standing.

The final step is evaluating the impact of advocacy efforts and adjusting strategies as needed. This requires tracking policy developments, gathering feedback, and assessing both short-term outcomes and long-term effects. Because policy advocacy is often an ongoing process, counselors must be prepared to refine their approach, demonstrating persistence and adaptability.

By following these structured steps, counselors can ensure that their advocacy is ethical, effective, and aligned with professional standards. However, different political and cultural contexts may require alternative approaches. For example:

- In regions where direct engagement with policymakers is limited, grassroots organizing and community education may be more effective.
- In cultures where personal narratives hold significant influence, qualitative data and case studies may play a larger role in advocacy efforts while still maintaining scientific rigor.

This flexibility ensures that advocacy remains ethical, culturally responsive, and impactful in diverse settings.

PROMOTING MENTAL HEALTH EQUITY

Mental health equity is a fundamental yet often overlooked aspect of counseling practice. It ensures that all individuals, regardless of socioeconomic status, race, ethnicity, or geographic location, have equal access to quality mental health care.

However, equity goes beyond equal access; it recognizes that different populations face unique challenges and barriers, requiring care that is tailored to their specific needs. Addressing these disparities is essential to improving the effectiveness of counseling interventions and fostering overall community well-being.

Root Causes of Mental Health Disparities

Mental health inequities are deeply embedded in societal structures, influenced by systemic barriers such as:

- **Institutional racism and discrimination** which contribute to mistrust in healthcare and underutilization of services.
- **Economic inequality**, which limits access to affordable mental health care.
- **Social determinants of health**, including education, housing, and neighborhood conditions, all of which impact mental well-being.

For example, individuals living in poverty often experience chronic stress and trauma, exacerbating mental health conditions while simultaneously facing financial and logistical obstacles to receiving care. Similarly, racial and ethnic minorities frequently encounter bias in healthcare settings, further discouraging them from seeking treatment.

Advocating for mental health equity presents several ethical challenges for counselors, including:

- **Fair allocation of limited resources** – How should scarce mental health resources be distributed to ensure the greatest impact while avoiding unintended disparities?
- **Cultural competence in care** – How can counselors provide services that respect diverse cultural backgrounds and avoid a one-size-fits-all approach?

Efforts to promote mental health equity have had mixed success. One promising approach is community-based participatory research, which actively involves underserved populations in shaping culturally appropriate interventions.

By fostering collaboration between researchers, practitioners, and community members, this method helps build trust and ensures that solutions are tailored to local needs. Another effective strategy is integrating mental health services into primary care settings. This can reduce stigma and make services more accessible, especially for those hesitant to seek specialized care. While both strategies show promise, they often struggle with scalability and long-term sustainability.

Counselors can play a crucial role in advocating for mental health equity through ethical, practical strategies. One approach is cultural competence training, which helps counselors provide more culturally responsive care by addressing implicit biases and improving communication with diverse populations. This training can raise awareness of cultural differences and lead to better patient outcomes. However, it also comes with challenges, such as the risk of oversimplifying cultures or struggling to measure its long-term impact on practice.

Another strategy is building strong partnerships with community organizations and leaders. Local knowledge and existing support networks are invaluable in addressing mental health disparities. By working together, counselors and community partners can identify barriers to care and develop culturally relevant, sustainable interventions. This approach fosters trust and leads to more effective solutions. However, it also requires balancing professional boundaries and navigating potential conflicts between clinical best practices and community preferences.

A third approach to promoting mental health equity is leveraging technology to expand access to resources. This includes teletherapy, mobile health apps, and online support groups designed for specific cultural or linguistic communities. Technology can make mental health services more accessible, especially for those in rural or underserved areas. It also allows for anonymous participation, which can help reduce stigma. However, there are challenges, such as bridging the digital divide, ensuring data privacy, and maintaining quality care in virtual settings.

Assessing the impact of these strategies requires a well-rounded evaluation process. Quantitative measures, such as service utilization rates, treatment outcomes, and population-level mental health trends, offer important insights. But numbers alone don't tell the full story. Qualitative assessments, including personal experiences and community feedback, are just as crucial. Longitudinal studies that track changes over time and across different demographic groups help reveal the lasting effects of equity-focused interventions. Involving community members in the evaluation process ensures that the chosen metrics are not only relevant but also culturally meaningful.

VALUES CONFLICTS IN ADVOCACY

A counselor navigating LGBTQ+ advocacy in a socially rigged community faces a complex ethical challenge, balancing personal values, professional responsibilities, and societal expectations. This example highlights the intricate nature of ethical advocacy in the counseling profession. It underscores the tension between the duty to support marginalized clients and the need to maintain effective therapeutic relationships within a diverse community.

One of the core challenges in this situation is reconciling professional ethics with community norms. The American Counseling Association's Code of Ethics emphasizes advocating for clients, especially those experiencing discrimination. At the same time, it calls for respecting diverse perspectives and avoiding the imposition of personal values. This delicate balance requires careful, thoughtful decision-making.

In response, the counselor chooses to provide safe and confidential support and resources to LGBTQ+ clients while addressing the broader impact of discrimination in discussions with all clients. This measured approach seeks to meet ethical obligations without alienating community members. It aligns with the principle of "do no harm" by prioritizing vulnerable clients' well-being.

However, this strategy raises a larger ethical question: How far should a counselor go in public advocacy? The counselor's anonymous contributions to a local LGBTQ+ support organization reflect an effort to create change beyond the counseling office while reducing professional risk and backlash from the socially rigged community. This approach illustrates the broader dilemma counselors face, finding ways to support social justice efforts while maintaining professional boundaries and objectivity. Should this counselor just leave the community? A new state? Or should they continue to find ways to change it, through their advocacy?

The approaches of open advocacy and complete neutrality represent two ends of a spectrum, each with distinct ethical implications. Open advocacy aligns more directly with the counseling profession's commitment to social justice but may strain relationships with clients who hold opposing views. On the other hand, complete neutrality may help maintain a broader client base but risks neglecting the needs of marginalized individuals and could be perceived as passively endorsing discrimination. Of course, it's a spectrum and counselors may find themselves moving through it depending on their community, setting and personal values.

This case study highlights several key principles for navigating conflicts between personal values, professional ethics, and community standards:

1. **Contextual Sensitivity:** Ethical advocacy requires an awareness of the cultural, social, and political landscape in which counseling takes place. The appropriate approach depends on weighing potential risks and benefits for clients and the wider community.
2. **Incremental Change:** In challenging environments, gradual advocacy, through small, consistent actions, can promote progress while minimizing resistance from opposing viewpoints.
3. **Ethical Prioritization:** When ethical obligations conflict, counselors must prioritize actions based on their potential impact.

In this case, supporting vulnerable LGBTQ+ clients took precedence while also considering the effects on other therapeutic relationships.

4. **Professional Boundaries:** Maintaining a clear distinction between personal activism and professional responsibilities is essential. The counselor's anonymous contributions illustrate a way to engage in advocacy while upholding professional objectivity.

5. **Continuous Reflection:** Ethical decision-making is an ongoing process. Regular self-reflection and consultation with colleagues help counselors navigate complex situations thoughtfully and responsibly.

6. **Client-Centered Focus:** Regardless of personal beliefs, a counselor's primary duty is to serve the best interests of all clients. This principle informed the balanced approach to discussing discrimination with different client groups.

7. **Systemic Perspective:** Effective advocacy operates at multiple levels, individual, organizational, and societal. The counselor's actions, from direct client support to community contributions, reflect this multi-level approach.

ETHICAL USE OF CLIENT EXPERIENCES

Using client experiences in advocacy efforts can be both impactful and ethically complex. While sharing personal stories can empower individuals and drive meaningful policy change, it also carries risks that require careful management.

Research supports the ethical and positive potential of this practice when proper safeguards are in place. A survey of clients whose stories were used in mental health advocacy campaigns found that 85% felt empowered by sharing their experiences. However, the 12% who later regretted participating highlights the need for strong informed consent processes and ongoing support.

Ethical concerns, particularly around confidentiality, require careful attention. Literature reviews and expert panel discussions emphasize key principles for ethical storytelling: informed consent, anonymity options, and the right to withdraw at any time. These safeguards help protect client welfare and ensure that advocacy efforts remain ethically sound.

By adhering to these principles, counselors and advocacy organizations can responsibly amplify client voices while minimizing potential harm. Thoughtfully incorporating personal experiences into advocacy can create meaningful change while respecting the dignity and autonomy of those who share their stories.

Despite its benefits, the use of client experiences in advocacy carries risks, including the potential for re-traumatization and exploitation. To safeguard client well-being, careful screening processes and comprehensive support systems are essential. Counselors must assess a client's emotional readiness before involving them in advocacy and remain vigilant in ensuring their ongoing well-being. Clear ethical guidelines and client-centered approaches are critical to preventing exploitation and ensuring that advocacy efforts prioritize the client's best interests.

These considerations have significant implications for counseling advocacy practices and ethical guidelines. They highlight the need for a thoughtful, client-centered approach that balances advocacy's potential impact with the responsibility to protect clients. Counselors and advocacy organizations should establish comprehensive protocols, including thorough informed consent procedures, ongoing emotional support, and strict confidentiality measures.

Additionally, these findings point to the importance of enhanced training for counselors involved in advocacy. Training should emphasize ethical decision-making, risk mitigation, and strategies for effectively supporting clients throughout the advocacy process. Developing specialized ethical guidelines for advocacy within counseling could further strengthen best practices, providing clear standards for the responsible use of client experiences in advocacy efforts.

ADVOCACY IN DIGITAL SPACES

Digital advocacy has become a powerful tool for counselors to promote social justice, raise awareness about mental health, and advocate for policy changes. Online platforms, social media, and digital campaigns allow counselors to reach broader audiences and drive change more quickly than traditional methods. However, the digital landscape also presents unique ethical challenges that require careful navigation to uphold professional integrity and protect client well-being.

The benefits of digital advocacy are significant. It enables counselors to share critical information rapidly, connect with diverse communities, and mobilize support for important causes. For example, a counselor might use social media to share suicide prevention resources, reaching individuals who lack access to traditional mental health services. Digital platforms also create opportunities for real-time engagement with policymakers and stakeholders, potentially accelerating systemic change.

However, the risks cannot be ignored. The speed and permanence of online communication mean that a poorly worded post or an ill-conceived campaign could harm vulnerable individuals or damage a counselor's professional reputation. Additionally, the blurred line between personal and professional identities in digital spaces can compromise client confidentiality and therapeutic relationships.

Beyond these concerns, ethical challenges in digital advocacy require careful consideration. Counselors must obtain informed consent before sharing client experiences, even when anonymized. The rapid spread of misinformation online also underscores the importance of fact-checking and responsible communication. Furthermore, counselors should remain mindful of their own biases and the risk of digital echo chambers that reinforce rather than challenge perspectives.

By approaching digital advocacy with ethical awareness and strategic caution, counselors can harness its potential for meaningful impact while minimizing risks to clients, themselves, and the broader mental health community.

Current approaches to ethical digital advocacy often focus on general guidelines for professional conduct online, emphasizing clear boundaries, client privacy, and information accuracy. While essential, these guidelines may not fully address the complexities of digital spaces or the nuanced ethical dilemmas that arise in advocacy work.

To enhance ethical practice in digital advocacy, three key strategies should be considered:

1. **Developing a Digital Ethics Framework for Counseling Advocacy**
   A profession-specific framework could provide clear guidance on challenges unique to advocacy work, such as balancing urgency with careful deliberation and managing the tension between personal conviction and professional objectivity. While this approach offers structured, relevant guidance, ensuring its consistent implementation across diverse counseling settings and keeping it updated in response to evolving technology would be challenging.

2. **Establishing Peer Review Mechanisms for Digital Advocacy**
   Creating a network of counselors to review advocacy content before publication could help identify ethical risks and enhance professional accountability. While leveraging collective expertise reduces the likelihood of ethical missteps, it may also slow down advocacy efforts and could unintentionally discourage individual initiative if not carefully managed.

315

3. Integrating Digital Literacy and Advocacy Ethics into Counselor Education

Providing training on evaluating online information, engaging responsibly in digital spaces, and anticipating ethical challenges could foster a more ethically aware profession. Though this approach has long-term benefits, it requires substantial resources and may take time to yield visible results.

Assessing the effectiveness and ethical integrity of digital advocacy is complex. Quantitative metrics like social media reach and engagement are easily accessible but fail to capture ethical nuances. Qualitative methods, such as stakeholder feedback and case studies, offer deeper insights but require more time and resources. A balanced approach incorporating both types of evaluation would provide a more comprehensive understanding of an advocacy initiative's impact.

Unlike traditional advocacy, digital platforms offer global reach, breaking geographical and cultural barriers. While this allows for rapid responses to emerging issues, it also increases the risk of hasty, ill-considered actions. Additionally, the viral nature of online content can amplify both positive messages and misinformation, placing a greater ethical responsibility on advocates to ensure accuracy and thoughtfulness in their messaging.

15

--------•⟨⟩⟨⟩•--------

BOUNDARIES AND MULTIPLE

RELATIONSHIPS

NAVIGATING DUAL RELATIONSHIPS

Counseling relies on clear boundaries, well-defined roles, and a singular focus on the client's well-being. However, dual or multiple relationships occur when a counselor takes on more than one role in a client's life, which can blur professional lines and create ethical challenges. Dual relationships, sometimes called multiple relationships, first introduced in Chapter 1, require careful boundary management. This chapter explores practical and contextual challenges.

The primary concern with dual relationships is the risk of harm or exploitation. When a counselor steps into multiple roles, such as also being a client's business partner or friend, it can lead to confusion, conflicts of interest, and a loss of objectivity (ACA, 2014, A.5.a.; AMHCA, 2020, I.C.3). For example, a counselor with a financial stake in a client's business might struggle to separate professional responsibilities from personal interests, potentially influencing therapeutic decisions in unintended ways.

Different types of dual relationships come with unique risks. Social connections, like friendships or community involvement, can compromise confidentiality and shift power dynamics. Business relationships may create financial conflicts that cloud judgment. Romantic or sexual relationships are especially problematic, as they breach ethical guidelines and can cause serious emotional harm to the client.

Maintaining firm professional boundaries helps ensure objectivity, protects confidentiality, and keeps the therapeutic relationship focused on the client's needs. This approach reduces the risk of ethical breaches and reinforces public trust in the counseling profession. However, in small or rural communities, complete separation between professional and personal lives may not always be practical, requiring careful ethical consideration.

In some cases, dual relationships are difficult to avoid, or may even be beneficial. In small communities or specialized fields, a counselor might be the only professional available with the necessary expertise. When that happens, the need for services may outweigh the risks of overlapping roles. Additionally, some therapeutic approaches or cultural traditions embrace more flexible boundaries, making certain dual relationships appropriate or even expected.

When a dual relationship is unavoidable, ethical management is key. Transparency is essential, counselors should openly discuss potential conflicts with clients and obtain informed consent. Establishing clear boundaries for each role helps prevent confusion and protects the therapeutic process. Regular consultation with colleagues or supervisors can also provide valuable guidance, ensuring ethical dilemmas are navigated thoughtfully.

Counselors must continuously assess how a dual relationship impacts therapy. This includes watching for signs of transference or countertransference, considering whether it affects the client's willingness to engage, and evaluating any risk of exploitation. If a dual relationship starts to compromise therapy or the client's well-being, the counselor must be ready to adjust roles or refer the client to another professional.

The ethical concerns surrounding dual relationships go beyond individual cases, they also shape public trust in the counseling profession. While maintaining strict boundaries reinforces professionalism, rigid rules can sometimes conflict with ethical principles like beneficence or respect for client autonomy. In certain situations, a dual relationship might provide unique advantages or align with cultural expectations, requiring a more nuanced approach.

Ethical decision-making in these cases should be guided by context, potential risks and benefits, and professional ethical codes. For example, the American Counseling Association's Code of Ethics discourages dual relationships but acknowledges that some are unavoidable. In such instances, it stresses the importance of informed consent, careful documentation, and ongoing evaluation of the relationship's impact on therapy.

ETHICAL IMPLICATIONS OF MULTIPLE ROLES

In small communities, counselors often face the challenge of managing multiple roles. Consider a counselor in a rural town who finds themselves providing therapy to a client who is also the parent of their child's classmate. This situation highlights the delicate balance between maintaining professional boundaries and navigating the social realities of a close-knit community. The potential for role confusion is significant, as interactions between counselor and client may extend beyond the therapy room into everyday social settings.

When handling such cases, several key ethical considerations come into play. The principle of nonmaleficence (avoiding harm) must be weighed against the limited availability of mental health resources in rural areas. A counselor's decision to discuss the potential dual relationship openly with the client reflects a commitment to transparency and informed consent, essential ethical standards that promote collaborative problem-solving and empower the client to make an informed decision about continuing therapy.

To maintain ethical integrity, counselors must proactively establish boundaries. Developing a clear plan for managing interactions outside of therapy can help prevent misunderstandings while preserving the therapeutic alliance. By involving the client in this process, the counselor supports the principle of client autonomy, fostering a relationship built on mutual trust and respect.

Confidentiality, a core ethical obligation, becomes even more critical in such scenarios. The likelihood of encountering clients in public settings requires counselors to have strategies in place for protecting client privacy. This could include discussing in advance how to handle accidental meetings or setting guidelines for communication in shared spaces.

Another crucial consideration is competence. Counselors must continuously assess whether they can provide effective treatment while managing the complexities of a dual relationship. Regular reflection, consultation with colleagues, and supervision can help ensure that professional objectivity is not compromised.

Possible alternatives, such as referring the client to another provider or enforcing strict no-contact rules outside of therapy, present their own ethical dilemmas. A referral might help avoid boundary complications but could also limit access to care in an already underserved area. On the other hand, strict no-contact rules may be impractical in a small community where social interactions are unavoidable.

This case underscores broader lessons about boundary management in counseling, particularly in rural or tight-knit environments. Transparency and informed consent are essential for ethically navigating dual relationships. Open conversations about potential challenges allow both the counselor and client to develop clear expectations and strategies for maintaining professional boundaries.

Ongoing self-assessment is equally important. Counselors must remain aware of how multiple roles impact therapy, client well-being, and their own professional judgment. Seeking peer consultation or supervision can provide valuable insight when facing complex ethical situations.

Several strategies can help counselors in small communities manage dual relationships effectively:

- **Clear Communication and Documentation** – From the outset, counselors should discuss potential boundary issues, risks, and agreed-upon guidelines with clients.
- **Robust Informed Consent Process** – Addressing the unique challenges of small-town practice helps establish mutual expectations.
- **Professional Support Network** – Building connections with colleagues for consultation or referrals can reduce isolation and provide alternative options for clients when needed.
- **Regular Ethical Audits** – Periodically reviewing boundary practices helps identify potential issues before they escalate, ensuring compliance with ethical standards.

By adopting these strategies, counselors can uphold ethical principles while acknowledging the realities of working in small communities. The goal is not only to protect clients but also to maintain the integrity of the counseling profession in all practice settings.

ROMANTIC AND SEXUAL BOUNDARIES

The strict ethical prohibition against sexual relationships between counselors and clients has deep historical roots. As psychotherapy professionalized in the early 20th century, Sigmund Freud was among the first to highlight the importance of maintaining boundaries. In his 1915 paper *Observations on Transference-Love*, Freud warned that therapists must resist acting on any romantic or sexual feelings that emerge during treatment, as doing so could compromise therapy and exploit vulnerable clients.

By the mid-20th century, professional organizations began codifying these ethical standards. In 1953, the American Psychological Association (APA) established its first formal ethics code, which included prohibitions against sexual relationships with clients. This was a turning point in solidifying what had previously been understood as an implicit professional norm.

The 1960s and 1970s brought heightened awareness of boundary violations, influenced by cultural shifts and high-profile cases of therapist-client sexual misconduct. One such case involved psychiatrist Jules Masserman, who was accused in the 1980s of drugging and sexually abusing patients. Public concern over cases like this led professional organizations to strengthen their ethical guidelines. In 1977, the APA revised its ethics code to explicitly ban sexual relationships with current clients. Other organizations, including the American Counseling Association (ACA) and the National Association of Social Workers (NASW), soon followed suit.

By the 1980s and 1990s, ethical standards became even more refined. Recognizing that power imbalances and risks of exploitation could persist after therapy ended, the APA introduced a two-year waiting period before therapists could engage in romantic relationships with former clients. Many other professional organizations adopted similar or even stricter policies.

Research during this period provided strong evidence of the harm caused by therapist-client sexual involvement. Studies linked these violations to increased risks of depression, suicide, and lasting emotional trauma for clients. This empirical data reinforced the need for strict boundaries and informed the creation of more comprehensive ethical guidelines.

The rise of the internet and social media in the late 20th and early 21st centuries introduced new challenges. Professional organizations have had to address ethical concerns related to online interactions, digital communication, and virtual therapy spaces. The ACA's 2014 Code of Ethics, for example, stresses the importance of maintaining professional boundaries in digital contexts, including social media.

Today, ethical guidelines regarding romantic and sexual boundaries are more detailed and stringent than ever before. Most professional codes enforce extended prohibition periods for relationships with former clients, typically ranging from two to five years. Some organizations, like the American Association for Marriage and Family Therapy (AAMFT), have implemented permanent bans on sexual relationships with former clients.

Beyond outright prohibitions, these guidelines also address related concerns such as romantic attraction, non-sexual physical contact, and the exchange of gifts. They emphasize the counselor's responsibility to proactively manage boundaries and seek supervision when faced with ethical dilemmas. The focus has shifted from merely banning sexual contact to fostering a deeper understanding of how subtle boundary violations can impact the therapeutic process.

Ethical discussions around romantic and sexual boundaries will likely continue evolving. Future considerations may include more specific guidelines for managing boundaries in online therapy, debates over absolute prohibitions versus case-by-case evaluations, and increased attention to cultural differences in boundary expectations. While ethical codes may adapt to new challenges, the fundamental principle remains the same: counselors must uphold professional integrity and prioritize the well-being of their clients above all else.

CULTURAL CONSIDERATIONS IN BOUNDARIES

Boundaries in counseling are universally recognized as essential, yet their interpretation varies widely across cultures. In Western societies, where individualism is emphasized, clear distinctions between personal and professional roles are seen as fundamental to ethical practice. In contrast, many non-Western cultures, particularly those with collectivist traditions, may view boundaries more fluidly, shaped by interconnected social structures and holistic healing approaches.

Western counseling models often stress strict professional boundaries, advocating for emotional distance and well-defined roles between counselor and client. These principles, rooted in psychoanalytic theory and formal ethical guidelines, are designed to protect both parties and ensure the integrity of the therapeutic relationship. However, in many non-Western traditions, counseling may naturally involve more flexible boundaries. Healers may also serve as community leaders, spiritual guides, or even familial figures, blending professional and personal roles in ways that would be considered inappropriate in Western practice.

Each approach has its strengths and challenges. Western boundary-setting helps maintain objectivity, safeguards against ethical violations, and creates a structured therapeutic environment. However, it may also introduce artificial barriers in cultures where interpersonal closeness is highly valued. In contrast, non-Western approaches may foster stronger therapeutic alliances and cultural alignment but may also carry risks, such as role confusion or potential power imbalances.

Historically, Western notions of boundaries have been shaped by the professionalization of mental health care and an emphasis on individual autonomy. In contrast, many indigenous and traditional healing practices see the healer as an integral part of the community, participating in everyday life and shared rituals. For example, in some African and Native American traditions, healers engage with clients beyond formal sessions, reinforcing trust and connection, an approach that might be viewed as a boundary violation in Western settings.

The challenge lies in balancing cultural sensitivity with ethical safeguards. In collectivist cultures, for example, gift-giving or participation in community events may be customary and even expected. Rather than imposing rigid Western boundary standards, counselors working in such environments may need to adapt while still upholding core ethical principles. On the other hand, as globalization influences traditional cultures, the adoption of more defined boundaries may become necessary to address evolving societal norms.

Developing a culturally responsive approach to boundaries requires a thoughtful, flexible mindset. Ethical guidelines should account for cultural variations while ensuring that client welfare remains the priority. Counseling training programs can incorporate cross-cultural competencies, helping future professionals navigate boundary dilemmas with awareness and sensitivity. Additionally, open discussions between practitioners from diverse backgrounds can lead to more inclusive ethical standards that reflect the complexity of real-world counseling practice.

Ultimately, while Western and non-Western perspectives on boundaries differ in their approaches, they share a common goal: to promote client well-being. By embracing a broader, culturally informed understanding of boundaries, the counseling profession can continue to evolve in ways that are both ethically sound and globally relevant.

BOUNDARIES IN THE DIGITAL AGE

The digital era has reshaped the way counselors navigate professional boundaries, introducing both opportunities and challenges. While online counseling has expanded accessibility, it has also blurred the lines between personal and professional spaces, raising complex ethical concerns. These challenges extend beyond virtual therapy sessions to include social media interactions, email communication, and the broader digital presence of both counselors and clients.

One of the most pressing concerns is the potential for personal and professional lives to intersect in online spaces. Many counselors maintain personal social media accounts, but the public nature of these platforms can lead to unintended disclosures. A client may, for example, come across a counselor's personal opinions, family photos, or social affiliations, information that would typically remain private in traditional in-person therapy. Such visibility can affect the power dynamic in therapy, potentially influencing the client's perception of the counselor and the therapeutic process itself.

Another major issue is the expectation of constant availability. The immediacy of digital communication can create a false sense of accessibility, with clients feeling entitled to instant responses to messages or emails. This can not only challenge professional boundaries but also contribute to counselor burnout, as work-life separation becomes increasingly difficult to maintain.

Beyond these concerns, digital interactions introduce new risks to confidentiality. Responding to a client's email over public Wi-Fi, using unsecured messaging apps, or even maintaining client records in cloud-based platforms can all pose security risks. Without strict protocols in place, client privacy, the foundation of ethical counseling, can be unintentionally compromised.

STRATEGIES FOR MANAGING DIGITAL BOUNDARIES

Counseling organizations have introduced guidelines to help therapists manage digital interactions, emphasizing secure communication, professional online conduct, and clear response-time policies. However, these guidelines often struggle to keep pace with rapidly evolving technology and shifting social norms. To address these gaps, several potential solutions have emerged:

1. Dedicated Therapeutic Platforms

Using secure, professional-grade platforms for messaging, video sessions, and document sharing helps maintain clear boundaries between professional and personal digital spaces. These platforms enhance confidentiality and structure client-counselor interactions. However, requiring clients to adopt specialized software may create accessibility barriers for those less familiar with technology.

2. Digital Literacy Training for Counselors

Training programs that teach counselors how to manage privacy settings, secure communication channels, and the psychological implications of digital interactions can help mitigate boundary risks. However, as technology continues to evolve, ongoing education will be necessary to ensure counselors stay informed about emerging threats and best practices.

3. AI-Assisted Boundary Management

Emerging technology could offer AI-driven tools that monitor digital communication patterns, alerting counselors to potential boundary concerns before they escalate. While this proactive approach could enhance boundary maintenance, it also raises ethical questions about data privacy, surveillance, and the role of technology in therapy.

Each of these solutions presents unique challenges. Secure therapeutic platforms require financial investment and client adaptability, while digital literacy training demands ongoing commitment from both individuals and institutions. AI-driven tools may offer convenience but must be carefully implemented to avoid ethical pitfalls.

Ultimately, the key to maintaining professional boundaries in the digital age lies in a balanced approach, one that integrates technology while reinforcing ethical principles. As new communication tools continue to emerge, counselors must remain adaptable, ensuring that their digital interactions uphold the same professional integrity as in-person therapy.

FOSTERING THERAPEUTIC ALLIANCE

The role of professional boundaries in shaping the therapeutic alliance is a central issue in counseling ethics. While maintaining clear boundaries is essential for professionalism and client safety, some argue that strict adherence may create emotional distance, potentially hindering the development of a strong, trust-based relationship. Striking the right balance between professional integrity and genuine human connection is a challenge that has significant implications for client outcomes and the overall effectiveness of counseling.

Advocates of strict boundaries emphasize their role in maintaining professionalism, protecting clients from exploitation, and ensuring ethical consistency. Research suggests that when counselors uphold clear professional boundaries, clients report higher levels of satisfaction and positive treatment outcomes. A meta-analysis by Smith and Glass (1977) found that therapists who maintained consistent boundaries experienced better therapeutic results. Adhering to structured guidelines also minimizes the risk of boundary violations that could compromise the integrity of the profession.

However, critics argue that rigid boundaries can create a clinical, detached atmosphere that may not meet the relational needs of all clients. In cultures that value personal connection and informality in relationships, a counselor's strict adherence to boundaries might be perceived as cold or uninvested, potentially weakening the therapeutic alliance.

A contrasting perspective advocates for more flexible boundaries, emphasizing that counseling is, at its core, a relational process. Research on therapist genuineness, such as Carl Rogers' (1957) work on the importance of authenticity in therapy, highlights that a counselor's ability to connect with clients in a sincere and empathetic manner is crucial to success. Allowing some flexibility, such as occasional self-disclosure or slight adjustments to session structures, may strengthen trust and engagement, particularly for clients from collectivist cultures who expect a warmer, more personal relationship with their counselor.

Despite these advantages, the flexible approach carries risks. A lack of clear boundaries can lead to role confusion, ethical dilemmas, and, in extreme cases, boundary violations. Critics worry that without clear guidelines, the line between professional care and personal involvement can become dangerously blurred.

Many experts argue that a middle ground, one that maintains essential ethical boundaries while allowing for culturally sensitive flexibility, may be the most effective approach. Kitchener's (1984) ethical decision-making model supports this perspective, emphasizing that boundary decisions should consider multiple factors, including the client's background, context, and therapeutic goals.

For example, while strict boundaries might be beneficial in some cases, minor adjustments, such as extending a session for a distressed client or carefully using self-disclosure, could strengthen rapport without compromising ethical integrity. An article by Speight et al. (2011) suggests that clients from diverse backgrounds may experience higher satisfaction with counselors who demonstrated flexibility in professional boundaries, suggesting that cultural factors play a key role in boundary expectations.

However, critics of this balanced approach argue that it introduces ambiguity, making it difficult to establish consistent ethical guidelines across the profession. If flexibility is interpreted too loosely, counselors may struggle to determine appropriate limits, potentially leading to inconsistent practices.

The ongoing debate over boundaries has significant implications for the future of counseling ethics and training. Strict adherence ensures professionalism but may alienate some clients. A more flexible approach fosters cultural responsiveness but requires careful ethical reasoning to prevent unintended boundary violations. A balanced model, while promising, necessitates sophisticated training in ethical decision-making, particularly for new counselors who may find boundary navigation challenging.

Ultimately, the question of how professional boundaries influence the therapeutic alliance is not a matter of choosing one approach over another but finding the right balance. As counseling continues to evolve, it is crucial to develop ethical frameworks that allow for both structure and relational depth, ensuring that professional integrity and genuine human connection coexist in ways that best serve diverse client populations.

MANAGING UNAVOIDABLE DUAL RELATIONSHIPS

In counseling, particularly within small or close-knit communities, unavoidable dual relationships present a complex ethical challenge. When counselors and clients share overlapping roles, whether as neighbors, colleagues, or community members, it becomes essential to navigate these relationships with transparency, professionalism, and ethical rigor. A structured approach can help counselors maintain ethical integrity while acknowledging the realities of their environment.

The first step in managing a dual relationship is recognizing its existence. Counselors must be vigilant in identifying potential overlaps between their professional and personal lives, even when these relationships seem minor. Ethical decision-making models and consultation with colleagues or supervisors can help counselors assess whether an interaction qualifies as a dual relationship. However, subtle overlaps may go unnoticed, so regular reflection on community involvement and client interactions is key to maintaining awareness.

Once a dual relationship is identified, the next step is evaluating its potential impact on the counseling process. Some dual relationships may be ethically manageable, while others pose risks such as conflicts of interest, power imbalances, or compromised objectivity. Counselors should use ethical guidelines and risk assessment frameworks to weigh both the potential benefits (e.g., increased trust and cultural appropriateness) and risks (e.g., boundary confusion and ethical dilemmas). Seeking external input from a supervisor or ethics consultant can provide an objective perspective, helping to mitigate personal bias.

If a dual relationship is deemed manageable, counselors must openly discuss it with the client. This conversation ensures informed consent and maintains the integrity of the therapeutic relationship. Using clear, non-technical language, counselors should explain the dual relationship, its potential impact, and the agreed-upon boundaries. Clients may initially feel uncomfortable or confused, so encouraging open dialogue and allowing questions can help ease concerns. Informed consent documentation can formalize the discussion, providing clarity and accountability for both parties.

Setting boundaries is crucial in managing dual relationships ethically. Counselors and clients should collaboratively define the limits of their interactions outside of therapy, ensuring that both parties understand appropriate conduct. Written agreements, boundary-setting techniques, and professional guidelines can support this process. However, balancing flexibility with ethical rigor can be challenging, counselors must avoid overly rigid boundaries that alienate clients while preventing situations that could lead to ethical breaches.

Thorough documentation is essential for accountability and ethical clarity. Counselors should record all discussions and decisions related to the dual relationship, including the rationale for boundary-setting choices, client agreements, and any consultations with supervisors. Secure record-keeping systems and structured documentation templates can ensure consistency. The challenge lies in maintaining records that are both comprehensive and concise, counselors should focus on recording key ethical considerations while avoiding unnecessary details.

Dual relationships are dynamic and require continuous evaluation. Regular check-ins with clients can help identify any emerging concerns or shifts in the therapeutic relationship. Supervision and client feedback mechanisms provide additional layers of accountability, helping counselors recognize subtle changes that may indicate the need for boundary adjustments. Scheduled reassessments ensure that ethical safeguards remain effective over time.

If a dual relationship becomes ethically problematic, counselors must be prepared to modify boundaries or, in some cases, terminate the professional relationship. Having referral options and termination procedures in place ensures a smooth transition for the client if necessary. Resistance to change, either from the client or the counselor, can make this process difficult, but ethical decision-making should always prioritize client welfare over personal or professional convenience.

Cultural context plays a significant role in shaping perceptions of dual relationships. In collectivist cultures, professional and personal boundaries are often more fluid, and strict Western ethical frameworks may not always be applicable. In these contexts, boundary-setting should be adapted to align with cultural expectations while maintaining ethical safeguards. Open conversations about roles and boundaries should be approached with cultural sensitivity, ensuring that ethical standards are upheld without disregarding social norms.

Managing unavoidable dual relationships requires a thoughtful, structured approach that prioritizes ethical transparency, client welfare, and continuous reassessment. By recognizing potential overlaps, evaluating risks, establishing clear boundaries, and maintaining open communication, counselors can navigate these complex situations effectively. While professional ethics provide a strong foundation, cultural adaptability and ongoing reflection are equally important in ensuring ethical and effective counseling practice in diverse settings.

16

———◦(੭◌〜◌੮)◦———

ETHICAL ASSESSMENT AND

DIAGNOSIS

UNDERSTANDING ETHICAL ASSESSMENT

E thical assessment is a crucial part of responsible and effective counseling. It helps counselors evaluate a client's needs, strengths, and challenges while ensuring ethical standards are met. A well-conducted assessment builds trust between counselors and clients, guiding ethical decision-making and effective treatment.

At its core, ethical assessment is grounded in key principles that shape a counselor's approach:

- **Respect for autonomy** – Clients have the right to make informed decisions about their care. Counselors must explain assessment procedures clearly, including their purpose and potential outcomes.

- **Beneficence** – Counselors should always act in the best interest of their clients, ensuring assessments contribute positively to their well-being.
- **Non-maleficence** – Assessments should avoid causing harm, requiring counselors to carefully weigh potential risks and benefits.
- **Justice** – All clients should be treated fairly and equitably, regardless of their background or circumstances.

These principles are reinforced by professional codes of ethics. Organizations like the American Counseling Association (ACA), American Mental Health Counselors Association (AMHCA), and American School Counselor Association (ASCA) provide guidelines to ensure assessments are conducted with competence, fairness, and cultural sensitivity. These codes help counselors navigate complex ethical dilemmas and uphold the integrity of the profession.

Ethical assessment extends beyond individual client interactions, it strengthens the credibility of the counseling profession. When done properly, it fosters trust, improves treatment outcomes, and prevents legal or ethical violations.

However, there are common misconceptions about ethical assessment. One is the belief that standardized tests are always objective and unbiased. In reality, factors like culture, language, and socioeconomic background can influence test results. Ethical assessment requires counselors to consider these influences and supplement standardized testing with clinical judgment and qualitative data. For example, an intelligence test given to a client from a different cultural background must account for variations in cognitive styles and educational experiences.

Confidentiality is another critical challenge. While client privacy must be protected, there are situations, such as working with minors or clients at risk of harm, where counselors must share information with healthcare providers or legal authorities. Ethical assessment helps counselors determine when and how to disclose information responsibly, balancing client rights with professional and legal obligations.

With advancements in digital assessment tools and telehealth, counselors have more ways to evaluate clients. These tools offer convenience and accessibility but also introduce concerns about data security, test accuracy, and potential barriers for clients who may struggle with technology. Ethical assessment in this context means staying informed about new technologies, ensuring their appropriateness for clients, and implementing safeguards to protect sensitive information.

CULTURAL COMPETENCE IN TESTING

Cultural competence in psychological testing has become an essential focus in counseling and assessment. Traditional standardized tests often assume a universal approach, applying the same methods across diverse populations. However, culturally competent assessment recognizes that cultural background significantly influences how individuals think, behave, and express emotions. This approach acknowledges that factors like language, values, and socioeconomic status can shape test performance and interpretation.

Unlike standardized testing, which prioritizes uniformity and broad normative data, culturally competent assessment emphasizes context, flexibility, and cultural awareness. For example, a culturally responsive approach might involve translators, culturally adapted test items, or even entirely new assessments designed for specific populations. In contrast, rigid standardized testing procedures can unintentionally disadvantage individuals from non-dominant cultural backgrounds.

The Evolution of Cultural Competence in Testing

The history of psychological testing shows a clear contrast between traditional methods and culturally competent approaches. Early standardized tests, developed by figures like Alfred Binet and Lewis Terman in the early 20th century, aimed to measure intelligence and aptitude but often reflected the cultural biases of their time. These tests assumed a single standard of cognitive ability, overlooking cultural differences in learning and reasoning.

The push for culturally competent assessment gained momentum in the latter half of the 20th century, particularly during the civil rights movement and the growing recognition of cultural diversity in psychology. Scholars like Derald Wing Sue and Stanley Sue emphasized the need for cultural awareness in both assessment and therapy, advocating for more inclusive testing practices.

To address cultural bias in assessment, two primary approaches have emerged:

- **Culturally Adapted Tests** – These involve modifying existing assessments to better suit specific cultural groups. Adjustments may include translation, item substitution, or norm adjustments to improve accuracy and fairness. However, these changes can sometimes make it difficult to compare results across diverse populations.
- **Culture-Fair or Culture-Free Tests** – These tests attempt to eliminate cultural content by focusing on abstract reasoning and non-verbal tasks. While intended to be universally applicable, they may still favor certain cognitive styles or cultural experiences.

The choice between these approaches depends on the purpose of the assessment. Culturally specific **tests** are particularly useful in clinical settings, where understanding an individual's cultural background is essential for accurate diagnosis and treatment. In contrast, universal measures are more appropriate for large-scale research or cross-cultural comparisons.

Integrating cultural competence into standardized testing remains both a challenge and an opportunity. Possible strategies include:

- Expanding normative data to reflect cultural diversity.
- Providing cultural competence training for test administrators and interpreters.
- Utilizing technology to develop more adaptive, culturally responsive assessment tools.
- Shifting assessment frameworks to view cultural factors as integral components rather than confounding variables.

ETHICAL COMMUNICATION OF RESULTS

Effectively communicating assessment results is a critical responsibility in counseling. It's not just about sharing information, it's about ensuring that clients understand their results while maintaining confidentiality and cultural sensitivity. Counselors must strike a careful balance between transparency and discretion, especially in cases where confidentiality intersects with mandated reporting or when third parties need to be informed.

One of the biggest challenges in ethical communication is making complex psychological or behavioral data accessible to clients. Many clients lack specialized knowledge, and if results are not explained in a clear and meaningful way, misunderstandings can occur. This can lead to misinterpretation, ineffective interventions, or even disengagement from the counseling process.

A major barrier to clear communication is the technical language often used in psychological assessments. Terms like *cognitive dissonance* or *executive functioning* might be second nature to professionals but can be confusing or intimidating to clients. If clients don't fully grasp what their results mean, they may misinterpret their own situation, which can undermine their progress in therapy.

Cultural differences add another layer of complexity. Many assessments are developed within specific cultural frameworks, which may not always align with a client's background. What is considered a psychological concern in one culture might be completely normal in another. Counselors must approach this process with cultural humility, being mindful that their own perspectives can influence how they interpret and present assessment results.

The way assessment results are communicated can have a profound effect on clients. Thoughtful, empathetic feedback can empower individuals by helping them recognize their strengths and challenges, leading to personal growth and improved coping strategies. On the other hand, poorly delivered or insensitive feedback can contribute to stigma, worsen existing mental health concerns, or even create new ones.

Different approaches to communicating assessment results vary in effectiveness and ethical soundness. Traditionally, counselors have taken an expert-driven approach, where they present findings with little client input. While this method ensures clarity, it has been criticized for being overly authoritative and potentially disempowering.

More collaborative approaches, such as using motivational interviewing techniques, encourage client engagement and understanding. However, these methods require time and skill to implement effectively, which can be a challenge in high-demand clinical settings.

Strategies for Ethical Communication

To improve how assessment results are shared, several strategies can be considered:

1. **Standardized Communication Protocols**

Developing structured guidelines for presenting results could help ensure clarity and consistency across different practitioners and settings. These protocols would offer a framework for explaining assessment findings in a way that is accessible and comprehensive. However, rigid guidelines may not always allow for the flexibility needed to tailor explanations to individual clients.

2. **Visual Aids and Interactive Tools**

Using graphs, charts, and digital tools can make complex assessment data easier to understand. Visual learning strategies are particularly useful for clients with diverse educational backgrounds or learning styles. The challenge here is creating tools that are both scientifically accurate and easy to use while ensuring that all clients have access to them.

3. **Multidisciplinary Team Collaboration**

Involving specialists, such as cultural consultants or language interpreters, can lead to more holistic and culturally sensitive interpretations of assessment results. While this approach provides valuable insights, coordinating a multidisciplinary team can be resource-intensive and may not always be feasible in every setting.

Each of these strategies comes with challenges, such as the need for research, funding, and logistical planning. However, investing in ethical and effective communication practices ultimately benefits both counselors and clients, fostering trust, engagement, and better outcomes in the counseling process.

INFORMED CONSENT IN ASSESSMENT

Obtaining informed consent for psychological assessment is more than a formality, it's an essential part of ethical practice that ensures clients understand the process and willingly participate. This involves clear communication, transparency, and respect for client autonomy.

The process begins with an open and thoughtful conversation. Counselors should introduce the purpose of the assessment in a way that is clear and free from jargon. Using visual aids or simple explanations can help clients feel more at ease, especially if they have concerns or anxieties about the process. Creating a welcoming and non-threatening environment encourages trust and open dialogue.

Once the client is comfortable, the next step is explaining the details of the assessment. This includes outlining the types of tests, how long they will take, and what the client can expect during and after the process. Counselors may provide sample questions or describe test formats in simple terms, avoiding unnecessary technical language. Analogies and real-world examples can also help clients grasp complex concepts without feeling overwhelmed.

A key part of informed consent is discussing potential risks and benefits. Clients need to understand how their assessment results could impact their treatment or daily life. Counselors should be honest about possible challenges while also emphasizing the potential for personal growth and positive change. Case examples or general statistics can help illustrate these points while maintaining a sense of hope and empowerment.

Confidentiality is another critical area to address. Clients should know how their assessment results will be used, stored, and shared. Counselors must also explain any legal or ethical limits to confidentiality, such as mandated reporting requirements. Being upfront about these boundaries builds trust and ensures clients understand their rights and protections.

To confirm understanding and voluntary participation, counselors should check that clients fully grasp the information presented. This can be done through simple comprehension checks, Q&A sessions, or the "teach-back" method, where clients explain the process in their own words. Some clients may face challenges, such as cognitive impairments or external pressures influencing their decisions. In these cases, additional support or adjustments may be needed to ensure true informed consent.

The final step is documenting consent in writing. Standardized consent forms or digital documentation systems are typically used, but counselors must also consider potential barriers, such as language differences or literacy issues. Offering consent forms in multiple languages or providing interpreter services can help ensure every client has a clear understanding before signing.

In some situations, such as working with minors or individuals with diminished capacity, informed consent may require a modified approach. This could include:

- Involving legal guardians or appointed representatives in the process
- Using simplified language, visual aids, or interactive explanations tailored to cognitive abilities
- Applying a supported decision-making model, where trusted individuals help the client without overriding their autonomy
- Seeking the individual's assent, even if legal consent must come from a guardian, to respect their personal preferences and involvement

ETHICAL CONSIDERATIONS IN DIAGNOSIS

Diagnosis in counseling is not just a clinical process, it carries ethical implications that can significantly impact clients. While diagnostic labels can help guide treatment and access to care, they also have the potential to contribute to self-stigma and limit how clients see themselves. Counselors must carefully balance accuracy in assessment with sensitivity to the broader effects of labeling.

Research highlights both the benefits and risks of diagnosis. A systematic review and meta-analysis examining interventions aimed at reducing mental health stigma among young people found that while diagnostic labels can increase self-stigma, they can also encourage treatment engagement (Song et al., 2023). Similarly, collaborative diagnosis between clinicians and patients has been shown to aid understanding of complex psychiatric symptoms, validate distress, and support shared decision-making regarding care and treatment (Hayne, 2003; Pitt et al., 2009). This suggests that involving clients in the diagnostic process fosters a sense of agency and trust.

Counselors themselves recognize the ethical complexities of diagnosis. While specific survey data on counselors' concerns about overdiagnosis and the importance of considering cultural factors in diagnosis are limited, the ethical challenges surrounding diagnostic labeling and the need for cultural competence in mental health assessment are well-documented in the literature (American Counseling Association, 2014). This underscores the importance of translating ethical awareness into everyday clinical practice.

Some argue that diagnostic labels are necessary for treatment planning and insurance coverage. While this is true from a practical standpoint, it must be weighed against the potential psychological and social impacts on clients. A nuanced approach is needed, one that ensures access to care while also considering the long-term effects of labeling (Corrigan et al., 2014). Another perspective suggests that a clear diagnosis can help clients better understand themselves. While this can be empowering for some, research indicates that labels don't always have a positive effect. The impact varies depending on the individual and their cultural or personal context, reinforcing the importance of discussing diagnosis openly with

344

clients rather than assuming a one-size-fits-all approach (Corrigan et al., 2014).

IMPACT OF DIAGNOSIS ON CLIENTS

As mentioned earlier, the impact of a diagnosis on clients in counseling is a complex issue that requires thoughtful consideration. While the American School Counselor Association (ASCA) states that school counselors do not diagnose, they acknowledge that a student's diagnosis and environment can greatly influence their academic, personal, and emotional success. This highlights the need to understand how diagnoses affect clients across various counseling settings.

A diagnosis can be beneficial, offering clients a clearer understanding of their experiences and access to targeted treatment. It can help reduce feelings of isolation and self-blame while opening the door to specialized services, insurance coverage, and evidence-based interventions. For example, a student diagnosed with Attention-Deficit/Hyperactivity Disorder (ADHD) may receive classroom accommodations, such as extended test time or preferential seating, leading to improved academic performance.

However, diagnoses can also have drawbacks. Stigmatization remains a major concern, particularly with mental health conditions. A diagnostic label may lead to discrimination, social exclusion, or a negative self-image. There is also the risk of self-fulfilling prophecies, clients might internalize their diagnosis and unconsciously conform to limiting expectations (Corrigan, 2007). For instance, someone diagnosed with Major Depressive Disorder may come to believe that chronic sadness is an unchangeable part of their identity, reinforcing depressive symptoms.

The effects of diagnostic disclosure vary based on factors such as age, cultural background, and the specific condition. Adolescents may benefit from disclosure by gaining a sense of autonomy and engagement in treatment, while younger children might need a simpler, more strengths-based explanation. Cultural considerations are critical, as different societies and communities perceive mental health diagnoses in unique ways, affecting how clients process and respond to them.

Historically, diagnosis was used primarily as a clinical tool for categorizing and treating mental health conditions. However, modern person-centered approaches involve clients more actively in the diagnostic process, promoting agency and recognizing their subjective experiences. Collaborative diagnostic practices enhance engagement and treatment adherence by giving clients a sense of ownership over their mental health journey.

Diagnostic systems such as the DSM-5-TR and ICD-11 provide standardized language for mental health professionals, facilitating communication and research. However, their categorical nature can sometimes oversimplify mental health experiences. The inclusion of the Cultural Formulation Interview (CFI) in the DSM-5-TR is a step forward in ensuring cultural sensitivity by incorporating clients' perspectives and social contexts into diagnosis and treatment planning.

Counselors must carefully determine when detailed diagnostic information benefits clients versus when a more general formulation is preferable. In cases where specific diagnoses are needed for accessing services or working with informed adult clients, detailed information can be empowering. In contrast, when working with young children or in environments where stigma is prevalent, a focus on specific challenges and strengths rather than diagnostic labels may be more appropriate.

To maximize the benefits of diagnosis while minimizing harm, counselors can adopt several strategies:

- **Frame diagnoses as tools, not labels**: Emphasize that diagnoses describe a set of experiences rather than define a person's identity, reinforcing the potential for growth and change.

- **Involve clients in the process**: Using collaborative assessment and shared decision-making fosters engagement and reduces feelings of helplessness.

Use mindful language: Discuss diagnoses in terms of specific symptoms and experiences rather than broad, potentially stigmatizing categories.

Implications for Counselor Education and Supervision

Given these ethical challenges, counselor education and supervision must emphasize more than just clinical accuracy, they must also focus on the holistic impact of diagnosis. Training programs should incorporate:

- **Collaborative Diagnosis Training:** Teaching counselors how to involve clients in the diagnostic process, ensuring transparency and shared decision-making.
- **Cultural Competence Development:** Recognizing how cultural backgrounds influence both the diagnosis itself and how clients perceive their labels.
- **Ethical Reflection in Supervision:** Encouraging counselors to critically examine their diagnostic decisions, considering long-term client outcomes.
- **Experiential Learning:** Using role-playing and simulations to help trainees navigate ethical dilemmas related to diagnosis.

Additionally, ongoing research is needed to further explore how diagnosis affects diverse populations. Future studies should focus on the cultural factors that shape the experience of being diagnosed and integrate these findings into training and supervision.

By fostering ethical awareness and a client-centered approach to diagnosis, counselors can ensure that their assessments support, rather than hinder, client well-being. Diagnosis should not be just a clinical label but a tool used thoughtfully to promote growth, understanding, and access to appropriate care.

MAINTAINING ASSESSMENT SECURITY

The concept of assessment security has evolved significantly since the early 20th century when standardized testing first became widespread in education and psychology. In the beginning, security measures were simple, primarily aimed at preventing blatant cheating during test administration. Proctors were assigned to oversee test-takers, and physical dividers were used to create separation between them. While these methods were basic, they laid the groundwork for more sophisticated security measures in later years.

By the mid-20th century, advancements in psychometrics led to stronger protocols for maintaining test validity and security. Standardized procedures for test administration, storage, and scoring became the norm. To deter cheating, test developers introduced multiple versions of exams with randomized question orders. The concept of test equating also emerged, allowing scores from different test versions to be compared fairly. These innovations were essential for ensuring the reliability of assessments, particularly in high-stakes settings.

The transition to computerized testing in the latter half of the 20th century brought both opportunities and challenges. Automated item selection, timed sections, and instant scoring improved security, but new risks arose. Protecting digital test materials and preventing unauthorized access became key concerns. This period saw the establishment of secure testing centers and stricter digital security protocols.

The rise of the internet in the late 20th and early 21st centuries introduced even greater challenges. Online testing made assessments more accessible but also more vulnerable. Issues such as test content leaks, identity fraud, and remote cheating became widespread concerns. In response, the field developed encryption technologies, secure browser software, and biometric authentication systems to safeguard online assessments.

Data security has also become a priority. As tests increasingly relied on digital platforms, protecting sensitive information became crucial. Cybersecurity measures were implemented to prevent data breaches, while ethical considerations regarding privacy and informed consent gained prominence. These concerns led to the establishment of comprehensive data protection policies in assessment security.

Today, assessment security integrates advanced technology and a comprehensive approach to test integrity. Remote proctoring, powered by artificial intelligence, now monitors test-takers using webcams and keystroke analysis to detect potential cheating. Suspicious activities are flagged for human review, improving the reliability of online exams.

Adaptive testing has also enhanced security. By adjusting the difficulty of questions in real-time based on a test-taker's performance, adaptive tests make it harder to predict or memorize test content, thereby reducing the risk of cheating. Additionally, encryption technologies, including end-to-end encryption and blockchain, are being explored to ensure secure storage and transmission of test data.

In counseling, assessment security is particularly critical due to the sensitive nature of psychological evaluations. Secure electronic health record systems protect client data, and professional organizations have established ethical guidelines for technology use in counseling assessments. These measures help ensure both the integrity of assessments and the confidentiality of client information.

New technologies will continue shaping assessment security. Artificial intelligence-driven anomaly detection is being developed to identify suspicious response patterns, potentially reducing the need for human proctors. These innovations promise to strengthen the integrity of assessments while making security measures more efficient.

As the digital options for testing evolves, maintaining strong security protocols will remain essential. By combining technology with ethical best practices, assessment security can continue to protect the fairness, accuracy, and confidentiality of evaluations across various fields, including counseling.

ETHICAL USE OF TECHNOLOGY IN ASSESSMENT

The rise of artificial intelligence in psychological assessment introduces a range of ethical challenges, as seen in the case of a counseling center implementing an AI-powered screening tool. This potential use highlights critical ethical concerns that go beyond a single instance, offering insights into the broader impact of technology in counseling.

As mentioned several times in previous chapters, one major concern in the use of artificial intelligence (AI) in mental health and counseling is algorithmic bias. While AI tools are often promoted for their potential objectivity, they can unintentionally reinforce existing societal and systemic biases, particularly when trained on non-representative data sets (Timmons et al., 2023). This issue is especially critical for minority clients, who may receive inaccurate assessments or recommendations if the AI systems do not account for cultural or contextual differences (Martinez-Martin, 2021).

As such, rigorous validation and testing across diverse populations are essential to ensure ethical and equitable outcomes. This reflects a larger issue in AI ethics: ensuring that technological progress supports inclusion and does not exacerbate existing disparities. As the American Psychological Association (2021) notes, while AI has the potential to improve mental health services, it must be implemented with careful oversight to avoid unintended harms and discrimination.

Data privacy and security are also crucial ethical considerations. Psychological assessments involve highly sensitive information, requiring strong safeguards. The rapid rollout of the AI tool, without proper protections, raises questions about whether the counseling center upheld ethical standards of confidentiality and informed consent. This situation illustrates the ongoing challenge of balancing technological innovation with the fundamental duty to protect client welfare.

Another key issue is integrating AI-assisted assessments with human clinical judgment. Staff confusion and mistrust highlight the importance of thorough training and clear guidelines for using AI-generated insights. This speaks to a broader debate in counseling: how to embrace technology without compromising the role of human expertise and the therapeutic relationship.

The counseling center's decision to implement the AI tool without a comprehensive ethical review serves as a cautionary tale. Prioritizing efficiency over ethical considerations can lead to biased assessments and a loss of trust. A more responsible approach would involve conducting a thorough ethical review before implementation. This aligns with the principle of non-maleficence, ensuring that new technologies do not unintentionally harm clients. Bringing together experts in counseling ethics, AI development, and cultural competence can help anticipate and address potential issues.

A gradual, carefully monitored rollout of AI tools is another ethical best practice. Continuous evaluation allows for real-time adjustments and fosters a culture of ethical awareness. Since both technology and ethical standards evolve, counseling professionals must adopt a flexible, responsive approach to integrating new assessment methods.

The lessons from this case apply to all forms of technology in counseling, from digital record-keeping to teletherapy platforms. Ethical considerations should always take priority over convenience. Above all, human oversight remains essential. While AI can enhance efficiency and provide valuable insights, it cannot replace the depth of understanding, empathy, and critical thinking that trained counselors bring to their work.

Applying these insights to similar situations, several key principles emerge:

- **Ethical foresight**: Anticipate and address potential ethical concerns before implementing new technologies. This requires engaging stakeholders, including clients, counselors, and technology experts.
- **Cultural competence**: Ensure that assessment tools are validated across diverse populations to prevent unintended biases.
- **Transparent integration**: Clearly communicate the role and limitations of technology in the assessment process to maintain trust and support informed consent.
- **Ongoing ethical evaluation**: Establish mechanisms for continuous monitoring and adjustment of technological tools, recognizing that ethical standards must evolve alongside advancements in technology.

Ultimately, technology should serve as a complement to, not a replacement for, the human elements of counseling. By prioritizing ethical considerations and maintaining human oversight, counselors can responsibly integrate AI and other technologies while upholding the core values of their profession.

17

—◦⟨◦⟩◦—

ETHICS IN CRISIS

INTERVENTION

NAVIGATING ETHICAL DECISIONS IN CRISIS COUNSELING

Ethical decision-making in crisis counseling is often a high-pressure balancing act. Counselors must make quick choices that prioritize client safety while upholding ethical principles and considering the broader impact on the community. In these moments, professional responsibility, time constraints, and resource limitations create complex challenges that require both critical thinking and compassion.

One of the biggest ethical dilemmas in crisis intervention comes from time pressure. In urgent situations such as when a client expresses suicidal thoughts, counselors may have to act immediately, even if it means making difficult trade-offs. For example, ensuring a client's safety might require breaking confidentiality or overriding their autonomy, which can feel at odds with core ethical values.

Many of these challenges arise from conflicting ethical principles. The American Counseling Association's Code of Ethics highlights key values like autonomy (respecting a client's choices), beneficence (promoting well-being), non-maleficence (avoiding harm), justice (fair treatment), and fidelity (maintaining trust). In crisis situations, these principles don't always align. A counselor may need to hospitalize a client against their will to prevent harm, prioritizing beneficence while compromising autonomy.

Safety often takes precedence in crisis counseling, but this can lead to tough ethical questions. If a counselor breaches confidentiality to protect a client or someone else, it may save a life but could also weaken trust in the therapeutic relationship. Balancing immediate safety with long-term ethical considerations is one of the most difficult aspects of crisis intervention.

The choices counselors make during a crisis don't just affect the immediate situation, they have lasting consequences for clients, counselors, and the community as a whole.

For clients, ethical decisions can shape their trust in the counseling process, their willingness to seek help in the future, and their overall mental health journey. A decision that prioritizes safety over autonomy, for example, might save a life but could also make a client hesitant to reach out again.

Counselors, on the other hand, often face moral distress and burnout from handling high-stakes ethical dilemmas. The emotional toll of making tough calls, especially when outcomes are uncertain, can affect both their professional effectiveness and personal well-being.

At a community level, these ethical choices influence how the public perceives mental health services. They can shape policies on crisis intervention, impact funding for mental health programs, and affect how society views the balance between safety, autonomy, and care.

Approaches to Ethical Decision-Making in Crisis Situations

Several structured frameworks help counselors navigate ethical challenges during crises. One example is the ETHIC model (Evaluate, Think, Hypothesize, Identify, Consult), introduced by Steinman, Richardson, and McEnroe (1998).

This model encourages counselors to consider different perspectives and seek consultation before making ethical decisions. However, in urgent crisis situations, time constraints often make it difficult to follow a step-by-step approach.

Given these challenges, alternative ethical decision-making models could be useful in crisis intervention:

- **Hierarchical Ethical Priority Model:** This approach would create a clear ranking of ethical principles specifically for crisis situations. Immediate safety and harm prevention would take priority over other considerations, giving counselors a structured framework for quick decision-making. However, such a rigid system might oversimplify complex situations and lead to overly paternalistic interventions.
- **Collaborative Crisis Ethics Network:** Leveraging technology, this model would create a real-time consultation platform where crisis counselors could connect with peers for immediate ethical guidance. While this could reduce individual bias and lighten the emotional burden of decision-making, challenges include ensuring data security, managing liability concerns, and responding quickly enough in urgent cases.

- **Adaptive Ethical Reasoning Model:** This approach would integrate artificial intelligence to analyze past ethical cases and professional guidelines, offering rapid, situation-specific recommendations. While AI could provide valuable support, it raises concerns about the role of human judgment and the risk of algorithmic bias in ethical decision-making.

Implementing any of these models would require comprehensive training, continuous evaluation, and strong support systems for crisis counselors. In the long run, these approaches could lead to shifts in counselor education, changes in professional liability, and updates to ethical codes that better reflect the realities of crisis intervention.

NAVIGATING SUICIDE RISK ASSESSMENT

Suicide risk assessment in counseling has evolved over time, with two primary approaches guiding practitioners: risk-based and protective factors-based assessments. While these methods differ in focus, they share the same goal, identifying individuals at risk and determining the best interventions. The risk-based approach, rooted in traditional medical models, emphasizes factors that increase a person's likelihood of suicide. In contrast, the protective factors-based approach, influenced by positive psychology, highlights strengths and resilience that can help safeguard against suicidal behavior.

Both approaches acknowledge the complexity of suicide risk but differ in their strategies. Risk-based assessments focus on warning signs, such as previous suicide attempts, mental health diagnoses, and significant life stressors. This method aligns with the medical model, which prioritizes identifying and treating pathology. Protective factors-based assessments, on the other hand, concentrate on coping mechanisms, social support, and personal strengths that can help mitigate risk. This perspective stems from positive psychology and emphasizes enhancing resilience rather than merely addressing threats.

In crisis situations, these approaches serve different purposes. Risk-based assessments offer a clear, quantifiable measure of immediate danger, making them valuable for rapid intervention. However, they sometimes overestimate risk, leading to unnecessary hospitalizations or interventions that might harm therapeutic relationships. Protective factors-based assessments, while less immediate in identifying danger, often encourage stronger client engagement. By focusing on strengths and resources, this approach can promote lasting well-being and long-term suicide prevention.

The historical development of these methods reflects shifts in mental health care. Risk-based assessments gained traction in the 1970s, influenced by Aaron Beck's research on hopelessness, which led to standardized tools for evaluating suicide risk. Protective factors-based assessments emerged later, shaped by the positive psychology movement in the late 1990s and early 2000s. Figures like Martin Seligman, with his work on learned optimism and resilience, played a key role in developing strength-based assessment strategies.

Each approach has advantages and drawbacks. Risk-based assessments provide clear, actionable data for crisis management, often including protocols for high-risk situations. However, over-reliance on hospitalization and restrictive interventions can strain therapeutic relationships. Protective factors-based assessments, while not always suited for urgent risk evaluation, contribute significantly to long-term prevention by reinforcing resilience and coping skills.

The choice between these approaches depends on the setting. In emergency departments or acute crisis situations, where immediate evaluation is essential, risk-based assessments may be the best option. In outpatient or long-term therapy settings, where rapport and resilience-building are priorities, a protective factors-based approach might be more effective. Increasingly, experts recognize that an integrated approach, combining both risk-based and protective factors-based assessments, provides a more comprehensive, ethical framework.

A practical way to integrate these approaches is through a two-phase assessment. The first phase could use a risk-based screening to assess immediate danger, followed by a deeper evaluation of protective factors. This method balances immediate safety concerns with long-term well-being, aligning with the ethical principle of beneficence, ensuring that clients receive the most appropriate and effective care.

Legal and ethical considerations further shape suicide risk assessment. The landmark case *Bellah v. Greenson* (1978) established that therapists have a duty to prevent suicide, even if it means breaching confidentiality. While laws vary by jurisdiction, this case underscores the ethical obligation to protect clients at risk. Counselors must carefully navigate this duty while respecting client autonomy and maintaining trust in the therapeutic relationship.

DUTY TO WARN: ETHICAL CONSIDERATIONS

Lets revisit that the duty to warn in crisis situations presents a complex ethical dilemma for counselors, balancing client confidentiality with the need to protect public safety. This challenge is particularly acute in crisis intervention, where decisions must be made quickly, often under intense pressure. Determining whether the duty to warn always outweighs client confidentiality requires careful consideration of ethical principles and practical consequences.

Some argue that the duty to warn should always take precedence, prioritizing public safety over privacy. This stance is reinforced by legal cases such as *Tarasoff v. Regents of the University of California*, which we previously discussed in Chapter 2. Note again that it established that mental health professionals have a responsibility to protect potential victims from harm. Preventing violence is a strong justification for prioritizing the duty to warn. However, critics caution that weakening

358

confidentiality might deter individuals from seeking help, potentially leading to more unaddressed risks.

A more nuanced perspective, the contextual approach, suggests that each situation should be evaluated individually. This approach recognizes the complexity of real-world cases and emphasizes professional judgment. Supporters argue that preserving a strong therapeutic alliance is crucial in crisis intervention and that breaching confidentiality should be a last resort. Skilled counselors can often work with clients to reduce risk without external warnings. However, opponents worry that this method may create inconsistencies in decision-making and increase legal liability for counselors who choose not to warn in unclear situations.

Another perspective, the client-centered confidentiality approach, prioritizes maintaining trust in the counseling relationship. Rooted in the ethical principle of client autonomy, this view holds that confidentiality is essential for effective therapy. Advocates argue that breaching confidentiality, even for safety reasons, can damage the client's willingness to seek help and may escalate crises. They suggest alternative strategies, such as safety planning and increased support, to manage risks without breaking confidentiality. Critics, however, question whether this approach sufficiently addresses counselors' broader ethical and legal responsibilities to prevent harm.

Mental health professionals and legal experts often diverge on this issue, reflecting their different priorities. Mental health professionals emphasize the therapeutic relationship and the client's long-term well-being, whereas legal experts focus on liability concerns and legal precedents. This divide can create challenges in developing consistent crisis intervention policies.

Each perspective on the duty to warn has broader implications for crisis intervention and public safety. An absolute duty to warn could standardize protocols and prevent some violent incidents, but it might also lead to over-reporting and discourage individuals from seeking help. A contextual approach allows for more flexible and effective interventions but could result in inconsistencies and unclear guidelines. A strong emphasis on client-centered confidentiality may enhance crisis counseling for individuals but could be criticized for prioritizing privacy over public safety.

The ethical considerations surrounding the duty to warn extend beyond the immediate counselor-client relationship. They raise fundamental questions about balancing individual rights with societal protection, the role of mental health professionals in public safety, and the limits of confidentiality in professional relationships. As crisis intervention practices continue to evolve, ongoing dialogue and research are essential to refining ethical frameworks that guide professionals in these challenging situations.

BALANCING AUTONOMY AND PROTECTION

The case of Alex presents a complex ethical dilemma that exemplifies the delicate balance counselors must strike between respecting client autonomy and ensuring client safety in crisis intervention scenarios. This situation underscores the multifaceted nature of ethical decision-making in counseling, particularly when confronted with acute suicidal ideation.

In analyzing this case, it becomes evident that the counselor's approach aligns with the principle of proportionality in crisis intervention. By negotiating a 24-hour safety plan and engaging a crisis support team for home visits, the counselor implements a measured response that addresses the immediate risk while preserving Alex's autonomy to the greatest extent possible. This strategy exemplifies the least restrictive alternative principle, an important part of ethical practice in mental health interventions.

The decision to avoid immediate involuntary hospitalization, despite its availability under local laws, demonstrates a nuanced understanding of the potential long-term implications of crisis interventions. While hospitalization might provide immediate safety, it could potentially erode the therapeutic alliance and exacerbate Alex's sense of powerlessness in an already vulnerable state. This consideration highlights the importance of weighing short-term safety against long-term therapeutic outcomes in crisis situations.

Furthermore, this case highlights the crucial role of risk assessment in ethical decision-making. The counselor carefully evaluates key factors, including Alex's history of depression, lack of previous suicide attempts, and limited social support. This thorough assessment guides an intervention strategy that balances risk management with respect for Alex's preferences.

The collaborative approach, seen in the negotiated safety plan, reinforces the importance of client involvement in crisis management. By including Alex in the decision-making process, the counselor helps maintain a sense of agency, which can improve adherence to safety measures. This aligns with the ethical principle of beneficence, which emphasizes doing good while minimizing harm.

More broadly, this case illustrates key ethical themes in crisis intervention:

- **Balancing protection and autonomy:** Counselors must navigate the delicate line between taking protective actions and respecting a client's right to self-determination.
- **Individualized risk assessment:** Ethical decision-making requires a case-by-case evaluation rather than a one-size-fits-all approach.
- **Collaborative crisis planning:** Engaging clients in their own safety plans can enhance effectiveness while preserving their dignity and autonomy.

- **Flexibility in interventions:** Crisis situations often demand creative solutions beyond standard protocols to best meet a client's needs.
- **Ethical use of legal options:** Just because involuntary hospitalization is available doesn't mean it's always the most ethical or appropriate choice.

When facing similar situations, counselors can apply the following key principles to navigate ethical decision-making effectively:

- **Prioritize safety while respecting autonomy:** Choose interventions that reduce immediate risks without unnecessarily infringing on the client's rights.
- **Conduct a thorough risk assessment:** Base decisions on a comprehensive evaluation of risk factors, protective factors, and the client's history.
- **Follow a stepped-care approach:** Start with the least restrictive interventions and escalate only when necessary, adjusting based on ongoing assessment.
- **Engage in collaborative decision-making:** Involve the client as much as possible in safety planning to foster a sense of control and responsibility.
- **Consider long-term therapeutic implications:** Weigh how crisis interventions may impact the therapeutic relationship and overall treatment progress.
- **Maintain clear documentation:** Record the reasoning behind all crisis intervention decisions to ensure ethical transparency and create a clear audit trail.
- **Seek consultation:** In complex cases, consult with colleagues or supervisors to ensure a well-rounded and ethically sound approach.
- **Regularly reassess the situation:** Crisis interventions should be dynamic, with ongoing evaluations and adjustments as needed.

TECHNOLOGY IN CRISIS ETHICS

The rise of technology in crisis counseling has introduced new ethical challenges that counselors must navigate carefully. Recognizing these complexities, state licensing boards have established guidelines to ensure ethical telehealth practices.

One key requirement in some states is assessing whether a client's mental health condition is suitable for telehealth. Not all crises can be effectively managed remotely, making this evaluation essential. Additionally, many licensing boards mandate that counselors confirm a client's physical location during each session. This ensures that, in an emergency, help can be dispatched promptly.

Ignoring these requirements can have serious consequences. Counselors who fail to comply with telehealth regulations risk disciplinary action, including suspension or loss of their license. More importantly, noncompliance can endanger client safety, potentially leading to delayed or inadequate crisis intervention.

Does Technology Improve or Compromise Ethical Practice?

The ethical impact of technology in crisis counseling is a complex issue with strong arguments on both sides.

1. **Potential Benefits**

Advocates argue that technology enhances ethical practice in crisis intervention by:

- **Expanding access to support:** Telehealth platforms, crisis hotlines, and text-based services allow individuals, especially those hesitant to seek in-person care, to receive immediate help.
- **Facilitating rapid intervention:** Counselors can respond quickly to crises, potentially preventing escalation.

- **Improving documentation:** Digital platforms can provide accurate and comprehensive records, ensuring continuity of care and legal protection.

2. **Ethical Concerns**

However, critics highlight several risks, including:

- **Confidentiality and data security:** If digital platforms lack proper safeguards, sensitive client information could be exposed.
- **Weakened therapeutic connection:** Physical distance in telehealth may make it harder to build trust and accurately assess distress levels.
- **Technical limitations:** Poor video quality, dropped calls, or misinterpreted text-based communication can affect the quality of care.

Finding a Balanced Approach

The ethical implications of technology in crisis counseling largely depend on how it is implemented. When telehealth systems are well-designed, with strong security measures, clear emergency protocols, and ethical oversight, they can expand access while maintaining high standards of care. However, poorly managed systems can introduce new risks and ethical dilemmas.

Counselors and technology developers often approach this issue from different angles. Counselors emphasize the importance of human connection, rapport-building, and real-time risk assessment. Developers focus on innovation, seeking ways to enhance virtual interactions through AI-driven tools or improved video conferencing. The future of ethical crisis intervention will likely depend on finding a balance, leveraging technology's benefits while ensuring it never replaces the human element essential to counseling.

BIBLIOGRAPHY

Alegría, M., NeMoyer, A., Falgàs Bagué, I., Wang, Y., & Alvarez, K. (2018). Social Determinants of Mental Health: Where We Are and Where We Need to Go. Current Psychiatry Reports, 20(11), 95. https://doi.org/10.1007/s11920-018-0969-9

Al-Krenawi, A., & Graham, J. R. (2000). Culturally sensitive social work practice with Arab clients in mental health settings. Health & Social Work, 25(1), 9–22. https://doi.org/10.1093/hsw/25.1.9

American Counseling Association. (2014). *ACA code of ethics*. American Counseling Association.

American Mental Health Counselors Association. (2020). *AMHCA code of ethics*. American Mental Health Counselors Association.

American Psychological Association. (2000). Guidelines for psychotherapy with lesbian, gay, and bisexual clients. American Psychological Association.

American Psychological Association. (2021). The promise and challenges of AI. Monitor on Psychology, 52(9). https://www.apa.org/monitor/2021/11/cover-artificial-intelligence

American Psychological Association. (n.d.-a). FAQ: Maintaining test security in the age of technology. https://www.apa.org/science/programs/testing/test-security-faq

American Psychological Association. (n.d.-b). APA guidelines for psychological assessment and evaluation. https://www.apa.org/about/policy/guidelines-psychological-assessment-evaluation.pdf

American School Counselor Association. (2022). *ASCA ethical standards for school counselors*. American School Counselor Association.

Anscombe, G.E.M. (1958). "Modern Moral Philosophy." Philosophy, 33(124), 1-19.

Aristotle (2009). Nicomachean Ethics (O. University, Translation). Oxford: Oxford World's Classics.

Baker, E. K. (2003). Caring for ourselves: A therapist's guide to personal and professional well-being. American Psychological Association. https://doi.org/10.1037/10482-000

Barnett, J. E. (2019). The ethical practice of psychotherapy: Clearly within our reach.Psychotherapy, 56(4), 431–440. https://doi.org/10.1037/pst0000272.

Barnett, J. E., & Scheetz, K. (2003). Technological advances and telehealth: Ethics, law, and the practice of psychology. Psychotherapy: Theory/Research/Practice/Training, 40, 86–93.

Barsky, A., Carnahan, B., & Spadola, C. (2021). Licensing complaints: Experiences of social workers in investigation processes. Journal of Social Work Values and Ethics, 18(2), 16–28. https://doi.org/10.55521/10-018-207

Beauchamp, T., & Childress, J. (2019). Principles of biomedical ethics: Marking its fortieth anniversary. The American Journal of Bioethics, 19(11), 9–12.

Bell, I. H., Nicholas, J., Alvarez-Jimenez, M., Thompson, A., & Valmaggia, L. (2020). Virtual reality as a clinical tool in mental health research and practice. Dialogues in clinical neuroscience, 22(2), 169–177. https://doi.org/10.31887/DCNS.2020.22.2/lvalmaggia

365

Bellah v. Greenson, 146 Cai. Rptr. 535, 81 Cal. App.3d 614 (1978).

Bentham, J. (1789) An Introduction to the Principles of Morals and Legislation. Clarendon Press, Oxford. http://dx.doi.org/10.1093/oseo/instance.00077240

Bernard, J. M., & Goodyear, R. K. (2019). Fundamentals of clinical supervision (6th ed.). New York, NY: Pearson.

Bhugra, D., & Bhui, K. (1997). Cross-cultural psychiatric assessment. Advances in Psychiatric Treatment, 13(2), 103–111. https://doi.org/10.1192/apt.bp.106.002105

Butcher, J.N., Perry, J.N. and Atlis, M.M. (2000) Validity and Utility of Computer-Based Test Interpretation. Psychological Assessment, 12, 6-18. https://doi.org/10.1037/1040-3590.12.1.6

Carson, M. (1992). Domestic Discontents: Feminist Reevaluations of Psychiatry, Women, and the Family. Canadian Review of American Studies 22(5), 171-192. https://muse.jhu.edu/article/682036.

Centers for Disease Control and Prevention (U.S.). Office of Science. (2022). U.S. Public Health Service Syphilis Study : syphilis study at Tuskegee timeline. CDC stacks.

Chadda, R. K., & Deb, K. S. (2013). Indian family systems, collectivistic society and psychotherapy. Indian journal of psychiatry, 55(Suppl 2), S299–S309. https://doi.org/10.4103/0019-5545.105555

Chen, S. W.-H., & Davenport, D. S. (2005). Cognitive-Behavioral Therapy With Chinese American Clients: Cautions and Modifications. Psychotherapy: Theory, Research, Practice, Training, 42(1), 101–110. https://doi.org/10.1037/0033-3204.42.1.101

Chung, R. C.-Y., & Bemak, F. (2002). The relationship of culture and empathy in cross-cultural counseling. Journal of Counseling & Development, 80(2), 154–159. https://doi.org/10.1002/j.1556-6678.2002.tb00178.x

Comas-Díaz, L. (2012). Multicultural care: A clinician's guide to cultural competence. American Psychological Association. https://doi.org/10.1037/13491-000

Cooper, M., & McLeod, J. (2011). Pluralistic counselling and psychotherapy. SAGE Publications.

Corey, G., Corey, M. S., & Corey, C. (2018). Groups: Process and practice (10th ed.). Cengage Learning.

Corrigan, P. W. (2007). How clinical diagnosis might exacerbate the stigma of mental illness. Social Work, 52(1), 31–39.

Corrigan, P. W., Druss, B. G., & Perlick, D. A. (2014). The impact of mental illness stigma on seeking and participating in mental health care. Psychological Science in the Public Interest, 15(2), 37–70. https://doi.org/10.1177/1529100614531398

Crenshaw, K. (1991) Mapping the Margins Intersectionality, Identity Politics, and Violence against Women of Color. Stanford Law Review, 43, 1241-1299.

Doi, L.T. (1973). The Japanese patterns of communication and the concept of amae. Quarterly Journal of Speech, 59, 180-185.

Dorociak, K. E., Rupert, P. A., Bryant, F. B., & Zahniser, E. (2017). Development of the Professional Self-Care Scale. Journal of counseling psychology, 64(3), 325–334. https://doi.org/10.1037/cou0000206

366

Ekmekci, P. E., & Arda, B. (2017). Interculturalism and Informed Consent: Respecting Cultural Differences without Breaching Human Rights. Cultura (Iasi, Romania), 14(2), 159–172.

Ewing v. Goldstein 15 Cal. Rptr. 3d 864 (Cal. Ct. App. 2004)

Feijt, M., de Kort, Y., Bongers, I., Bierbooms, J., Westerink, J., & IJsselsteijn, W. (2020). Mental Health Care Goes Online: Practitioners' Experiences of Providing Mental Health Care During the COVID-19 Pandemic. Cyberpsychology, behavior and social networking, 23(12), 860–864. https://doi.org/10.1089/cyber.2020.0370

Fernando, S. (2010). Mental health, race and culture (3rd ed.). Palgrave Macmillan.

Figley C. R. (2002). Compassion fatigue: psychotherapists' chronic lack of self care. Journal of clinical psychology, 58(11), 1433–1441. https://doi.org/10.1002/jclp.10090

Frame, M. W., & Williams, C. B. (2005). A model of ethical decision-making from a multicultural perspective. International Journal for the Advancement of Counselling, 27(1), 131–141.

Freud, S. (1912/1958). The dynamics of transference. In The standard edition of the complete psychological works of Sigmund Freud (Vol. 12, pp. 97–108). London: Hogarth Press.

Freud, S. (1915). Observations on transference-love: technique of psycho-analysis., S.E., 12:159-171.

Garcia, J. G., Cartwright, B., Winston, S. M., & Borzuchowska, B. (2003). A transcultural integrative model for ethical decision making in counseling. Journal of Counseling & Development, 81(3), 268–277.

Gilligan, C. (1982). In a different voice: Psychological theory and women's development. Cambridge, MA: Harvard University Press.

Glueckauf, R. L., Maheu, M. M., Drude, K. P., Wells, B. A., Wang, Y., Gustafson, D. J., & Nelson, E.-L. (2018). Survey of psychologists' telebehavioral health practices: Technology use, ethical issues, and training needs. Professional Psychology: Research and Practice, 49(3), 205–219. https://doi.org/10.1037/pro0000188

Goldenberg, H., & Goldenberg, I. (2012). Family therapy: An overview (8th ed.). Brooks/Cole.

Gone, J.P. (2010). Psychotherapy and Traditional Healing for American Indians: Exploring the Prospects for Therapeutic Integration. The Counseling Psychologist, 38, 166 - 235.

Guy, J. D., Poelstra, P. L., & Stark, M. J. (1989). Personal distress and therapeutic effectiveness: National survey of psychologists practicing psychotherapy. Professional Psychology: Research and Practice, 20(1), 48–50. https://doi.org/10.1037/0735-7028.20.1.48

Ha Dinh, T. T., Bonner, A., Clark, R., Ramsbotham, J., & Hines, S. (2016). The effectiveness of the teach-back method on adherence and self-management in health education for people with chronic disease: a systematic review. JBI database of systematic reviews and implementation reports, 14(1), 210–247. https://doi.org/10.11124/jbisrir-2016-2296

Hall, E. T. (1976). Beyond culture. New York: Anchor Press/Double day.

Hardy, K. V., & Laszloffy, T. A. (1995). The cultural genogram: Key to training culturally competent family therapists. Journal of Marital and Family Therapy, 21(3), 227–237.

367

Hayne, Y. M. (2003). Experiencing psychiatric diagnosis: Client perspectives on being named mentally ill. Journal of Psychiatric and Mental Health Nursing, 10(6), 722–729. https://doi.org/10.1046/j.1365-2850.2003.00692.x

Held, Virginia (2006). The Ethics of Care: Personal, Political, Global. New York: Oup Usa. Edited by David Copp.

Herlihy, B., & Corey, G. (2015). Boundary issues in counseling: Multiple roles and responsibilities (3rd ed.). American Counseling Association.

Hobbs, N. (1948). The development of a code of ethical standards for psychology. American Psychologist, 3 80-84.

Homrich, A. M. (2009). Gatekeeping for personal and professional competence in graduate counseling programs. Counseling and Human Development, 41(7), 1–24.

Homrich, A. M., & Henderson, K. L. (Eds.). (2018). Gatekeeping in the mental health professions. American Counseling Association.

Hook, J. N., Davis, D. E., Owen, J., Worthington, E. L., Jr., & Utsey, S. O. (2013). Cultural humility: Measuring openness to culturally diverse clients. Journal of Counseling Psychology, 60(3), 353–366. https://doi.org/10.1037/a0032595

Houser, R., Wilczenski, F. L., & Ham, M. (2006). Culturally relevant ethical decision-making in counseling. Sage Publications, Inc.

Hsiung R. C. (2001). Suggested principles of professional ethics for the online provision of mental health services. Telemedicine journal and e-health : the official journal of the American Telemedicine Association, 7(1), 39–45. https://doi.org/10.1089/153056201300093895

Jaffee v. Redmond, 518 U.S. 1 (1996)

Jordan, A. E., & Meara, N. M. (1990). Ethics and the professional practice of psychologists: The role of virtues and principles. Professional Psychology: Research and Practice, 21(2), 107–114. https://doi.org/10.1037/0735-7028.21.2.107

Kant, Immanuel (1785). Groundwork for the metaphysics of morals. New York: Oxford University Press. Edited by Thomas E. Hill & Arnulf Zweig.

Kant, I. (1993) [1785]. Groundwork of the Metaphysic of Morals (3rd ed., p. 30). Translated by James W. Ellington, Hackett.

Kitchener, K. S. (1984). Intuition, critical evaluation and ethical principles: The foundation for ethical decisions in counseling psychology. The Counseling Psychologist, 12, 43–55. https://doi.org/10.1177/0011000084123005

Kitchener, K.S, & Anderson, S. K. (2011). Foundations of ethical practice, research, and teaching in psychology and counseling (2nd ed.). Routledge/Taylor & Francis Group.

Koçyiğit Özyiğit, M. (2022). Challenges and Ethical Issues in Counseling Supervision from Faculty Supervisors' Perspective. Participatory Educational Research, 9(5), 305-329. https://doi.org/10.17275/per.22.116.9.5

Ladany, N., Friedlander, M. L., & Nelson, M. L. (2005). Critical events in psychotherapy supervision: An interpersonal approach. American Psychological Association. https://doi.org/10.1037/10958-000

Lawson, G., & Myers, J. E. (2011). Wellness, professional quality of life, and career-sustaining behaviors: What keeps us well? Journal of Counseling & Development, 89(2), 163–171. https://doi.org/10.1002/j.1556-6678.2011.tb00074.x

Leach, M. M., & Harbin, J. J. (1997). Psychological ethics codes: A comparison of twenty-four countries. International Journal of Psychology, 32(3), 181–192.

Leiter, M. P., & Maslach, C. (2009). Nurse Turnover: The Mediating Role of Burnout. Journal of Nursing Management, 17, 331-339.

Lester, D. (1974). Supports crisis phone services: Lester replies. American Psychologist, 29(2), 149–150. https:// https://doi.org/10.1037/h0038127.

Luxton, D. D. (2014). Artificial intelligence in psychological practice: Current and future applications and implications. Professional Psychology: Research and Practice, 45(5), 332–339. https://doi.org/10.1037/a0034559

Lynn, D. J., & Vaillant, G. E. (1998). Anonymity, neutrality, and confidentiality in the actual methods of Sigmund Freud: A review of 43 cases, 1907–1939. American Journal of Psychiatry, 155(2), 163–171.

MacIntyre, Alasdair (1981). After virtue: a study in moral theory. Notre Dame, Ind.: University of Notre Dame Press.

Martinez-Martin, N. (2021). Minding the AI: Ethical challenges and practice for AI mental health care tools. In F. Jotterand & M. Ienca (Eds.), Artificial intelligence in brain and mental health: Philosophical, ethical & policy issues (pp. 111–125). Springer. https://doi.org/10.1007/978-3-030-74188-4_8

Maslach, C., & Leiter, M. P. (2016). Understanding the burnout experience: recent research and its implications for psychiatry. World psychiatry : official journal of the World Psychiatric Association (WPA), 15(2), 103–111. https://doi.org/10.1002/wps.20311

McGoldrick, M. (2005). Ethnicity and family therapy (3rd ed.). Guilford Press.

Mill, J. S. (1863) Utilitarianism. London, Parker, son, and Bourn. [Pdf] Retrieved from the Library of Congress, https://www.loc.gov/item/11015966/.

Mittal, M., Morgan, A. A., Du, J., Jiang, J., Boekeloo, B., & Fish, J. N. (2023). "Each week feels like a mountain": The impact of COVID-19 on mental health providers' well-being and clinical work. Professional Psychology: Research and Practice, 54(1), 103–113. https://doi.org/10.1037/pro0000501

Moodley, R. (2007). (Re)placing multiculturalism in counselling and psychotherapy. British Journal of Guidance & Counselling, 35(1), 1–22. https://doi.org/10.1080/03069880601106748

Moodley, R., & Palmer, S. (Eds.). (2006). Race, culture and psychotherapy: Critical perspectives in multicultural practice. Routledge.

National Commission for the Protection of Human Subjects of Biomedical and Behavioral Research. (1979). The Belmont report: Ethical principles and guidelines for the protection of human subjects of

369

research. U.S. Department of Health and Human Services. https://www.hhs.gov/ohrp/regulations-and-policy/belmont-report/read-the-belmont-report/index.html

Nichols, M. P., & Schwartz, R. C. (2004). Family therapy: Concepts and methods (6th ed.). Allyn & Bacon.

Noddings, Nel (1984). Caring: A Feminine Approach to Ethics and Moral Education. University of California Press.

Norcross, J & Guy, J.D. (2007). New York, Guilford Press.

Norcross, J. C., & Wampold, B. E. (2011). Evidence-based therapy relationships: research conclusions and clinical practices. Psychotherapy (Chicago, Ill.), 48(1), 98–102. https://doi.org/10.1037/a0022161

Orlinsky, D. E., Schofield, M. J., Schroder, T., & Kazantzis, N. (2011). Utilization of personal therapy by psychotherapists: A practice-friendly review and a new study. Journal of Clinical Psychology, 67(8), 828–842. https://doi.org/10.1002/jclp.20821

Owen, J. J., Tao, K., Leach, M. M., & Rodolfa, E. (2011). Clients' perceptions of their psychotherapists' multicultural orientation. Psychotherapy, 48(3), 274–282. https://doi.org/10.1037/a0022065

Patel, V., Saxena, S., Lund, C., Thornicroft, G., Baingana, F., Bolton, P., Chisholm, D., Collins, P. Y., Cooper, J. L., Eaton, J., Herrman, H., Herzallah, M. M., Huang, Y., Jordans, M. J. D., Kleinman, A., Medina-Mora, M. E., Morgan, E., Niaz, U., Omigbodun, O., Prince, M., … UnÜtzer, J. (2018). The Lancet Commission on global mental health and sustainable development. Lancet (London, England), 392(10157), 1553–1598. https://doi.org/10.1016/S0140-6736(18)31612-X

Pedersen, P. (2003). Culturally biased assumptions in counseling psychology. The Counseling Psychologist, 31(4), 396–403. https://doi.org/10.1177/0011000003031004002

Pedersen, P. B., & Marsella, A. J. (1982). The ethical crisis for cross-cultural counseling and therapy. Professional Psychology, 13(4), 492–500. https://doi.org/10.1037/0735-7028.13.4.492

Perez-Foster, R. (1998). The power of language in the clinical process: Assessing and treating the bilingual person. North Bergen, NJ: Jason Aronson.

Perle, J.G., Zheng, W. A Primer for Understanding and Utilizing Telesupervision with Healthcare Trainees. J. technol. behav. sci. 9, 46–52 (2024). https://doi.org/10.1007/s41347-023-00322-5

Pitt, L., Kilbride, M., Nothard, S., Welford, M., & Morrison, A. P. (2009). Researching recovery from psychosis: A user-led project. Psychiatric Bulletin, 33(5), 161–163. https://doi.org/10.1192/pb.bp.108.020248

Pugh, M. A., & Vetere, A. (2009). Lost in translation: An interpretative phenomenological analysis of mental health professionals' experiences of empathy in clinical work with an interpreter. Psychology and Psychotherapy: Theory, Research and Practice, 82(3), 305–321. https://doi.org/10.1348/147608308X397059

Ratts, M. J., Singh, A. A., Nassar-McMillan, S., Butler, S. K., & McCullough, J. R. (2016). Multicultural and social justice counseling competencies: Guidelines for the counseling profession. Journal of Multicultural Counseling and Development, 44(1), 28–48. https://doi.org/10.1002/jmcd.12035

Rawls, J. (1958). Justice as fairness. The Philosophical Review, 67(2), 164-194

Richter Herlihy, B., & Watson, Z. E. P. (2007). Social Justice and Counseling Ethics. In C. C. Lee (Ed.), Counseling for social justice (2nd ed., pp. 181–199). American Counseling Association.

Rogers, C. R. (1957). The necessary and sufficient conditions of therapeutic personality change. Journal of Consulting Psychology, 21(2), 95–103. https://doi.org/10.1037/h0045357

Rønnestad, M. H., & Skovholt, T. M. (2003). The journey of the counselor and therapist: Research findings and perspectives on professional development. Journal of Career Development, 30(1), 5–44. https://doi.org/10.1023/A:1025173508081

Rousseau, Jean-Jacques (1947). The social contract. Harmondsworth,: Penguin Books. Edited by Charles Frankel.

Rubin, M., Arnon, H., Huppert, J. D., & Perry, A. (2024). Considering the Role of Human Empathy in AI-Driven Therapy. JMIR Mental Health, 11, e56529. https://doi.org/10.2196/56529

Schueller, S. M., Glover, A. C., Rufa, A. K., Dowdle, C. L., Gross, G. D., Karnik, N. S., & Zalta, A. K. (2019). A Mobile Phone-Based Intervention to Improve Mental Health Among Homeless Young Adults: Pilot Feasibility Trial. JMIR mHealth and uHealth, 7(7), e12347. https://doi.org/10.2196/12347

Seligman, M. E. P., & Csikszentmihalyi, M. (2000). Positive psychology: An introduction. American Psychologist, 55(1), 5–14. https://doi.org/10.1037/0003-066X.55.1.5

Skovholt, T. M., & Trotter-Mathison, M. (2016). The resilient practitioner: Burnout and compassion fatigue prevention and self-care strategies for the helping professions: Third edition. Taylor and Francis Inc. https://doi.org/10.4324/9781315737447

Slote, M. (2001). Moral Sentimentalism and Moral Psychology. Philosophical Explorations, 4(1), 30–42.

Smith, M. L., & Glass, G. V. (1977). Meta-analysis of psychotherapy outcome studies. American Psychologist, 32(9), 752–760. https://doi.org/10.1037/0003-066X.32.9.752

Song, N., Hugh-Jones, S., West, R. M., Pickavance, J., & Mir, G. (2023). The effectiveness of anti-stigma interventions for reducing mental health stigma in young people: A systematic review and meta-analysis. Global Mental Health, 10, e39. https://doi.org/10.1017/gmh.2023.34

Speight, S. L. (2011). An Exploration of Boundaries and Solidarity in Counseling Relationships. The Counseling Psychologist, 40(1), 133-157. https://doi.org/10.1177/0011000011399783

Steinman, S. O., Richardson, N. F., & McEnroe, T. (1998). The ethical decision-making manual for helping professionals. Brooks/Cole Publishing Company.

Sue, D. W., Arredondo, P., & McDavis, R. J. (1992). Multicultural counseling competencies and standards: A call to the profession. Journal of Counseling & Development, 70(4), 477–486. https://doi.org/10.1002/j.1556-6676.1992.tb01642.x

Sue, D. W., & Sue, D. (2016). Counseling the culturally diverse: theory and practice. 7th edition. John Wiley & Sons, Inc.

371

Tarasoff v. Regents of the University of California, 12 Cal.3d 425, 131 Cal. Rptr. 14,551 P.2d 334 (1976).

Thakkar, A., Gupta, A., & De Sousa, A. (2024). Artificial intelligence in positive mental health: a narrative review. Frontiers in digital health, 6, 1280235. https://doi.org/10.3389/fdgth.2024.1280235

Thomas, J. T. (2005). Licensing board complaints: Minimizing the impact on the psychologist's defense and clinical practice. Professional Psychology: Research and Practice, 36(4), 426–433. https://doi.org/10.1037/0735-7028.36.4.426

Timmons, A. C., Duong, J. B., Simo Fiallo, N., Lee, T., Vo, H. P. Q., Ahle, M. W., Comer, J. S., Brewer, L. C., Frazier, S. L., & Chaspari, T. (2023). A call to action on assessing and mitigating bias in artificial intelligence applications for mental health. Perspectives on Psychological Science, 18(5), 1062–1096. https://doi.org/10.1177/17456916221134490

Toporek, R.L., Lewis, J.A., & Crethar, H.C. (2009). Promoting Systemic Change Through the ACA Advocacy Competencies. Journal of Counseling and Development, 87, 260-268.

Tribe, R. & Thompson, K. (2009) Exploring the Three Way Relationship in Therapeutic Work with Interpreters. International Journal of Migration, Health and Social Care, 5,2, 13-21

Tu W. (1998). Confucius and Confucianism. In W.H. Slote G.A. DeVos (Eds.), Confucianism and the family. 3-36. Albany, NY: State University of New York Press.

United States Holocaust Memorial Museum. (n.d.). The Nuremberg Code.

VanLandingham, M. J., Nguyen, T., Tran, C.-T., Pham, N. K., Bui, B., & Anglewicz, P. (2023). Building Bridges and Mending Fences: Cultural Conflict and Cultural Brokering between Academic and Immigrant Communities. Journal of Applied Social Science, 17(3), 324-337. https://doi.org/10.1177/19367244231171530

Warrier, U., Warrier, A. & Khandelwal, K. (2023). Ethical considerations in the use of artificial intelligence in mental health. Egypt J Neurol Psychiatry Neurosurg 59, 139. https://doi.org/10.1186/s41983-023-00735-2

Wilkinson, T., Smith, D., & Wimberly, R. (2019). Trends in ethical complaints leading to professional counseling licensing boards disciplinary actions. Journal of Counseling & Development, 97(1), 98–107. https://doi.org/10.1002/jcad.12239

White, M. and Epston, D. (1990) Narrative Means to Therapeutic Ends. W. W. Norton, New York.

World Medical Association (2013). World Medical Association Declaration of Helsinki: ethical principles for medical research involving human subjects. JAMA, 310(20), 2191–2194. https://doi.org/10.1001/jama.2013.281053

Zhang, Z., & Wang, J. (2024). Can AI replace psychotherapists? Exploring the future of mental health care. Frontiers in Psychiatry, 15, 1444382. https://doi.org/10.3389/fpsyt.2024.1444382

Zhao, J.-B., Ji, J.-L., Yang, X.-L., Yang, Z.-Z., Hou, Y.-F., & Zhang, X.-Y. (2011). "National survey of ethical practices among Chinese psychotherapists": Correction to Zhao et al. (2011). Professional Psychology: Research and Practice, 42(5), 374. https://doi.org/10.1037/a0025703

Zur, O. (2007). Boundaries in Psychotherapy: Ethical and Clinical Explorations. American Psychological Association. https://doi.org/10.1037/11563-000

SUBJECT INDEX

www.ingramcontent.com/pod-product-compliance
Lightning Source LLC
Chambersburg PA
CBHW072045020426
42334CB00017B/1394